# SANC

# THE ꞆPIRIT

## BY
## JULIA BEACROFT

SANCIO
BOOKS

# SANCTIFYING THE SPIRIT

*Published by Sancio Books*

*40 Innerbrook Road, Chelston, Torquay, Devon TQ2 6AQ*

*Tel +44(0)1803 607678.* www.sanciobooks.com

© Julia Beacroft, 2016.

*julia.beacroft@sanciobooks.com*

ISBN 978-0-9935935-0-5

Edited and produced by *Adrian Wardle*. Typeset in 11pt Caslon.
Illustrations by *Joseph Hanrahan* © 2016.

*Printed & bound by Latimer Trend & Co. Ltd, Estover Road,
Plymouth, Devon PL6 7PY. Tel. +44 (0)1752 201930*
*www.latimertrend.com*
Printed on environmentally friendly *Edixion* woodfree paper
FOREST STEWARDSHIP COUNCIL (ISO 14001).

# SANCTIFYING
# THE SPIRIT

Take a look at how we interact with God
in everyday situations.

---

**A M D G**

---

*A personal guide to catechesis and the*
*New Evangelization*

Joseph Hanrahan

*Illustrated by Joseph Hanrahan*

# ~ *Contents* ~

# ~ *Introduction* ~

I suppose you could say that I was moved by the Spirit to write this book. At least, that's what I would like to think, and what I hope and believe to be the case. Although possibly not always in the most orthodox of ways, I realized that I was spending a considerable amount of time reflecting upon the Lord, not only in church but also when cooking or washing up, or gardening or walking and when in the car (as a passenger, I hastily add!). And after a while I began to realize that although rather unconventional, my reflections and prayers were possibly not only becoming more sincere, but were decidedly becoming more spiritual in character: divine or awe-inspiring – call it what you may. This recognition guided me to an awareness that spontaneous spiritual reflection and prayer (wherever, whenever), was not only acceptable, but could be deeply satisfying. I soon realized that not only did I want to capture some of these thoughts and feelings for my own personal spiritual benefit and growth, but, if possible, I would like to share some of them with other people.

It was my idea that this book could be quite diverse and read in a variety of ways and for a number of purposes. God is at work in each one of us in our daily lives, but we're not always aware of this, especially at that specific time or place where and when the 'action' is. This book looks at everyday situations and how God is evident in these. Those who would like to deepen their understanding of their faith and see how our lives are so deeply interlinked with God that we co-exist with him in every sense, would, I hope, derive a clearer insight into this from reading this book. Each chapter deals with many different situations and aspects of life which help to further illuminate this. In short, no theological qualification or expertise is required to read this book, just an enquiring mind, a love of the Lord and a desire for a deepening closeness to him and for a more profound understanding of how our actions, speech and behaviour affect not only ourselves, but our relationships with God and others.

### A Complete Work

In a similar way to the Bible itself, where each book contained within it can be read in isolation from the others, in *Sanctifying the Spirit* each chapter can be read and reflected upon as a separate entity. Alternatively, this book can simply be read from beginning to end. Every chapter is a complete work in itself, dealing with its own subject matter, so the book doesn't have to be read sequentially. Footnotes identify any source references and the bibliography gives more details at the end.

During the *Rite of Christian Initiation of Adults* (RCIA) in the Catholic Church, many topics are covered which relate either directly or indirectly to the structure and origins of the Church, as well as the faith journey which most of us find ourselves upon. The chapters largely deal with the kind of life situations which are encountered on these faith journeys. This means the material could be used for discussion and to help give more clarity to the RCIA sessions.

### *Personal Encounters*

Not all the topics may be appropriate but those which are found to be so can easily be used in conjunction with the catechetical sessions. Moreover, the role of catechist, although mainly a joyful and privileged one, is not always an easy one. Self-discovery is equally important when helping to lead others to know Jesus Christ. Indeed, some of the insights found in the following pages may even help the catechists themselves to discover their own true nature, gifts and spirituality.

Although most Christians are conscious of the importance of prayer, vocation, spreading the Gospel message and reconciliation, there are many other factors which are significant in the lives of practising Christians. On the other hand, there's often an *unawareness* of some of these less obvious aspects of the Christian life. This book aims to improve comprehension of the importance and value of these particular aspects and thus offer a springboard for deep reflection and prayer on these topics.

Guided by the prompting of the Holy Spirit, *Sanctifying the Spirit* delves into some of the many facets of Christian life. It also draws upon some of my own personal encounters and events, in an attempt to provide greater illustration and insight for the reader. By the grace of our Lord may you be able to perceive yourself, your faith journey and your personal relationship with Christ, with ever greater love and clarity as you continue through life.

If this book can in any way support and help you, then my work has been done.

*Julia Beacroft*
Pentecost 2016.

# ~ *Chapter One* ~

## Vocation, Vocation, Vocation!

*'If our hearts have heard the voice of the Lord
Let us open our lives to the calling.'* [1]

The beauty of these lyrics will not fail to stir even the strongest soul especially when combined with a really haunting melody. However, while one's spirit is

---

[1] Lyrics taken from 'Let us open our lives' from *Gather Us In* – Marty Haugen.

surely moved, how often do we truly 'open our lives' to God's call? Marty Haugen, liturgical composer and performer, uses this text from one of the psalms; a psalm essentially of praise and worship. In so doing, he highlights an idea which is well known to most people, but not always acted upon. Interestingly, the concept of opening our lives to the Lord, having 'heard' his voice, is the key to the whole mystery of our faith – something which we hunger to unlock, yet which can elude us for much of our mortal life.

The idea of opening our hearts, minds, souls and ears to tune in to the voice of the Lord is by no means new. In fact it's a state most Christians aspire to. Yet, like so many of life's opportunities, many of us find it difficult, to say the least. Now if people were to be entirely honest, they're often not really sure if they've heard or recognized the Lord's voice at all! We may assume that apart from a very few notable exceptions over the centuries, the chance of receiving a 'road to Damascus' conversion experience [2] such as St Paul underwent, is really slim. The 'showings' of Julian of Norwich in her divine revelations, which have fascinated scholars and theologians alike since the fourteenth century, may have been a similar type of

---

[2] *Acts of the Apostles* 9:1 - 9.

experience. The evidence of her short text, which was written immediately after the 'showings', and her long text, which was recorded more than 20 years later, give a detailed account of her divine experiences, and her narrative describing those encounters with the Lord has an authenticity which cannot be denied. It's also obvious however, that such remarkable events as these are not only extremely rare, but definitely not for the faint hearted! Anchoress [3] Julian of Norwich suffered from a severe, unspecified illness while experiencing her divine revelations. She had astonishingly hoped to become mortally sick just to have a greater closeness with God. Be that as it may, few Christians would adopt such extreme measures!

### *Recognizing God's Voice*

So, if the idea of an encounter like this is a non-starter for us, then how can we expect to experience the action, movement or voice of the Lord in our lives? Undoubtedly, the voice of our conscience is one such way. It's a reminder when we least expect or want to hear it, of what we should or perhaps *shouldn't* do. Certainly conscience plays an enormous part in our

---

[3] A woman who makes an active decision to withdraw from the world to live a solitary life of prayer, devotion and mortification.

relationships with one another and with God. So if we exclude the voice of our conscience, how else can God communicate with his 'holy people?' [4] Maybe when something 'just feels right' – could that be the Lord's prompting or guiding hand?

How often do we feel a spontaneous urge to take some sort of action, quite unplanned and unexpected? A religious sister I knew was fond of recalling a particular incident. While carrying out the simple task of filling her car with petrol, she had felt an overwhelming urge to visit a friend she hadn't seen for some time. She had actually made other plans for after her visit to the petrol pumps. However, she was adamant that the compulsion to see the lady in question remained so urgent that it was impossible to ignore. On arriving at the home of her friend, she was greeted with the words: "God must have sent you to me. My son has just died." While this is an outstanding tale, there are many of us who have experienced a compulsion to act or speak in an unexpected way. And we can be very surprised by the result!

---

[4] Paragraph 11 - 12 in The Dogmatic Constitution on the Church, *Lumen Gentium,* one of the documents produced as a result of the Second Vatican Council of the Roman Catholic Church, promulgated 21st November 1964.

### *A God who is Subtle yet Persistent*

An overpowering impulse may be balanced on the other
hand, by a gentler, more subtle approach from the Lord;
an approach fortified however, by a steady persistence.
We're never forced by God to do or say anything. Sacred
scripture clearly illustrates this when various characters
were *requested* by God to perform particular tasks. The
most notable is Mary the Mother of God, who was given
the option as to whether she would carry out the most
supreme task of all: to become the mother of Christ. So,
how often in *our* lives have we felt God's gentle
persistence?

Some years ago my family and I relocated to
another part of Britain. For two or three years prior to
the move, I had given very serious consideration to
becoming a Catholic and when I had recovered from the
chaos of the house move, my thoughts and attention
returned to this yet again. Although my father was a
'cradle Catholic', sadly he was non-practising and so my
upbringing hadn't included or embraced the Catholic
tradition. However, despite this, my Dad had always
spoken freely of his Catholic roots and background,
including his convent school education and all this
entailed. There can be little doubt that his explanations
played a distinct part in my desire to be received into

the Catholic Church and to foster a closer relationship with God. However, when I reflect upon all this today, I am struck by the movement of God's gentle encouragement to take the appropriate action and initiate the process. Incredibly, while shopping, working or carrying out everyday tasks, my thoughts would return to this matter over and over again in a really persistent manner. It was only in hindsight that I fully recognized the prompting of God.

Abbot Christopher Jamison in his discussion on communication with the Lord [5] makes a profound observation in stating that the noise and busyness of our everyday lives are definitely not conducive to communication with God. He recommends serious periods of silence, whatever our lifestyle, to help facilitate this. Clearly this is copied from none other than Jesus himself who 'went off to a lonely place and prayed there'.[6] There can be little doubt about the wisdom of Abbot Jamison's approach when trying to listen to the Lord. But in my experience, when God wants to get our attention and speak to us, he will soon have a way to make himself heard regardless of the noise and clutter in our lives.

---

[5] *Finding Sanctuary – Monastic Steps for Everyday Life –* Christopher Jamison.
[6] *Mark 1*: 35.

How many of us have suddenly become aware of a song, tune or melody that appears to be stuck in our heads and simply won't fade away? We often have no idea where it came from. More often than not we've heard it very dimly or softly in the background, way below the noise level and it has penetrated not only our ears but our mind as well. I would guess that most people have experienced this at some time or another. In fact, the retail trade has taken advantage of the fact that our subconscious mind can affect our decision making. Supermarkets now cunningly adjust background music to boost spending. Faster music subliminally induces speedier buying.

The experience of a tune that won't leave the mind is an effective analogy for this type of communication from the Lord – a quiet, subconscious message or urging. We gradually become aware of it and then realize that we've been experiencing it for some time. God is definitely never forceful, but he can surely be extremely persistent!

Acknowledge it or not, our hearts, souls and minds undoubtedly hear the voice of the Lord – whether we oblige him to become repeatedly insistent, or whether we recognize it and listen to him. Thomas Groome reminds us of God's all-embracing contact by stating that '...each person is alive by God's Spirit and has constant access into the heart of the Divine.'[7] How true, and yet how often are we inclined either to overlook it, or feel that this astonishing gift is not for us, but for others who are far more deserving?

God also communicates through sacred scripture, which can always fascinate us and offer us something new and fresh each time we read or listen to it, while providing a welcome safe anchor in today's rapidly changing world. Have you noticed how other people are often used by the Almighty to get through to us, although we don't always recognize the true value of this? It can be especially difficult if we hear a painful fact or truth from someone else.

God is ever present and ready to use others who are in the right place at the right time to get his message across. Into the bargain, he very often chooses intermediaries who we may consider to be the least likely candidates for the job. We really shouldn't be surprised by this, since the Bible – particularly the Old Testament – is littered with most unlikely heroes who are entrusted by God to carry out a mission of some sort for him.

---

[7] *What Makes Us Catholic* – Thomas Groome, p. 272.

## *How do we Fulfil the Lord's Work?*

Having accepted that the voice and guidance of the Lord can be discerned in our lives; does it necessarily follow that our calling will spontaneously be revealed? If again we take as a model those characters in the Bible that were addressed by the Lord – and there were by no means a few – they were each allocated a special task which then became their individual mission. There are numerous examples such as Abraham, Moses, Jonah, Samuel and the prophets.

According to the Oxford English Dictionary the word 'calling' can be defined as a 'profession or occupation' and also 'a strong feeling that you are suitable for a particular occupation; a vocation'.[8] If we think about vocation in the Lord, it can be divided into two categories, namely a disciple or follower and also an evangelist.

If we open our hearts and admit the presence of the Lord, then every Christian is instantly bestowed with the vocation of becoming a follower of Jesus Christ – whether they've always been a disciple – or have

---

[8] *Oxford English Dictionary*, Third Edition, Ed. Sara Hawker, 2006.

experienced a form of conversion at some point in their life. They've been given a vocation of *faith*.

At a conference I attended, a keynote speaker made quite a simple observation, yet it stuck in my mind because it contained a profound truth. She explained that her moment of conversion had occurred when she became aware that God was not at the centre of her life as he should be, but that she herself was instead. She said that she had minimised him to something that she could produce as and when the need arose – in other words when the going got tough. Not to put too fine a point on it, she went on to explain, her own selfish ego was firmly in control, as she was not really listening to God at all, let alone trying to follow his ways. However, as she came to realize this, she most definitely recognized and took heed of the voice of the Lord. She then re-affirmed her vocation to the Christian lifestyle. Interestingly, this led her to an occupation involving evangelization, the second vocational category. And so it is that the second category for vocation could be described as the execution of that particular work for which people are uniquely qualified by their own personal gifts. The gifts which we receive, which are in themselves pure gift from God, are wide-ranging and variable, and miraculously tailor-made for each person's character, abilities and talents to fit the work which the Father has in store for them.

'Every Christian receives potentially – or really, over a lifetime – a calling to some ministry. Speaking about one's faith, evangelizing others, being a parent, and serving others is life from the Spirit', rationalizes the Rev Thomas O'Meara at a symposium in 2004[9] where the life of the Spirit – our guiding hand of the Lord, helps kick-start our vocation, which in turn initiates community, service and grace.

Every free gift from God should be received with joy, alacrity, and gratitude. Every free gift should be used to its best advantage in the service of others. However, in a world that's very far from ideal, this is all too often not the case. Some individuals can, on occasion, act like spoilt children who don't appreciate the gifts they get at birthdays or Christmas. They feel they're never good enough. Similarly, it's quite commonplace to hear such remarks as "I'm too fat/thin/tall/short" or "I'm no good at maths/music/languages." These comments may well be true but do we really have to highlight our

---

[9] Quotation acquired from *Lay Ministry in the Catholic Church* pp. 70 - 71, which contains the transcript of the addresses from the keynote speakers and edited by Richard W. Miller II.

shortcomings, rather than appreciate our virtues and talents? Rightly or wrongly, this common self-deprecation is usually to give a false impression of modesty.

Although some years ago, when listening to a priest's homily, it was explained that there are definitely some people who have a great need to be affirmed in their gifts and talents. It's not enough for such people to be in possession of them, he went on to explain, they need to be told that they really are gifted, skilled and accomplished in, or at, particular activities or abilities. They then need to be encouraged and exhorted to use those skills for the benefit of others and for the Lord's work. Quite clearly, he concluded, they won't manage to do this without that initial vital affirmation and that should come from us.

So it would seem that we're in constant danger of hiding our light under a bushel,[10] which on its own is bad enough. However, we're also totally at risk of foregoing the beautiful joy and grace that we receive when we use our gifts, and fulfil our own personal ministry in the service of others. For it's evident that this is a further gift. Little could replace the peace, happiness and grace that accompany the act of serving

---

[10] *Matthew* 5: 15.

others to the best of our ability, in any capacity. Furthermore, how wonderful it is to get a 'Thank You' – far better than any wage or salary!

## *A Diversity of Gifts*

Our gifts can sometimes lie dormant for years, or even for a large part of our lives. We may have been denied the opportunity to explore and use them. It's quite a common occurrence to discover a late vocation and in so doing reveal those God-given abilities which make it our own unique calling. In a Catch 22 situation, it's equally true then, to say that abilities or gifts are often latently discovered, which in its turn uncovers vocation. Surely gifts and skills can gradually unfold, grow and develop over a lifetime, often bringing surprise revelations along the way? Whether our gifts are discovered early or later on in our life journey, they are always needed for the good of our neighbour and for God's holy Church. We encounter St Paul, in his letter to the inhabitants of Corinth describing in no uncertain terms that the body is made up of many parts... all needed to function together effectively... and each 'part' to use its own talent to the best of its own ability.[11]

---

[11] 1 *Corinthians* 12: 4 - 13.

Furthermore, vocations are as vastly diverse as we are, and sometimes we recognize our calling from God, and sometimes we fail to do so. In my own experience, I not only felt called by God to enter the Catholic Church, but afterwards to become an active participant in church life and particularly to catechesis in the parish. I found to my amazement that I had a gift for this, yet I had been totally unaware of this before. In fact, I would go so far as to say that for most of my adult life up until this point, I had felt that I had no particular gifts whatsoever. To make matters worse, I was also guilty of being one of the bemoaners of physical features ("I'm too tall, I have to wear glasses" being a favourite complaint of mine.) Therefore, like so many of Christ's initiatives, gifts and talents are revealed as and when the Lord sees fit to do so according to his plan for us.

Father Christopher Jamison's reflections additionally include the question of whether Christ had specifically called *him*. To this question he replied, "Of course," but he then went on to ask himself the hypothetical question as to whether Christ had left him a voicemail? Unsurprisingly, the answer was "Of course not!" [12] This would suggest that it's equally likely that

---

[12] *Finding Sanctuary,* p. 6.

our calling can sometimes seem to be somewhat vague and undefined. When this *is* the case we can only patiently await further revelations from God, using the time profitably in prayer to discern God's plan for us.

When we consider characters such as Mother Teresa of Calcutta, Sister Helen Prejean and Bob Geldof we contemplate prime examples of vocational diversity. These giants of charitable works can be recognized as people who found their vocation in life. They simply appear to have a natural aptitude for doing the right thing, at the right time, in the very best way that they could. These high profile celebrities are, of course, well known to most of us, but vocation is important no matter how lowly or unimportant we may feel ourselves to be. Taking this into consideration, what of a young mother who despite her busy schedule of housework, child care and part time employment, still has the time, inclination and knack of being able to listen to her elderly neighbour? She provides her with some much needed company, and generally makes her day appear much brighter by just being there. Would this not be termed a vocation? Or the middle-aged 'friend to all' who dispenses help and advice at the office where they work? Those around her are always certain of a sympathetic ear and sound, sensible guidance. Could this be deemed a vocation? Or James who has been imprisoned more than once for working to promote human rights in Burma?[13] Could it be said that James also has a vocation? Obviously they all have vocations of varying types. Basically, providing a person uses their skills or aptitudes for the good of others, with a fundamental love of Christ in their hearts, they've a vocation whether they are priest, religious sister, or any of the above – or for that matter, you or I.

So finally, when you do 'get the call', *don't hang up!* Don't be scared or get cold feet or be too self-effacing. Your loving God will never ask more than you can give. Your faith and prayers will fortify you and give you courage and peace of mind. Well, really, what's the worst that could happen anyway?

---

[13] *Faith Builder – A basic Guide on how to live as a Christian today,* p. 58.

# ~ *Chapter Two* ~

## So What on Earth is Prayer all About?

This is a question which I have often asked myself from time to time and yet in reality the answer is quite straightforward; prayer is simply a tried and tested way to get the best out of life.[14] In general terms, those who don't believe in the Trinity (Father, Son and Holy Spirit) have my sympathy because they therefore have to face the world 'unarmed' and to some extent 'unaided'. Prayer is the way that Christians fulfil the First Commandment:

'You must love the Lord your God with all your heart, with all your soul, and with all your mind.' [15] So you've got to have faith in the first place. However, faith without hope and charity is of little use. This is where prayer comes in. Because when we pray we don't just call on our faith but we're driven by hope and overwhelmed by love. This love is not only our love of God but also his unlimited love for us as individuals for mankind and all of his creation. Nonetheless, all things being equal, one still wonders how it all works...

In the film comedy *Bruce Almighty* we see Jim Carrey playing lead role Bruce Nolan, a hapless TV reporter who's given the opportunity, for a time, to undertake God's role and all this entails. In one particularly comical but thought-provoking scene we encounter Carrey as God, having to deal with the

---

[14] 'I have come so that they may have life and have it to the full.' *John* 10: 10.
[15] *Matthew* 22: 37.

problem of not only receiving, but having to answer millions of prayers, and his subsequent droll desperation as to how to do this. The reason the scene worked so well is probably because this entire episode must surely be something that many of us have wondered about at some time or another. Indeed, how *does* the Lord deal with the demands of such heavy prayer 'mail'? Obviously we don't know, and we can't attempt to understand. But even so, what we do know is that prayer is essential to foster and maintain our relationship with Jesus Christ. In fact, to learn about him, to become acquainted with him, and to try to understand him is absolutely critical for our own faith journey.

Not only that, but, if our lives lack the sustenance of prayer, where else will we find the power which supports and guides us in our chosen ministry, job or way of life? Or to put this another way, it will be much harder to succeed in our own personal mission, especially one which has been chosen for us by the Almighty, if we don't spend time with him in prayer. We believe we're more likely to reach these goals through the providence of our Lord. In my own parish ministries, I am only too well aware of my own human frailty, and of needing the Lord's daily help. When it's my turn to read the Word *(Lessons)* at Mass, I try to take time beforehand to ask God to grant me the gift to make his words alive to those who will listen to them. When I embark on catechesis,[16] I pray that God will help to place the right words in my thoughts and in my mouth, so that others may come to know and understand Christ. In short, I understand that the strength of my ability comes from God and that without his help I can seldom succeed.

Even so, how many of us take any time out of our busy lives and jobs to spend time with the Lord in prayer? Once, when sharing confidences with a friend, she said some wise words namely that although many of us have hectic lifestyles which can wreak havoc with our prayer life, this will only take place if we allow it to. She assured me that there were methods of dealing with this problem. At one of the most difficult and demanding periods of her own life she made a conscious decision to find time for prayer. She felt it was, if anything, more necessary than ever. Finding no other way to do so, she would allow herself an extra half an

---

[16] 'Catechesis is an *education in the faith* of children, young people and adults which includes especially the teaching of Christine doctrine imparted, generally speaking, in an organic and systematic way, with a view to initiating the hearers into the fullness of Christian life.' From *The Catechism of the Catholic Church,* p. 8, Paragraph 5.

hour in the car when she had to collect someone each day, and spend that time with the Lord in prayer. Occasionally, she admitted, she had been recognized and spotted "just sitting there with her eyes closed", but she felt this to be a small price to pay for the sheer pleasure and benefit of being able to pray in solitude!

## *Constructive Distractions*

Many people find prayer easier said than done. Having the desire to pray, and actually doing so can very often be two very different things. We often refer to someone as 'deep in prayer' when they are observed kneeling or sitting, hands together or slightly held out in supplication, with eyes closed and a reflective expression on their face. I have often wished I could be inside that person's head at that juncture, not out of curiosity, but just to hear how they pray and how that prayer develops. This is purely because I speculate that those around me pray more effectively and with fewer distractions than myself.

I have heard from many people, and know myself, that distraction is all too common during our prayers. But far from it becoming a worrying burden, it can, at times, be surprisingly constructive. You may find it hard to believe, but we sometimes see that God is even present in the distractions themselves. Diversions in prayer can vary from those tedious, mundane thoughts which, unbidden, intrude upon our prayer, to, on the other hand, an anxiety that we're struggling with. Either way, God seems keen to be informed of, and share our worries, or just to listen to our everyday conversation. Rather like a parent who attends to a child who has returned home after a day at school and is eager to relate all of the day's events.

Prayer distractions can also crop up in various other ways. Paradoxically, prayer in church doesn't necessarily mean prayer without distraction. Praying before the start of Mass or any service can almost certainly be challenging as arrivals, conversation, movement, general noise and particularly remarks or conversation aimed at ourselves, are a huge distraction which all too often can entirely preclude prayer.

Some time ago a parishioner at a nearby church was clearly praying when an acquaintance tried to gain his attention. Eventually she resorted to tapping him on the arm two or three times. The man who had been praying snapped crossly at her as a result. But when I thought about it afterwards, I really came to the conclusion that the scene which I had witnessed was perhaps more complex than I had at first realized. The person at prayer was clearly trying to build and maintain his relationship with the Lord. In so doing, it follows that he should have been attempting to emulate the model that Christ gave to us during his time on earth. Ronald Rolheiser, in his work *Seeking Spirituality* explains in some detail how the concept of personal prayer and one's life in Christ should be put into practice:

'Private prayer and personal moral integrity in things, even in the smallest private affairs, is one of the things that Jesus makes non-negotiable within the spiritual life. He asks us to 'pray in secret'…to have a private, personal relationship with him and, through him with God. Moreover, in Jesus's mind the test as to whether or not we are in fact doing this, having a personal relationship with God, is not a question of whether we feel we are having one or not, but of keeping the commandments.'[17]

Accordingly, if we take Rolheiser's statement as valid, bearing in mind the basis for it is taken from the Gospels,[18] then we begin to get an insight into what happened when the man's prayer was interrupted in church. If his prayer was sincere, then we can have some sympathy for his plight. However, because he was

---

[17] *Seeking Spirituality* p. 59.
[18] 'But when you pray, go to your private room.' *Matthew* 6: 6.

disagreeable to his fellow parishioner – although he may have had some cause to be, that's contrary to the teaching of Jesus, and therefore almost cancels out any benefit of his personal prayer. In fact, Jesus himself said, 'Love your enemies, do good to those who hate you, bless those who curse you, pray for those who treat you badly. To the man who slaps you on one cheek, present the other cheek too…'[19]

When discussing distractions in prayer, it's worthwhile exploring the role of self-discipline in trying to overcome them. Of course, many types of prayer are a discipline in their own right, especially in the case of formal prayer or the repeated use of prayer words, which effectively becomes a mantra to clear the mind of extraneous matter. These may help to achieve that closeness to God which all those who pray consciously seek. The Jesus Prayer is one such example, and effectively fits into this category with the words: 'Lord Jesus Christ, Son of God, have mercy on me, a sinner', repeated over and over again. Likewise, the Rosary uses a similar formula with the Our Father and Hail Mary repeated, interspersed with reflections on some of the sacred mysteries. Help is therefore at hand for those who may find themselves unable to concentrate during

---

[19] *Luke* 6: 27 - 29.

prayer, and find it awkward or challenging to place themselves in the Lord's presence for any length of time.

In Thomas Merton's work *New Seeds of Contemplation*, he encourages the use of a meditative approach to prayer. His critique on this method encompasses the usefulness of this tool which enables someone to 'enter into a conscious and loving contact with God in which he is disposed to receive from God the help he knows he needs so badly, and to pay to God the praise and honor and thanksgiving and love which it has now become his joy to give.'[20]

However, Merton expands on this by explaining that in so doing we must explore the state of unknowing, darkness and emptiness, which those who are called to a life of contemplative prayer must undertake in order to reach out blindly to God. To put it another way, to become 'useless and silent in the presence of our God' which 'belongs to the core of all prayer.'[21] What does Merton actually mean by his assertion of unknowing, darkness and emptiness which we must become familiar with, in order to achieve meditative prayer? He claims this state is not arrived at

[20] *New Seeds of Contemplation,* p. 221.
[21] *Reaching Out,* Henri Nouwen, p. 103.

by rational reason but by simply letting go and 'just being', a state which is definitely not easy to attain. Nonetheless, he states that to achieve this desirable state one must die to oneself, as this type of 'death' leads to a higher mode of being.

This concept of becoming detached from the self, as a means to thus know God, involves becoming divorced from the ego, that innate selfishness which so often dictates our thoughts, words and deeds. Even after this self-emptying, we are, according to Merton, then in a situation where self-denial still requires God's recognition of that person's soul. Many of us would like to achieve this higher state of being to which Merton refers, I am sure. Many of us recognize that our ego can be a force to be reckoned with and one which must surely be kept under control for the sake of our own spiritual well-being. However, the idea of passing through the 'dark night, the crisis of suffering',[22] so called by Merton to describe this struggle to die to one's self, is somewhat daunting, and can take any amount of time before we may come even close to achieving it. Yet in spite of this, there will be those who are blessed with this particular spiritual gift of selflessness to aid them in their communication with

---

[22] *New Seeds of Contemplation,* p. 213.

God. Even so, to obey Christ's command to love others as we love ourselves, we must first therefore love and nurture ourselves to be truly free to love others.[23]

Most of us have a preference for a type of prayer. There's nothing wrong with that as all prayer is beneficial in that it helps to keep us 'rooted' in Christ,[24] but also because it ultimately changes us. God cannot change. God is the eternal, everlasting God who has always been and who always will be. We glimpse this quite clearly when God says to Moses, "I am who I am." [25] Informal, private prayer does, however, give us an opportunity to genuinely open our hearts and minds, and tell the Lord how we're feeling – happy, sad, worried, angry or indignant – and to have a frank and honest dialogue about our lives. Only by engaging in prayer with God are we gradually transformed.

### *Self-Discipline in Prayer*

We're not necessarily changed by any action on God's part but often, when struggling with personal issues,

---

[23] Maslow's hierarchy of needs identifies our need for love and belonging as a stage of growth and motivation which we move through towards self-actualisation.
[24] *John* 15: 1 - 17 – *'The True Vine.'*
[25] *Exodus* 3: 14.

we're eventually able to discern the right path. So we also get power, confidence and strength through prayer, available nowhere else, to help us make sometimes even radical changes (for the better). Moreover, continually introducing ourselves into God's gentle, comforting presence cannot fail to transform us and affect us favourably.

Self-discipline in our prayer life can also be understood from the perspective of actually disciplining the mind not to stray when we're trying to communicate with our Lord. Through personal experience I have found that by continually leading my thoughts back to God, and by contemplating some specific event in connection with him, such as the Crucifixion, I am eventually able to stay focused on my prayer and reflection.

Every Maundy Thursday the Catholic Church traditionally celebrates the Mass of the Lord's Supper, in common with other traditions of the Christian faith. After Mass, the Blessed Sacrament is exposed for adoration and we, the congregation, are invited to 'watch' with Jesus, present in the Blessed Sacrament, in the same way that Jesus's disciples were asked to stay awake and watch with him, in the garden of

Gethsemane, on the night before he was arrested and taken before the Sanhedrin.[26]

The 'watching' time lasts for three hours in my own church, and during that period parishioners can choose whether they want to stay for the entire time, some of the time, come and go within the period, or indeed watch for none of the time. Having reached a conscious decision some years ago to spend time with the Lord in adoration, which was also the last unselfish act I could achieve during the Lenten period, I chose to keep an open mind, 'see how it went', and not set myself a time limit in advance as to how long I could 'keep watch' with Jesus. In the event I lasted about half an hour! This was not due to boredom, or any desire to get out of the church, but merely because I felt I was wasting my time as my mind was continually distracted. On later reflection, of course, I have realized that the distractions were part of my prayer and contemplation, and that it was I who had a problem with these – not God. However, the following year I achieved two hours of reflective prayer before the Blessed Sacrament, and the third year was able to 'stay the course' in its entirety. Was I distracted during those periods of time? The truthful answer to that is a little. By focusing my

---

[26] *Mark* 14: 32 - 40.

mind on the Lord, and his works in my life and in other people's, I was able to pray and reflect in a way which I sensed made the Lord's presence ever stronger to me and within me.

### *"Dear God, Can you fix it For Me?"*

The notion of private or personal prayer is exactly what it says – personal and private. This means that most of us pray wholly unobserved and in a manner that's unique and distinctly our own. Nevertheless, there does appear to be a common denominator in everyone's prayers, namely that at some point or another God will be asked to grant a request, or more likely, requests. I would find it very difficult to believe anyone who told me that they had never asked God for something. Indeed, our requests are hardly surprising since Jesus himself said: "Ask, and it shall be given to you."[27]

Unfortunately, this statement can easily be misinterpreted. We can be fairly confident that when Jesus spoke those words he was referring to inviting God's love, especially when he continues with "Search, and you will find; knock, and the door will be opened to you."[28] In reality though, to pray in a 'shopping list'

---

[27] *Matthew* 7: 7.
[28] *Matthew* 7: 7.

fashion doesn't allow us to give the best of ourselves to God. Having on occasion listened to children's prayers, it's interesting to note that they pray in a decidedly similar way to this. For example, a child's prayer may basically go along the lines of:

"Dear God, Please look after all of us. Please look after Mummy and Daddy and my brother Andrew (I suppose!) Please could you help Mummy to arrange for me to go to tea with Rosie tomorrow night? Thank you, God. Amen. P. S. I almost forgot to mention, but do you think Mummy and Daddy could book that holiday in France that I heard them talking about?"

The immaturity of this prayer is predictable since it comes from a child. Regrettably however, many adults appear to pray in a similar fashion. Between 1975 and 1994 the BBC broadcast a long running, well-known show entitled 'Jim'll Fix It'. Quite simply, the show, in response to letters from young viewers, attempted to act as fairy godmother and make their dreams come true.

The catchphrase "Jim'll Fix It" came from the fact that the late Jimmy Savile[29] hosted the show. The letters always began "Dear Jimmy, Can you fix it for me to have/ get/ be able to..." So it is that the type of prayer that merely makes request after request to God is somewhat immature and has a decidedly 'Jim'll Fix It' theme to it – "Dear God, can you fix it for me to...!"

This is not to say that we're not at liberty to ask our Father in heaven for help, in whatever way, shape or form we may need. Certainly we may do so, but I feel a far more wholesome method of prayer is to use the prayer that Jesus himself gave us – the 'Our Father' – as a template for our own prayer. If we carefully examine

---

[29] **Author's Note:** Jimmy Savile was investigated approximately a year after his death and sadly found to have been responsible for numerous cases of sexual abuse. However, the show 'Jim'll Fix It' is merely quoted here to give an analogy regarding the prayer of some people. No other reference or intimation is in any way intended.

the Our Father, we can understand how we could effectively compose this.

The Our Father or Lord's Prayer begins with the words, 'Our Father, who art in Heaven.' This explains to us that we should acknowledge that God is the Father of all, who seeks an intimate relationship with each and every one of us, and who delights in caring for his children with love. Bearing this in mind, therefore, we should first thank him for his solicitous love, and convey that we too are seeking the same intensely loving and intimate bond with him. An expression of our awe and wonder should follow, because the words 'who art in heaven' invite us to proclaim this, and furthermore remind us that we're so greatly loved that God sent his only Son to live among us: a fact to which we should respond with joy and thankfulness. 'Hallowed be thy name' again invites us to register our wonder of the living God, and 'thy kingdom come' acts as a reminder of the kingdom of God which is always close at hand – here on earth where God is ever present, and also in heaven where we will come face to face with him after death. We should pay homage to the Lord during our lives, and tell him that we eagerly await the day when we shall see the glory of his face and should then continue by placing our lives and our will into his hands. He is, after all, so much more able to put our lives in order, and alleviate the chaos of them, than we are. As it is stated by the prophet Isaiah, 'we (are) the clay, you the potter, we are all the work of your hand.'[30] The basis for this is found in the words, 'thy will be done on earth as it is in heaven.' Then, and only then, are we given an opportunity to place our needs and desires before the Lord, and ask for his unfailing help. Jesus allows us to give voice to our own personal petitions by giving us the phrase 'give us this day our daily bread.'

Finally, we register and humbly admit our own shortcomings, faults and failings and ask for God's loving help and patience in attempting to overcome these, and accordingly place them into his hands. More importantly, we genuinely ask for his forgiveness with a contrite heart. Equally, we request the grace to be able to forgive those who have hurt us. And we ask this for a very good reason, because holding onto our own anger and pain can be so self-destructive. Indeed, when we're able to let go of this, we're completely liberated to be able to live out our lives in the way that Christ desires. The prayer that Jesus gave us concludes with the declaration 'and lead us not into temptation but deliver us from evil.' Our own prayer therefore should take into

---

[30] *Isaiah* 64: 8 - 9.

account a plea to the Lord for resistance to temptation, and recognition of our own weaknesses and areas of denial. Alongside this, we must pray to resist evil, in all its forms and be ready and willing to actually change our sinful ways, otherwise what's the point?

If this prayer was good enough for our Lord Jesus Christ, then it most certainly should be good enough for us to not only pray it in its 'pure' form, but also to apply its format to our own prayers, in the way that has just been described. Not surprisingly, some of the notions in the Lord's Prayer decidedly put us to the test in themselves. The hypothesis of forgiving others, even if they've personally harmed us in whatever way, is challenging in the extreme. For others, myself included, the concept of completely surrendering our will to that of the Lord, and effectively letting him 'take charge' can, in the words of Timothy Radcliffe mean that one can 'remain nervous that God may take me at my word and ask more than I wish to give... One might like to check out what God had in mind before signing this blank cheque.'[31] Not only that, but when we're overburdened with anxieties or worries and place these into the Lord's hands in prayer, how often do we then continue to worry anyway? Yet, if we truly relinquish our

---

[31] *Why go to Church?* p. 105.

will to God's, there should be no further rational point to our anxiety, because our total trust in the Lord should mean that we hand it all over to him. We can be confident that he will deal with it in the best possible way and with the best possible outcome.

As always, however, God understands our reservations, struggles and temptations and only asks that we try to do our best. It seems reasonable therefore, that adult, mature prayer should embrace all these aspects of the 'Our Father' yet with an honest admission that we may not always be able to accomplish them!

### A God who Thinks Outside the Box

There's also the very salient question of whether the Lord will agree to grant our petitions or not. It's obvious to most of us that there are frequent occasions when the answer to our requests will seem negative. In other words, God has not perhaps agreed to our requests. We can only guess at the reasons, but in my own experience with the advantage of hindsight, I have seen that my original petition would have probably been detrimental. There's a well-known expression 'things always work out for the best' that we recognize and frequently hear. I have come to realize the profound truth of this statement. I have come to believe and accept that things work out for the best not by mere chance, but because God wills that they should do so. In fact, we're assured and believe that God always works for our good, and shapes our lives and plans, especially when we consider the words of the prophet Jeremiah:

'I know the plans I have in mind for you – it is Yahweh who speaks – plans for peace, not disaster, reserving a future full of hope for you. Then when you call on me, and come to plead with me, I will listen to you.'[32]

Indeed, as I said at the start, hope is the second essential for prayer after faith. It's so powerful that hope in the providence of God and the greater good of mankind can swiftly and actually reduce stress. Hope is astonishingly healing for body, mind and spirit. So when we ask God for help – and hope for the outcome, that alone helps us to 'live the good life'. Arguably, the only reason that The National Lottery is so successful is that for a brief moment, it gives millions of people a bit of hope in their lives. However, it's only through prayer that everyone is a winner! Indeed St Paul reminds us:

---

[32] *Jeremiah* 29: 11 - 13.

'We are God's work of art; created in Christ Jesus to live the good life as from the beginning he had meant us to live it.'[33]

So when God doesn't grant our petitions it's because he can see – and we obviously can't – that we're probably mistaken in those requests; namely that they wouldn't be good for us or others in the long run. In this light, it's not difficult to perceive God as the responsible Father, who can see the errors of his beloved children, and sometimes has to say "no" to them for their eventual own good. We could refer to this as 'tough love', which any parent would understand. However, we must not overlook the loving Father who alternatively can see the long-term wisdom of our prayerful petitions, and helps us to attain them. Personally I am often fascinated by God's *modus operandi* when our prayer requests are approved; when God has said "yes". This is because God appears to frequently 'deliver the goods' but in a method that we least expect.

How many times, when we look back over past events, can we recognize that the Lord has indeed bestowed upon us a gift or blessing that we really needed? Not only does the gift come to us in an

---

[33] *Ephesians* 2: 10.

unexpected way, but has ultimately been seen to be far more beneficial than we could ever have anticipated? It's hardly strange then that our Lord has been dubbed on occasion, 'God of surprises!' [34] Indeed, when God does dispense his own mercy and favours, the sheer volume, magnificence and abundance of these can sometimes be quite over-whelming. God certainly doesn't do things by halves, especially when supporting a prayerful or consecrated endeavour.

To rationalize the way that God 'thinks outside the box' can, of course, only be pure guesswork. Traditionally, the Church considers Christ to be the bridegroom, the Church his bride,[35] and Jesus is often thought of as Christ the lover. When contemplating this metaphor we can consider his relationship with us to be like that of a marriage or partnership. In an earthly relationship of this nature, it can sometimes 'run dry' after a long period of time.

One way for a relationship to stand the test of time and not descend into familiarity and boredom could be when one or both of the partners are occasionally a bit unpredictable. This can keep the

---

[34] *God of Surprises* – Gerald W. Hughes.
[35] *Lumen Gentium* – The Dogmatic Constitution on the Church, Paragraph 7.

relationship fresh and alive, and keep the other person 'on their toes'; interested or even fascinated. Could it be therefore, that God's unpredictability keeps us interested and 'on *our* toes'? For centuries we've always wanted more, and all of us – saints, scholars and the faithful – have all tried to understand him.

On the other hand, a more likely explanation could be the easily accepted definition of a God who simply thinks in a completely different way to mankind; a way which we cannot comprehend.[36] I have already mentioned that some years ago my family and I relocated. To my surprise, I found the fact that I had left all my friends behind in a different part of the country very difficult indeed, especially as we knew no-one at all in our new location. Furthermore, running a new business gave me little opportunity to make new friends. Despite a happy marriage, and the company of my children, I felt lonely and quite bereft, and particularly so since I had never been in this situation before. So I asked for God's help, explaining to him that I really had no idea how he was going to bring me new friends, considering my lifestyle.

---

[36] 'For my thoughts are not your thoughts, my ways not your ways...' *Isaiah* 55: 8.

About that time, I was thinking of joining the Catholic Church and after a period of instruction[37] I was received into the Catholic Church, much to my great joy. As a result of this I became actively involved in parish ministry, (made easier for me as we had decided to shut down our business) and soon acquired a whole number of new friends. God, therefore, answered my prayer as regards friendships, but in a way that I had certainly never anticipated. It definitely did not occur to me when I arrived for my first R.C.I.A meeting that new friendships would be one of the fruits of this prayerful endeavour.

### *Trivial Pursuit*

It's a strange phenomenon that although most people realize, and generally embrace the fact that they can pour out their thoughts and hearts to God, they appear to be reluctant to pray about the little things. Maybe they feel that our Lord is too awesome and mighty to be concerned with trivia. There may even be some truth in this. Nevertheless, if we're to surrender our will to that of the Lord, it must surely follow that we must ask for his help with our decision-making, and lay our thoughts

---

[37] The period of instruction in the Catholic Church is known as R.C.I.A. – *The Rite of Christian Initiation of Adults.*

and anxieties before him, no matter how inconsequential they may seem to us.

I have to admit to feeling most impressed when I heard that a well-known celebrity was known to 'pray about everything'. To agonise over a tough decision can certainly be difficult, but when that dilemma is placed before God, and his help is sought in faith, hope and prayer, it's quite incredible how quickly our personal well-being increases as a result. Besides which, persistent prayer of this nature does indeed yield results. There's the evidence, if needed, of many a saint who has never given up in pursuit of God's providence and help through prayer. When faced with a quandary, the intuitive urge to make a decision one way or another will eventually be realized, and this imperative comes from God. Added to this, if that decision then rests easy on the mind and soul, we can take this as confirmation that God has indeed ratified our decision; arguably for the greater good.

It's strange to relate that there's a genuine concern, shared by many who treat their prayer lives with great seriousness, that they don't pray often enough, or for long enough. Surely this could be because we're uncertain about exactly what God requires from us? I would suggest that love and sincerity are probably of greater importance to him than length of time in prayer, although prayer should be a regular practice. To maintain any valuable relationship it requires a two-way dialogue with listening and talking in equal measure. Moreover, if we consider the occasions when we're thinking about Jesus Christ – what he means to us, his influence on our lives, his time on Earth, and his Gospel message – this could surely be considered to be a prayer in itself.

During a day out with my husband when he was driving, I was left to my own thoughts, which turned to God after a while. It was only at this point that I underwent a defining moment as I realized how often this happened and essentially how powerfully prayerful it was. If our thoughts turn to the Lord under any circumstances, than we're almost certainly striving towards a really close, prayerful and loving communion with him.

### Love is... Taking the Time to Listen to God

Although offloading our thoughts, worries, desires and giving a general update on our lives is a habit that most of us are apt to fall into in prayer, there's certainly no cause for concern in so doing, as the Father delights in this dialogue with his children. But there must also be a time for *listening* to the Lord. Unfortunately, in the busy, noisy world in which we live, listening seems to have become something of a dying art, perhaps because it calls for us to be less self-centred. Personally speaking, I realize that I am guilty of waiting for an opportunity to jump in with my own conversational gambit when talking to someone. This usually means I'm not really listening to them properly. I am sure that this is a fairly common practice for many of us.

Obvious though it may sound, if we never stop to listen, how can we possibly hear what is being said? This applies equally to our everyday encounters with others and also in our prayer life. When we listen to someone attentively, it's an act of charity – maybe even an act of love. And it is love, after faith and hope which is the third and last 'foundation stone' on which we build our prayers. Love is never unkind or selfish. So it is that God speaks to us only if we lovingly make the space and time to listen. But there's no doubt that there will be times when we can discern no response from our Lord. The reasons for this may soon be quite clear. Certainly a lack of listening on our behalf, or not listening to others when God is speaking through them could account for some of our failure to hear God. On the other hand, we may not be in a frame of mind in which we can hear the Lord reply to our prayer.

Certainly anger can obstruct this process, and acute anxiety can play its part also. Worst of all, when we actually hear from God and discern his will for us, we may reject it. Maybe we don't want to repent and change our lives. Maybe we can't or won't forgive someone. Perhaps we won't pay what we owe. How then can he help us?

Listening to God is not easy by any means. Especially in the midst of a world where, for example, commuters have to constantly use laptops, mobile phones and iPods; where people walk down the street with earphones in and gaps in conversation are considered taboo. Seeing that contemporary society appears to have a fear of quietness – a quietness into which God may intrude.

So we must remember to pray with faith, hope and love in equal measure. Without faith our prayer is meaningless, without hope it's insincere and without love it's selfish and undeserving of a response. But despite all complexities, failures and trials, prayer is the sure and certain way to a deep and lasting relationship with Christ. In the words of Kim Kasali whose cartoons were popular in the 1970's, 'Love is…' spending time with the Lord in prayer.

*Fishers of Men*

*(Note that the Greek translation of St Mark's gospel uses the word* ánthropoi [άνθρωποι] *meaning people, i.e. 'fishers of people' not 'fishers of men' – more inclusive, really…)*

# ~ *Chapter Three* ~

## How do we Become
## Fishers of Men?

The words of Jesus to the Galilean fishermen[38] that he encountered on his travels are generally well recognized in a Gospel passage that's frequently read and quoted. Maybe these simple fishermen had already heard of Jesus and his new style of preaching, teaching and healing. Perhaps they had already thought about what it would mean to be a follower of his. And if their meeting with Jesus was completely new to them – both his words to them and their immediate response – are in their own way, remarkable. It's probably safe to assume that Simon and Andrew would have been unsure of what Jesus intended when he invited them to become 'fishers of men'. Indeed, they were all too often described as confused and uncertain of the implications of his words! Even so, they were prepared to give it a go and put their trust in the Lord. If we're to follow in their footsteps, we too should put our own trust in the

---

[38] "Follow me and I will make you into fishers of men" – *Mark* 1: 16 - 20.

Lord, and give him a blank canvas on which to paint saying without reservation "Here I am Lord, use me!"

Jesus, in fact does really offer each of us an open invitation to follow him in the same way as his disciples. It's a recurring theme in the Gospel message, and it's certainly a message that unfailingly gives us hope in the future of the Church. Some time ago I purchased a beautiful picture of Jesus in an attitude of welcome. The picture was appropriately entitled 'Come to me', and evokes his all-embracing and inviting call of welcome. Holman Hunt's well known portrayal of Christ as the Light of the World shows Christ preparing to knock on an overgrown door seeking admittance. It's another illustration of the constant loving request that Jesus makes: namely to be an essential part of our lives, and for us to be a part of his. In short therefore, we're all called by the Lord to 'Come and see' [39] what the Good News is all about.

We read that the disciples experienced a bumpy ride in their encounter with the living Lord, a roller-coaster of peaks and troughs, joys and tears, confusion and comprehension. As followers of Jesus Christ our faith journeys may be marked by the same obstacles or frustrations as well as periods of gratification and

---

[39] *John* 1: 35 - 39.

glorious enlightenment. Jesus did not leave us an easy path to follow, and neither did he promise that we would have one. In fact, our Christian faith comes with a high price tag for most of us who give it the serious commitment it deserves and requires.

In common with his disciples, we're also commissioned to become 'fishers of men' and make evangelization part of our faith journey and our life journey too, but what exactly does this mean, and how do we achieve it?

### *Actions Speak Louder than Words*

St Francis of Assisi is thought to have said 'Preach the Gospel, if necessary use words.' While there appears to be some doubt as to whether this spiritual titan actually uttered this by now famous quotation or not, the underlying principle is sound, and still applies just as effectively nowadays as it did in his lifetime.

Not only that, but Jesus makes it quite clear that even those actions which benefit other people should be performed with the utmost graciousness and discretion, and if praise is to be given it should never be self-praise:

'Be careful not to parade your good deeds before men to attract their notice; by doing this you will lose all reward from your Father in heaven...' [40]

If we have a desire to know God, then the answer is simple: read the Gospel accounts of the life of Jesus Christ and this will be the result. The Jesus to whom we have become accustomed, is a person who's all about love, compassion, healing, forgiveness, understanding and empathy. These qualities set every one of us today a target and a benchmark for living. To become fishers of men we have to adopt and display these qualities in all our contacts and relationships with others. But this is neither easy nor comfortable. Certainly when we encounter unpleasantness for no good reason, we must remind ourselves that generally we've no inkling as to what is taking place in that other person's mind. They may simply be anxious, stressed or even feeling unwell. All too often our natural instinct in this type of situation is to be defensive and react with a retort that can be equally unkind.

If we're genuinely to follow the path that Jesus has set for us, we should try to take the time to find out more about the other person, and try to discover if there's some underlying cause for their hostile

---

[40] *Matthew* 6: 1.

behaviour. However, even this course of action can be fraught with problems. While we may be congratulating ourselves upon our patience, tolerance and understanding, we may appear to them in a somewhat different light. Well-meaning we may be, concerned with someone else's well-being we may surely be, but with the best will in the world this can seem to be pure intrusiveness. To put it simply, we could be accused of 'sticking our noses in someone else's business!' In fact, being able to deal effectively with this type of situation could be regarded as a gift. This means not getting annoyed, and still being able to gain that person's trust and confidence.

Naturally, those of us who have been given this particular gift find it a much less difficult task to become fishers of men, than those of us who have to really work hard to display these particular attributes and skills. Similarly, we need to take care – in our words and deeds – that we're not accused of piousness, when we're merely trying to reach out to that other person's anger or pain. In present society being a 'bible-bashing do-gooder' is a common or a direct insult from those who lack the joy of faith.

In brief, Jesus bade us to try and understand, tolerate and sympathize with others, but we should remember that every situation can be different. Most of us will therefore need to learn the 'tools of the trade' for managing certain situations, circumstances and people. But some people will never actually manage this juggling act of tact, understanding, empathy and consideration successfully, and others will almost certainly struggle with it, but try we must, if we're going to be an effective modern disciple. As Jean Vanier explains 'Compassion is a difficult thing for us to live' [41], however, it's critical that 'we must, by our voice, by what we say, bring the Spirit to people. We must bring them the peace of Jesus by the way we talk and by the way we act... this must become a reality.' [42]

### The Good News – Cast it out then Reel it in

Trying to understand 'what makes another person tick' even under adverse circumstances appears to be a basic requirement for evangelization and for the care of others, especially if we want to imitate the non-judgemental attitude of Christ himself. Yet when Jesus invited his disciples to become fishers of men, their mission included witnessing and broadcasting of the Good News of life after death to the world. Jesus himself actually issued them with a precise instruction:

---

[41] *Followers of Jesus* – p. 59 – Jean Vanier.
[42] *Followers of Jesus* – p. 89 – Jean Vanier.

'And he said to them, "Go out to the whole world; proclaim the Good News to all creation'.[43]

There's no doubt as to the success of this commission. Since the death and resurrection of Jesus Christ more than two thousand years ago, Christianity has spread throughout the whole world. In a sense, the mission of the apostles and the early Church to do this was simultaneously challenging and yet simple. But this contrast seems to be the opposite of our experiences today. Clearly, to give witness to the 'way'[44] of Christ, would have been extremely perilous during the period of Roman occupation in Judaea, and surely only an unshakeable faith compelled followers to endanger their lives for this cause, yet this was indeed the case. Conversely, their ability to believe in Christ as the Son of God was made easier by their being in 'the right place, at the right time'. In fact, the apostles met, conversed, and even shared a meal with the resurrected Christ. There was also the action of Thomas who actually experienced touching Christ's wounds to satisfy himself of Jesus's resurrection.[45] Added to this, the vow of Jesus which proclaimed that he would be with them

---

[43] *Mark* 16: 15.
[44] A term for early Christianity.
[45] *John* 20: 27 - 29.

'always…to the end of time'[46] further strengthened their faith and courage. The apostles' encounter with the Holy Spirit at Pentecost endorsed his divinity and was the ultimate revelation of his vow.[47] Of course, the Holy Spirit was not only bestowed upon the apostles, but upon every human being for eternity.

So it is that the challenges which face us as fishers of men in today's society are in direct contrast to those facing the early Church. Unlike Peter, John and others who were always in fear of persecution for their Christian beliefs, we're usually free to express our Christian affiliation without fear of reprisal and punishment, even though there are times when we're challenged, criticized and mocked for our own Christian beliefs. When spreading the Good News of Christ however, our task is a bit more difficult than that of the apostles. They had been given the evidence of their own eyes to lend credibility to their public witness. We rely upon our faith – a gift in itself – to give authenticity to our certainty in the life, death and resurrection of Jesus. Not only that, but when the strength of our faith and our love of Jesus shine through in our interactions with others in our everyday lives, although we may be unaware of it, little by little our joy is transmitted to

---

[46] *Matthew* 28: 21.
[47] *Acts of the Apostles* 2: 1 - 4.

other people, and they soon want to share it and 'have life to the full.' [48]

## *The Essential Mission of the Church*

Most of us are aware of our need to evangelize: to help others in their search for Christ. The Church itself, of course, holds the concept of evangelization in the highest esteem. *Evangelii Nuntiandi* – The Apostolic Exhortation of Pope Paul VI explains in the clearest possible 'church-speak' the vital importance of evangelization in society: 'The duty of confirming the brethren – a duty which with the office of being the Successor of Peter we have received from the Lord and which is for us a "daily preoccupation", a program of life and action ... seems to us all the more noble and necessary when it's a matter of encouraging our brethren in their mission as evangelizers, in order that, in this time of uncertainty and confusion they may accomplish this task with ever increasing love, zeal and joy.' [49] Although it can be said that St Francis of Assisi had an intention that was of sound principle when he

---

[48] *John* 10:10.

[49] Paragraph 1, *Evangelii Nuntiandi* – 'Evangelization in the Modern World', the Apostolic Exhortation of Pope Paul VI, given in Rome at St Peter's, on the Solemnity of the Immaculate Conception of the Blessed Virgin Mary, 8th December, 1975.

advocated actions not words to spread the Gospel message, eventually there's always a time when we're actually called to speak out to others about our faith. We can feel uncomfortable about this, especially as the risk of being labelled pious or even unrealistic is ever-present. Yet it's as if the Holy Spirit is working in us when there are times, often by chance, when the conversation turns toward religion.

There can be a surprising interest and absorption in the subject from those to whom we're speaking. There are often bystanders who to start to listen and then become fascinated by the subject. They may interject, and very often put forward quite profound questions and observations.

People such as these are trying to share our experiences of God, understand our joy, confidence and peace of mind and so learn about Christ from us. Surely if God sees fit to use us in this way, then who are we to refuse?

### Resounding our Faith

Jesus Christ was the 'first and supreme evangelizer. He proclaimed the Kingdom of God as the urgent and definitive intervention of God in history, and defined this proclamation "*'the Gospel'*", that is, the Good News.' [50] He was our first model catechist, who continues to invite men and women today to follow his example, become 'fishers of all mankind' and teachers in the ways of the faith. His call to catechesis invites those who have been graced with a natural charism for this, to *resound* the faith so as to introduce others to Jesus Christ. In common with all forms of service to others, whether in a secular or ecclesiastical role, catechesis brings about changes in both those to be catechised and in the catechists themselves.

Broadly speaking, formation, growth in outlook and faith, and increased understanding and empathy for others are natural by-products for the catechized. For the catechist there's an increased developing love and understanding of others as well as of catechetical undertaking itself. Obviously those seeking a greater understanding of the Good News and the doctrine of the Church, experience a learning curve of information, comprehension and love. Nevertheless, there can be little doubt that the catechists are also engaged on a learning curve of their own. It's often both surprising and satisfying how both catechist and catechised constantly learn from each other as their own life

---

[50] *General Directory for Catechesis* – Congregation for the Clergy, p. 45.

experiences are shared, and they tell their own particular story. Indeed, this particular process can take place over a complete lifetime. It can be summarized as saying that:

> 'A catechist is one who shares his or her faith, one who shares what he or she is experiencing in Christ. As the catechist shows others the way of Christ, those others see in the catechist the very faith, charity, love, and hope which they themselves seek.' [51]

It's entirely possible that in catechesis those involved can undergo a 'fishers of men' experience *par excellence*. In the 'Walk to Emmaus' event, [52] Jesus as supreme catechist explained all things written about himself in the Scriptures and eventually his true identity was revealed to the disciples. Similarly the catechist helps reveal the nature of a person's relationship with God. Only by becoming intimately acquainted with those to be catechised can any catechist hope to achieve this. And this is not all. Perhaps even more astonishingly, in so doing, both catechist and catechised gradually learn to understand

---

[51] *The General Directory for Catechesis in Plain English –* Bill Huebsch, p. 43.
[52] *Luke* 24: 13 - 32.

many other previously unexplored aspects of their own personalities. Personally speaking, I can vouch for the legitimacy of this. The RCIA experience, apart from generating a more profound love and understanding of Jesus, also facilitates a greater care and concern for others and also a better understanding of oneself. In essence, if the catechists can achieve these objectives then they are irrevocably closer to the two great commandments that Jesus gave to all:

> *'You must love the Lord your God with all your heart, with all your soul,* and with all your mind. This is the greatest and first commandment. The second resembles it: *You must* love your neighbour as yourself.'* [53]

When we've little or no understanding and love for ourselves, then it becomes extremely difficult to have this for other people. The catechist therefore, who can achieve self-understanding and love is not only blessed with a talent for this ministry, but can be classified as a true 'fisher of men', and would probably closely correspond to the profile of a catechist given by Liam Kelly:

---

[53] *Matthew* 22: 37 - 39.

'Formation seeks to mature an educational capacity in the catechist which implies: an ability to be attentive to people, an ability to interpret or respond to educational tasks or initiatives in organizing learning activities and the ability of leading a human group towards maturity.' [54]

Unsurprisingly, the Church regards catechesis as of equal importance to (and part of) evangelization. The Apostolic Exhortation *Catechesi Tradendae* explains in its opening sentence that catechesis holds a uniquely important function within the Church and is the initiative attributed to 'the whole of the efforts within the Church to make disciples, to help people to believe that Jesus is the Son of God.' [55] Yet how often in our parish churches do we hear of parishioners who decline the role of catechist, very often on the grounds of unworthiness, lack of knowledge or lack of commitment?

We're all unworthy to some lesser or greater extent to carry out God's work, this is fairly obvious to most of us. There has only ever been, and can only ever

---

[54] *Catechesis Revisited* – Liam Kelly, p. 133.

[55] Apostolic Exhortation *Catechesi Tradendae,* Catechesis in our Time, of Pope (St) John Paul II at St Peter's, Rome on 16th October 1979.

be one perfect catechist, and that is Christ himself. However, if we're called to be 'fishers of men' then we have a sacramental commitment (by our baptism and confirmation) and duty to accept this role, even if this means committing to it from time to time, according to our own personal circumstances. No potential catechist should consider themselves unworthy since *all* are considered worthy in the eyes of God. He himself appeared to make some unusual, surprising and unexpected leadership choices from among his followers.

Lack of knowledge, of course, can always be improved upon – that so-called learning curve on which catechist, catechised and every one of us embark. Indeed, it's safe to say that love, caring, understanding and of course, faith are the leading requirements for the catechetical role, while Church doctrine, although important, may need to follow later. Essentially, doctrine is a taught experience, something which every one of us is capable of absorbing, understanding, recalling and subsequently adopting as a lived experience. Undeniably, although there are times when most of us have to provide patience, consideration and understanding for others, love, caring, respect, empathy, sympathy and gentleness are not qualities that can be learned from a resource, or any guidebook. They are attributes which we, as humans, and as potential catechists and evangelists, receive as a gift from God. We as Christians, that is followers and *practitioners* of the teachings of Christ, learn from him how to use them as building blocks to improve our own natures and achieve holiness and the prize of everlasting life. If we're to follow that model and supreme catechist and become 'fishers of men', we must then surely share these gifts for the benefit of others in our everyday lives and bring new souls to our Father in heaven.

# ~ *Chapter Four* ~
## To Be or Not to Be Reconciled?

*'Lord how often must I forgive my brother if he wrongs me?*
*As often as seven times?' Jesus answered, 'Not seven, I tell you,*
*but seventy-seven times.'* [56]

J esus' reply to Peter's question is perhaps as astonishing and thought provoking for us today as it must
have been for Peter at the time. Peter, disciple and
companion to Jesus and fully aware of some of the

---

[56] *Matthew* 18: 21 - 22.

teachings of Jesus, was therefore definitely on the right track when he asked about forgiveness. It was not by accident that he used the number seven to try and fix a level of forgiveness for his 'brother', but in so doing he was already clearly aware of the priority which reconciliation must take in his life and in others too.

Both during the lifetime of Jesus Christ, and indeed before this, as evidenced in the Old Testament, numerology was held in high esteem. The number seven was believed to be a significantly 'perfect' number representing wholeness or holiness, perfection and completion. It symbolized God's great perfection, and indeed we're told that God created the world in seven days; the seven day week ensues as a result of this, and the seventh day should be sacred and a day of rest and reflection, as directed by God himself. So the number seven was seen to add weight to any discussion.

Therefore, when Peter considers forgiving his brother seven times this would have represented to him a reasonable number for complete reconciliation. Yet, Jesus's response to this explains that seven times falls far short of the response Peter must make. He must forgive seventy-seven times – in other words he must forgive again and again and again. In fact, he must do whatever it takes to reach that perfect pinnacle of forgiveness to which we must all aspire.

In terms of today's society, this still represents an equally huge expectation, which we, like Peter, are expected to fulfil, because the advice, lessons, parables and teachings of Jesus which are given in the Gospels are just as relevant to each and every one of us today. So, how do we fulfil this expectation? Generally speaking we're aware of the need to forgive, but in practical terms how do we accomplish this momentous task of forgiving repeatedly, and what help is there for us to achieve this?

## *The Tools of the Trade*

When we've been hurt by another person various emotions come into play. These are usually pain, distress and anger. Unfortunately, when we become angry with someone else it makes it harder to forgive them. Certainly some time is needed to let our emotions settle and subside; to allow us to review the situation in a more objective manner, and for our anger to abate. The amount of time this can take varies, depending upon factors such as our own personality, the cause of our hurt and distress and very often how much we like or even love the person who has caused us this pain. Of course these things influence how easily or how difficult it is to make amends with that other person.

From my own experience, I am acutely aware that when the hurt goes very deep, forgiving someone can be incredibly difficult to do, even though I know this should be done. We all come to reconciliation at different times and in different ways. Luckily, there are ways and means which help us not only to try and achieve this 'mission impossible', but which also give us food for thought about our actions and interactions with others. This in itself will be for many of us a valuable life experience. However, these words and actions could, by no means, be described as fool-proof procedures, but we're foolish if we don't try them because, after all, they are from the teachings of Christ himself.

To start with, it's important to be sensitive to the other person's situation or state of mind. Anyone who's unduly troubled or anxious is much more likely to be 'on a short fuse' and when 'wound up' will give vent to their anger, distress and hurt without restraint. It's worth emphasizing that none of us are ever fully aware of what the other person is experiencing in their life at that moment. Indeed, how can we know what takes place 'behind closed doors'? Of course, it's equally true to say that this may not be the case at all and that someone could be completely unjustified in hurting another person. Even so, it's the right and proper course of action to try and look at their point of view first of all, no matter how challenging this may be.

When we've been hurt – in whatever way – we naturally have a tendency to feel indignant. In spite of this we need to carefully consider our *own* actions, faults and failings. By doing this we're able to review the situation in a somewhat different light and 'think before we react'. The result of this is quite simple: the injury that we've suffered will not have undergone any change. However, various questions such as: "Have I ever said or done something like that to anyone in my past?" will soon spring to mind. It's really most surprising how often we find that we've committed that self-same offence at some time, and expected to be forgiven for it. Not only that, but we probably need to replay the scene in our own mind, including asking ourselves further questions such as: "Was I really blameless in all this?" and "Should I have really said that?" I firmly believe that in any argument no-one is ever completely innocent and no-one is ever completely guilty either. Wherever there is conflict, both parties often carry some share of the blame. It may even be as heavily weighted against one person as ninety per cent to ten per cent, but even ten per cent of blame holds some significance in these circumstances. Once we do begin to bear in mind our own shortcomings – those which have led us into trouble in the past and those which have contributed to the present situation, we will instantly find it so much easier to forgive.

Finally, and most importantly, prayer is of vital importance in our quest to be able to forgive others, and equally essentially, for them to forgive us. Our on-going prayer – it's even an integral part of the 'Our Father' - should be to appeal to the Lord to grant us help in seeking forgiveness. Our own private prayer should automatically include this petition, because without doubt, we need as much divine help with this difficult task as we can possibly get! Not that God is unaware of this human need. He understands and realizes that for frail and weak humans we may try to imitate our Lord Jesus Christ who could forgive everyone, but we often fail despite having the best of intentions. Prayer is, of course, particularly crucial when we're caught up in a situation where forgiveness is called for. And this prayer shouldn't only be for ourselves, but also for that other person who we need to forgive. If our prayer is made with genuine charity then with God's grace that other person will be empowered to understand what went wrong in their relationship with us. Furthermore, they will be granted the grace to admit fault themselves and to accept an apology from us. Although difficult, the prayer should also include an appeal to God for that person to be happier, closer to God and critically for God's help in preventing them from committing the same offence again. This type of prayer for someone who has hurt and wounded us is very hard to do, but if we can manage it, then surely are we not more than half way towards complete reconciliation already?

### *Poison for the Soul*

I was fascinated to hear an expression which related to being unable to forgive someone. The expression claimed that it was 'like drinking poison and hoping the other person would die.' This struck me as being particularly profound. After my husband and I started running our own hotel, we found ourselves in competition with the neighbouring establishment. Sadly, the owners of this hotel seemed to regard this competition as a personal vendetta, and one which had no limits or end. I very quickly realized that I was becoming obsessed by our highly competitive rivals and a game of one-upmanship was soon under way. The game went something like this. We had new lighting; they had new lighting. We advertised in a tourist guide;

they did likewise. They had new outside signs; we had to follow suit.

In itself this would have been harmful enough, but intense dislike can so quickly get out of hand. During the course of a typical day, when I was peering out of one of my windows to 'see what they were up to' at the hotel next door, my mother who was visiting at the time, seemed to be studying me. She made an observation that thankfully brought me to my senses and restored my equilibrium, to say nothing of my sanity. She observed that, "I had let those people not only get under my skin, but allowed them to get into my head." My first thoughts on hearing her say this was 'not only into my head but into my heart and my soul.' In effect I was drinking the poison and waiting for them to die. All the anger and all the pent-up emotions that I had been generating were not hurting our rivals. They were probably quite unaware of what I was thinking and feeling, but it was hurting and destroying me.

Luckily, I heeded my mother's wise words, which had come not a moment too soon, and that day marked a turning-point and a change of attitude on my behalf. But looking back, I was appalled by how easily I had fallen prey to this state of mind and I have never forgotten what occurred and how I felt at the time. Nor do I actually want to forget; it helps to keep me balanced if and when things go awry with those I encounter in day-to-day life.

In fact we all have the capacity to poison our own minds this easily. Many of us find it very simple to demonise a person who has hurt us and completely lose sight of the context in which the initial problem arose. Suddenly, there's a shift in our perception of the other person. Instead of someone with whom we could rub along with, but who had injured us in some way, they had, in our minds, quickly developed into a monster for which no sin was too big or too bad for them to commit! It appears, in fact, to be all too easy for humans to make this massive leap in judgement.

Our minds, hearts and souls are delicately and finely tuned and can easily be stained, tarnished or harmed. We so often say a hurtful word, or gossip, or jump to a wrong conclusion, which can be so destructive, both to the person concerned and likewise to ourselves. I have been trying to control my dreadful temper for all of my adult life, and to a certain extent I have succeeded. However, usually without any adequate warning, it erupts and the consequence of this can often be harmful, in that another person can be wounded in my verbal attack. And there are yet further consequences to this action. I too feel damaged by that onslaught, in that I feel defiled and dirtied because I have cast the shadow of someone else's pain onto myself. In a way this is even more painful because I have myself, been the cause of this. Although there is some benefit. This painful awareness definitely helps me to seek reconciliation with that person, even though this is by no means as simple as it sounds, as so much depends upon their response and why I was angry in the first place. What I can be sure of though, is that I am never comfortable with feeling that I have contaminated my innermost being; that which is closest to the Lord – my soul.

### *Change of Attitude, Change of Heart*

In their book 'Finding Forgiveness', *Stephanie Thornton* and *Jim McManus* point out that when we forgive we're transformed:

> 'In forgiving, we undergo a benevolent change in our attitudes and intentions towards our enemies and transgressors, a change that involves a willingness to let go of resentment and grievance and revenge.' [57]

---

[57] *Finding Forgiveness* – Jim McManus & Stephanie Thornton, p. 56.

Although I totally agree with this statement, I would however, like to take it one step further. In actual fact, it's quite possible to be transformed; to change our attitude, *before* we even reach the point where we're in the position of having to ask someone for forgiveness; that point where we want and need to forgive them.

We all at times encounter people that we don't particularly get on with, have nothing in common with, or even dislike more or less straightaway. This is probably due to the fact that we're all unique individuals, and therefore, although not desirable, not at all unusual. However, those first impressions can remain unaltered in our minds as Matthew McKay explains:

'Inaccurate first impressions often go uncorrected. Research indicates that roughly two-thirds of your first impression of another person will remain unchanged after months of regular interaction. In short, you are likely to freeze your first impression of a person with only minor modifications.'[58]

Conversely, I have heard that nearly always when we meet new people, a third like us straight away;

[58] *Messages – The Communication Skills Book –* Matthew McKay.

a third are neutral and a third actually dislike us for no apparent reason. These 'inaccurate first impressions' can probably give us problems in dealing with others and unfortunately I found myself facing this difficulty some time ago. A new couple started attending my parish church and my first impressions of them were certainly not favourable. In fact, I became rapidly aware that there were various aspects about them which quite simply irritated me. At this point I would like to state unequivocally that this was probably due to my own intolerant attitude. However, be that as it may, relations appeared to be always strained if I found myself in their company. The situation continued in this vein until a confrontation arose between them and my husband and I. It would be irrelevant at this point to go into detail over the subject of the argument, but what is relevant is that the situation had now reached crisis point. Thankfully the dispute itself was short-lived, but for some time afterwards both parties stubbornly refused to acknowledge each other.

How long this ridiculous stand-off would have continued for I really can't hazard a guess, but circumstances changed remarkably quickly and easily as the result of one small incident. Shopping in town one day, I was about to enter a shop when I realized that Sonia – the woman in question, was already inside and looking around. The shop was small. Once inside it would have been impossible to avoid each other. At this point I was faced with a dilemma. Basically, I had three choices of action to choose from: I could either walk on and therefore not go in the shop at all, I could enter the shop and in close proximity refuse to acknowledge Sonia, or go in and speak to Sonia, and possibly run the risk of a rebuff.

Very much to my surprise, I quickly reached a decision and without giving myself any time to change my mind, I walked in, said hello, and asked Sonia how she was. She may have been surprised – she certainly appeared to be, but she answered pleasantly enough, and after this incident thankfully hostilities ceased.

This whole episode had made a huge impact upon me. I gradually began to realize that the problems had begun way before the argument had taken place, which was really the climax to the situation and not the cause of it. My own contribution was my irritation and dislike of Sonia and her husband, which had begun some time ago. In retrospect, I became aware that had I managed to keep this under control it would have really helped the situation.

As an 'add-on': after a while Sonia and her husband moved away and left the parish community. I didn't encounter either of them for some years until I took a job and found to my surprise that Sonia was already employed there. Although slightly hesitant – because, after all, we did have 'history' – I was able to chat with her in a fairly relaxed manner and to my delight we became very friendly work colleagues. I was so thankful that I had been able to put our situation on a correct footing some years earlier and that Sonia had responded so well. It could have been deeply distressing to have been in a situation of tense anxiety due to a situation of un-forgiveness while starting a new job. I had God to thank for his loving providence in this matter.

Subsequently, there have been occasions when others have annoyed or irritated me, especially as tolerance is most definitely not one of my strong points! However, since the incident I have described, I do now try to 'think myself into a different state of mind.' In other words, I try to tell myself that I *don't* necessarily dislike someone, they are *not* annoying me, and to try to remember some incident, pleasantry, or nice comment they've previously made.

The effect of these thought processes are fairly astounding. Without any exaggeration, the irritation, anxiety and stress appears to roll away like a troublesome burden, and the feeling of liberation is enormous. The sense of well-being is remarkable. For followers of Jesus Christ it's certainly not difficult to assume that this happiness and well-being is a natural by-product of trying to obey God's will, and that God will be rejoicing with us, and for us, because we've managed to successfully accomplish this.

## *The Problem of Covetousness*

Lack of forgiveness can be caused by any number of reasons. But one primary motive for this appears to be that many people are unable to forgive others for being in possession of things which they themselves are unable to have. Unfortunately the list of things to be coveted by others can be fairly exhaustive. People can even be disliked on first acquaintance because they are more beautiful, handsome or attractive than we ourselves are. We live in a society, moreover, which appears to place an ever greater importance on material possessions. Our status symbols have become the property we own, the car we drive, the amount and type of holidays we take each year and the way our homes are furnished. Our status symbols have become, for many of us, a way of life. Even our clothes and accessories are often judged, criticized, and sometimes found inadequate, especially among the younger generation.

Sadly, it's often the case that bad feeling and un-forgiveness are created in schools by pupils who don't possess, for example, a pair of trainers with the correct label and this can also be accompanied by peer pressure and bullying. There can be little doubt, in fact, that materialism has become a 'God' for this age, and this God, like all Gods, has to be worshipped. However, in the worshipping of this false God, people invariably become hurt.

When God gave Moses the Ten Commandments, it was with very good reason that he included the tenth commandment: 'You shall not covet your neighbour's house. You shall not covet your neighbour's wife, or his servant, man or woman, or his ox, or his donkey, or anything that is his.'

Becoming obsessed by another person's possessions can never be desirable, but in this commandment God was trying to help us to understand that when this does occur it could only lead to greed, envy, dislike and unforgiveness. It's a sobering thought that we might desire something to such an extent, that we're unable to forgive another human being for possessing it.

## *Peace Be With You*

Transformative peace can be brought about by forgiveness. Likewise, happiness and peace can be achieved when we're able to think positively about other people and not allow ourselves to get into a downward spiral of dislike and discord. Yet for many of us this type of peace frequently eludes us. When we go to Mass or a church service, we come before Jesus Christ just as we are, with all our positive attributes and all our imperfections and failings. We know that Jesus, of course, is already aware of these as he knows that 'all my thoughts lie open to your gaze' and 'before a word is on my tongue you have known it's meaning through and through.'[59] However, although Jesus may know us both inside and out, he still asks that we try to follow his teachings.

Before we receive Holy Communion, the Body and Blood of Jesus Christ, we're asked to give a sign of peace to those around us. However, if one of those around us has caused us hurt, pain or misery and we've not been reconciled to them, and they to us, how do we

---

[59] *Psalm* 139.

make the sign of peace with them at this point in the Mass? Jesus was quite specific in his instruction on this point when he said that:

> 'If you are bringing your offering to the altar and there remember that your brother has something against you, leave your offering there before the altar, go and be reconciled with your brother first, and then come back and present your offering.' [60]

To refuse to offer the sign of peace to another person at this stage of Mass is unthinkable. To ignore someone's outstretched hand and their words wishing us peace is similarly out of the question. There are, of course, certain precautions which could be taken. An avoidance strategy of sitting in a different position to anyone you are currently not on good terms with, while hoping that they might do the same, is a solution of sorts. Yet it's patently obvious that if we go down this route we're most definitely not carrying out that instruction Jesus gave us in St Matthew's Gospel, about leaving our offering and being reconciled with our brother. Moreover, surely we should naturally baulk at such a course of action when we come to church? So, in view of this we may find ourselves being offered the sign of peace by the last person we would want to

---

[60] *Matthew* 5: 23 - 25.

receive it from. So, if we make the required response, "Peace be with you" but we don't mean it in our hearts, then we're basically hypocrites or liars. So it seems that the only way to deal with this circumstance is to give the sign of peace *and to mean it*.

We really need to be able to have reached the stage where we can forgive someone, before we reach the sign of peace. In so doing we can then regard this as a fresh start in our relationship with that person, and gladly take the opportunity to move on and be at peace with them, with God and with ourselves. Ideally, we should long for peace and seek it at all times, and also remember that peace and forgiveness go hand-in-hand. After all, if we believe in Jesus, how can we not believe that what he instructed and taught us really works – and works so well for us, too?

## The Taint of Hypocrisy

In the same way that proclaiming 'Peace be with you' and not truly meaning it could be deemed an act of hypocrisy, so would apologizing and not having a genuine intent when this was said. Although it may appear somewhat cynical, I do sometimes wonder how many people say they are sorry to someone because they feel it's considered the right course of action, but deep down they are possibly not really repentant, or at least not as sorry as they should be. As we know, Jesus gave us an extraordinarily difficult task when he asked us to be reconciled to one another. However, we can certainly be in danger, especially in 'church circles' of making the correct gesture without the true intent to accompany it.

Jesus himself was intensely derogatory towards hypocrites, [61] and indeed sometimes used the term without restraint when he expressed his frustration towards those who appeared to follow the Law, and yet were spiritually far removed from the way of life that God asked them to follow. The *Catechism of the Catholic Church* therefore places the highest degree of importance on honesty and integrity when it states that:

> 'Truth or truthfulness is the virtue which consists in showing oneself true in deeds and truthful in words and guarding against duplicity, dissimilation and hypocrisy.' [62]

When we bear this in mind we should become ever more convinced that we're always in need of the grace of God to enable and empower us to be true to

---

[61] *Matthew* 23: 13 - 32.
[62] *Catechism of the Catholic Church,* Paragraph 2505.

ourselves and to others. *Bona fide* forgiveness should spring from the heart and soul – an authentic desire to seek forgiveness from someone, not just a role to be played out in an attempt to impress others. In addition, we need to remember that when someone is gracious enough to ask for our pardon and forgiveness, we should not only express our acceptance of their apology, but make every effort to mean it in our hearts. As a rule of thumb, the greater the grievance that has been inflicted upon us, the more taxing it is to be genuinely reconciled to that person. However, unless we've sincerely forgiven them, our words in response to their apology will be empty and meaningless, and we will be at risk from the taint of hypocrisy.

St Augustine reminds us that:

> 'There are many kinds of alms the giving of which helps us to obtain pardon for our sins: but none is greater than that by which we forgive from our heart a sin that someone has committed against us.' [63]

Ultimately we should consider this: By God's grace, if we open our hearts, we're able to forgive. *But only because we ourselves have been forgiven.* This is why so

---

[63] *St Augustine* (354 – 430), Bishop of Hippo and Doctor of the Church.

many of us rely on the great gift of the Sacrament of Reconciliation (Confession). Because sometimes we can only forgive ourselves and others with the help of God.

## *Reconciled to the Father*

A novel I read some years ago had a moving storyline of a man who was struggling with an extreme trauma during one stage of his life. I am sure many of us can perhaps identify with his desperate prayers asking God for help and guidance and his subsequent frustration when that help and guidance didn't appear to be forthcoming. When in prayer one day, kneeling before his crucifix which hung on his wall, and most definitely having reached the end of his tether, he cried out in anguish to Christ on the Cross: "Don't just hang there – do something!" To be honest, when I first read these words I was slightly shocked as I felt they seemed a bit blasphemous.

However, I later became aware of a whole new depth of meaning that lay behind this simple cry of pain. Its superficial meaning, of course, is abundantly clear: he was awaiting an affirmative action from Christ to solve his problems. At that moment he was not impressed with a God who hung and suffered and who yet appeared deaf to his cries for help. And yet the very action of Christ's hanging on the Cross was doing more than anyone had ever done, before or since, for the human race:

> 'Redemption refers to the penalty or price for our sin being paid for us by Jesus's sacrifice on the Cross... Let's put it simply: Jesus death on the Cross has paid the penalty for our sin. He rose again and is alive today, so through repentance and faith in him we can receive forgiveness and cleansing from our sin. That means an end to all the consequences of sin – in part now and when Jesus returns...' [64]

In other words, Christ willingly forgave our sins and opened the gates of everlasting life to all. Therefore, who are we to refuse to forgive others, or indeed, refuse to accept their forgiveness? We're called to try to absolve 'the people who have abused, rejected, abandoned, ignored or offended us. It will include the people who falsely accused or betrayed or lied to us. The list of people we need to forgive also include the ones who called us names or made fun of us. Parents who did not protect us or who did not do a very good job of parenting also need to be included on this list. It will

---

[64] *The Fragrance of Jesus* – Patrick Coghlan, p. 13.

include all the people who have misunderstood us or attributed motives to us that were not ours.' [65]

Every single one of these people merits our forgiveness because we merited Christ's. Furthermore, forgiveness is on hand each day for every repentant sinner who gives a promise not to sin again. Some of us, in our human frailty will fail, but providing that we try, we shall continue to be forgiven again and again by God's mercy and grace which is available to all.

Sadly, too few of us take advantage of the wonderful Sacrament of Reconciliation. Perhaps we prefer to be a prisoner of our own hatred so that by not loving our enemies, we need not love ourselves and so remain trapped by a fear of love.

### And not the Least of Which is to Forgive Ourselves

Our God-given human task is to forgive others no matter how difficult and how much pain we've suffered at their hands, and we, in turn, are to accept the forgiveness offered to us by other people. Furthermore we believe and accept that we've all had our sins atoned for by Jesus Christ on the Cross, who continues to provide love and unconditional reconciliation for his

---

[65] *Thy Kingdom Come* – Dee Alei, p. 109.

people every time they sin and are sorry. Therefore, if we accept and encompass this, surely it must also follow that we must forgive ourselves as and when the need arises. Purely and simply – if God can forgive us, then who are we to question this by not forgiving ourselves? I have known people who have become imprisoned in their own guilt, anguish and unforgiving attitude which they aim at themselves. If we allow this to happen it becomes impossible to 'move on' in our thoughts, hearts and lives. We cease to be whole people created in the image and likeness of God, unable to carry out the unique vocation with which God has granted us.

Under these circumstances guilt dominates and colours our lives, and this in turn affects how we perceive others. And if we perceive others in this incorrect way, then we're unable to know them as the people God created them to be. Eventually, our discernment of other people and ourselves can become distorted.

Additionally, how much more difficult is it to forgive others if we cannot even forgive ourselves? How much more difficult is it to love others if we cannot even love ourselves? The answer to that is that although it becomes tremendously challenging, the way of Christ never fails, that is if we follow his teachings with a pure heart. When we attempt to live out the two great commandments of Jesus Christ: [66] to love the Lord our God with essentially every part of us, and to love our neighbour as ourselves, we must realize that to equally forgive ourselves has to be a part of this equation.

By forgiving and loving ourselves and our neighbour – and loving God – we shall always find the true peace of God.

---

[66] *Matthew* 22: 37 - 40.

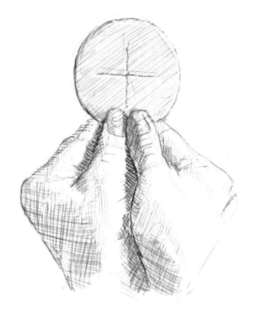

# ~ *Chapter Five* ~

## Church + Faith = Christian?

One of the aspects of our faith that my father and I couldn't agree on was about going to church. He felt that his relationship with God was essentially a private one, so therefore why was there any need for him to go to church? He had, moreover, a strong faith and lived out his life as a Christian to the best of his own ability.

When he sinned, he confessed those sins directly to God, and asked for forgiveness. Therefore, he reasoned, what was the point in attending a service which most people have learnt by rote, and very few actually understand or appreciate? Strangely, despite my own love of the Mass, my regular church attendance and my strong belief in community, I have a little sneaking sympathy for some of my father's opinions. So how do we, the laity, experience the Church in our lives? Each of us differently, I believe.

The liturgy changes in November 2011 in the Catholic Church were considered to be an opportunity for clergy, religious, and especially the laity to invest some much needed time in order to understand the new translations of parts of the Mass. They were definitely, by their very nature, ripe for discussion. They generated renewed interest and gave everyone the opportunity to actually consider and rediscover the full impact of the words which they were saying at every celebration of Mass. So it would appear that my father's initial argument was not unfounded and could even be said to be supported to some extent by the clergy themselves.

He also did not always fully appreciate those who were regular church attendees and were involved in parish ministries, roles and duties. Although he found it easy to make allowances for the frailty of our own human natures, he simply could not understand why we, as laity, should be so committed to spending our own free and precious time assuming various 'church' tasks.

## *Service or Disservice?*

As part of an academic discipline, I recently carried out research regarding lay ministerial duties in parishes, in connection with how roles are initiated and distributed in general. The results of this were interesting. Regardless of those who were already happily engaged in church ministries, it seemed, overwhelmingly, that most of us have to be actually *asked* to undertake them. Indeed, many people seldom volunteer of their own volition. The reasons for this seem significant. Apart from a general feeling of lack of worthiness and knowledge, the greatest excuse by far was a reluctance to 'muscle in on someone else's job or territory' – saying: "Someone might object to the way I'm doing it. They might not like what I'm doing." Alternatively, there was a profound resistance to change: "We've done it this way perfectly well for years," was a frequent comment. Furthermore, this research exposed the fact that we can all become so attached to a role or ministry that it quickly becomes really precious to us.

Personally, I too have shared this experience. And yet we need to be careful how we live out this aspect of our 'church' and Christian lives. One of the first actions of Jesus's public ministry was to gather some disciples around him [67] to help him with his ministry, to form them, teach them, and to enable them to pass on the Gospel message after Christ's ascension. However, there's no evidence of Jesus allotting distinguishing roles. In fact, on the contrary, we find him gently rebuking the mother of Zebedee's sons for making a request that would give James and John an exalted position in his kingdom. [68] Additionally, 'Paul's writings are explicit...' explains Bernier: 'There is a constant stress of sharing, unity and concern for one another.' [69] The Christ that we know and recognize today is a God of equal measure and value, a Messiah who saw the merit in all people, and who by his teaching tried to enable and empower all others to understand and reach his kingdom.

---

[67] *Matthew* 4: 18 - 22.   *Luke* 5: 1 - 11.   *Mark* 1: 16 - 20.

[68] *Matthew* 20: 20 - 23.

[69] *Ministry in the Church* – Paul Bernier, p. 17.

It could, of course, be argued that the pyramid structure of the Catholic Church contributes to lay members becoming attached to their roles and ministries. The historic structure of Bishop, Priest and Deacon lays a firm foundation stone for leadership status within the Church. And why not? After all, there are benefits to be gained from the huge numbers of active, hard-working, generous and conscientious volunteers without whose selfless service our church communities would soon grind to a halt.

In fact, Donald Cozzens points out that the laity, although now granted roles and ministries within the structure of the Church, which in its turn provides the help and support required, still have no 'meaningful voice in shaping decisions that touch directly … in the making of rules or in the exercising of church governance.'[70] The documents of the Second Vatican Council attempt in no small measure to try and equate this balance of power, giving credibility to the importance of lay roles within the Church, and although still a work-in-progress, a measure of advancement has most definitely been made. On the other hand, even though these are without doubt marvellous Church documents, it's an unfortunate fact that lay ministerial

_____

[70] *Faith that Dares to Speak* – Donald Cozzens, p. 82.

roles, which have developed as a consequence of such documents as *Lumen Gentium,* can still be fairly undefined; sometimes leaving lay volunteers overly anxious about their own particular task and what it entails.

## *The 'Extraordinary' Laity*

It's hardly surprising that tension has arisen regarding both lay and clerical roles and how they fit together in today's Church. Despite their declining numbers, and the fact that over fifty years have elapsed since the Second Vatican Council documents were produced, some clergy appear to still have anxiety about the role and leadership status of the lay faithful. Indeed, some Church documents even appear to highlight this tension with the Post-Synodal Apostolic Exhortation on the Formation of Priests in the Circumstances of the Present Day, *Pastores Dabo Vobis*, [71] stating that the 'priest is placed...in the forefront of the church', while on the contrary the Catechism of the Catholic Church states unequivocally that 'lay believers are in the front line of church life.' [72] So it's hardly surprising that confusion regarding roles can arise!

---

[71] *Pastores Dabo Vobis,* March 25th 1992, Paragraph 22.
[72] *Catechism of the Catholic Church,* Paragraph 899.

Furthermore, clerical apprehension is not eased by references such as the one in the Post Synodal Apostolic Exhortation on 'The Vocation and the Mission of the Lay Faithful in the Church and in the World', *Christifideles Laici*, which states when referring to lay ministries within the Church that 'the exercise of such tasks does not make Pastors of the lay faithful'.[73] This statement perhaps underscores niggling doubts which some clergy may have about their own role and position, since the lay faithful were issued with a new directive for their life in the Church, by the Second Vatican Council. It hardly seems worth mentioning that the lay faithful don't normally envisage themselves in a clerical role (and wouldn't wish it either).

A further confusion could lie in the fact that the Church documents quite clearly recognize that the laity, by virtue of their baptism are incorporated into Christ, according to the 'Dogmatic Constitution on the Church,' *Lumen Gentium*,[74] 'and are able to automatically use the gifts which they have received'[75], and yet have, at times, to be especially commissioned by the Church before being able to fulfil certain tasks, such as Extraordinary Ministers of the Eucharist or appointed as

---

[73] *Christifideles Laici,* December 30th 1988, Paragraph 23.
[74] *Lumen Gentium,* Paragraph 31.
[75] *Lumen Gentium,* Paragraph 33.

Readers of the Word. Therefore, when taking these types of tensions into account, it can come as little surprise that misunderstandings and confusion are all too often prevalent in both clergy and laity alike. Yet, if we can put aside the problems caused by our own human failings, we can then appreciate that the Church is in fact a wonderful institution in which we're all called to be active participants.

### *Hear the Word of God*

So once we've sorted out how we should function as 'church', we surely need to know our faith and live our faith so we can go out and share our faith too. In both the Liturgy of the Word, and the Liturgy of the Eucharist, Christ is present with his people. In fact Christ is always present in his Church. The Liturgy of the Word which historically was virtually overlooked for many years has now been granted its due reverence. For it is, after all, God speaking to us through Holy Scripture and the simplest way to learn and know your faith. I feel sure that there must be many people, like myself, who have listened to the readings at Mass, and most especially the Gospel, and have marvelled at how a particular piece of scripture appeared to be directed towards them and especially at that particular moment in their lives; whether it be connected with joy, sadness, or trauma.

This never fails to amaze me and to re-affirm my faith in the Lord. I remember most particularly one Sunday morning when my father had died in the early hours.. I went to Mass later that same morning full of grief and desperately fighting to retain my composure. The entrance hymn was 'I am the bread of life' with the refrain of 'I will raise you up on the last day', and the entire theme of the liturgy for that particular Sunday was being raised to new life after earthly death.

I remember feeling distinctly dumbfounded, but at the same time incredibly comforted. My daughter turned to me and whispered "God is telling us, Mum, that we have believed in him, and he in turn is keeping faith with us. Granddad has been raised to eternal life." I don't think I will ever forget those words.

The best way to know our faith is to hear the word of God. Moreover, one of the marvels of Scripture is the way that it can be discovered and then re-discovered over and over again. It resembles the peeling of an onion: as one layer is peeled away, it's followed by another and another and another... and every time there's the discovery of something new and exciting and thought-provoking that we've not appreciated before. This is, in itself, surely nothing less than astonishing. Even some very well-known passages can still offer a new and unexplored dimension, a meaning which we've missed, or a subtlety which had been previously overlooked.

There are, of course, arguments for and against the reading of a written text at Mass while the Word is being proclaimed by the reader. Those in favour of doing so explain that they can concentrate on what is being said more effectively by reading it, to say nothing of the fact that sometimes hearing the reader is not always easy! Those against reading the text claim that it's better to just listen and absorb what is being said without the distraction of having to read at the same time. Personally, I am of the opinion that it really doesn't matter which method is chosen as long as that person understands the reading, and more importantly, can hopefully *feel* what God is trying to teach us – what he is all about.

Next we need to live our faith and the most evident way to do this is to receive Holy Communion regularly. In fact, the Liturgy of the Eucharist still remains for all Catholic Christians the sacrament *par excellence*, the source and summit of our Christian faith.

We don't know and we can't explain how bread and wine are transformed into the Body and Blood of our Lord Jesus Christ, but we believe that this happens at every celebration of the Eucharist and that Jesus is made real and present for us each time. Timothy Radcliffe beautifully explains about this great gift that we're given and receive, as follows: 'We come to the altar with empty hands having placed our lives upon the altar. And the one whom we receive has emptied his hands too, entrusting himself into ours.'

For every time we go to the Eucharist, every time we receive Jesus under the species of bread and wine, we bring all of ourselves before him. At the offertory, when the collection is obtained from the congregation, and then solemnly processed to the priest along with the un-consecrated hosts and wine, it's not just these objects which are placed on the altar. It is all of our joys, sorrows, anxieties, hopes, fears and dreams as well – and all part of our living faith. For all of this is poured out to God at this time, and offered up as part of our sacrifice to him, and laid bare before him. And when we consider all this, it's difficult to imagine how we could not wholly desire to attend Mass.

A friend of mine once stated that, 'If we really believe that Jesus is made truly present for us in the

Eucharist, then how could we wish to abstain from it unless we absolutely have to?' In the end, it's really all a question of faith, and certainly 'in order that the liturgy may be able to produce its full effects it is necessary that the faithful come to it with proper dispositions, that their minds be attuned to their voices, and that they cooperate with heavenly grace.'[76]

### *A Mission Shared*

As we receive the gifts of the Word and the Body and Blood of Jesus Christ, we're also offered a further grace from our Lord. As we gather to receive these riches, we gather together as one people, as one community, to praise and worship, and we're united in our faith and love of the Lord. Every parish community has its ups and downs, but as Jesus gathered his disciples around him, so we too gather in the same way. We try to overcome our failures and dislikes, and we try to genuinely understand one another, and accept this challenge for exactly what it is – a challenge. The hierarchical structure of the Catholic Church will remain with us for the foreseeable future, after all it is apostolic and episcopal by its very nature – like it or not. We also cannot help but be aware that Church and faith are sometimes put into two separate 'boxes' by

---

[76] *Sacrosanctum Concilium,* Paragraph 11.

some of the faithful, and we may have some appreciation of the reasoning behind this. Theism – or – faith is, on the one hand, that personal and private belief that we carry with us at all times, which involves our own innermost thoughts, prayers and love of the Trinity. Church, on the other hand, should represent each and every one of those who are bound together by their faith belief.

However, for some 'church' can actually represent the bricks and mortar edifice which they attend on a weekly basis; that place where they receive the Sacraments. Yet, whatever our own feelings on this matter, it remains an inescapable fact that Jesus's own ministry was not undertaken in a solitary manner. Moreover, it was perfectly apparent that as we are gathered by him each time we attend Mass, so too are we sent out in the same way – to share our faith and spread the message of the Gospel by our words and actions. In the closing rites of the Mass, it is explicitly emphasized that we must:

'Go and announce the Gospel of the Lord' or 'Go in peace, glorifying the Lord by your life.' This urges and commissions each of us to go out into the marketplace to make a difference both to our own and other people's lives.

I would, nevertheless, question whether our 'sending' is as effective as our 'gathering'. Some of the lay faithful may appear to be attending Mass out of a sense of duty, obligation or habit, but they are, at least, still gathered together in church – with one another – as part of their community. But whether or not they realize the full extent of Christ's directive, to be sent out to be witnesses to their Christian faith beliefs, remains to be seen. For Christ did actually leave us with a most difficult mission to follow at times. After my own reception into the Catholic Church I have become more and more aware of this. In my whole life, in my dealings with others, nothing appears simple and straightforward any more. The days when I could say something hurtful, lose my temper, or tell a lie without being overly concerned, are now long gone. Nowadays I usually feel guilty and ashamed as a result, if this occurs. I have often thought that it seems as if once you have 'let God into your heart and soul' then everything changes forever and you alongside it. I assume this to be a symptom of conversion!

This sending out into the world has an intrinsic value and importance that cannot be underrated. For unless we go out and try to overtly live out our Christian faith, we're plainly only attempting a part of the commission that was given to us by our Lord Jesus

Christ. When we come to church we come as fragile beings who sin despite our best efforts. I often hear people say, "I don't go to church because I do too many things wrong in my life!" However, Christ does not gather, or even attempt to gather, the righteous around him, but those who have imperfections and are in need of his healing help and forgiveness. In fact, Christ gave an assurance of this when he explained that:

> 'I have not come to call the virtuous, but
> sinners to repentance.'[77]

Thus, every time we gather together and receive Christ in the Eucharist we're both directed and empowered to become more like him in our daily lives.

### *A True Christian needs both Church and Faith*

We can most certainly live out our lives adhering to our Christian beliefs, pursuing our own faith journey, and spending times of reflection and prayer alone with our God. But in following the Christian way – the path illuminated by Christ himself, we also need to gather together as a community (as 'church') in unity with one another by our faith and to praise and worship the living God. Furthermore, each and every one of us needs to be

---

[77] *Luke* 5: 32.

regularly nourished by the Word of the Lord and by his Body and Precious Blood in Holy Communion. In so doing we're following the command to do this as a memorial to the Lord.

And so it is that we consider whether our involvement with 'church' and our faith belief make us into what would be described as Christian. The experience of 'going to church' varies enormously from person to person and a typical congregation can be segmented by factors such as age, status, wealth or lack of it, obligation, indifference, sanctity, health or illness, state of mind, language and others. In fact research has shown that it's indeed a very small percentage of attendees who are there for truly selfless or holy reasons. Therefore we must take into consideration that each and every one of us are different. We were made that way by the Lord and this is a fact that we should accept. Added to which, we're all at different stages on our faith journeys.

Both 'church' and faith are a lived experience – something which we grow into and which grows in us. At some times in our lives our faith may be stronger than at others, depending upon our circumstances and in a similar way we may sometimes find going to church of more help and comfort than at other times.

In essence, both our 'church' participation and our faith are important elements of our life journey. However, the road for a true Christian is clear: to follow Christ's ways in all matters, taking him as our perfect example. Our faith may be rock solid and our church attendance –whatever category of parishioner we may fall into –may be exemplary, but if we ignore the teaching of our Lord and live out our lives dictated by our own desires, we will not truly and fruitfully fulfil the criteria which we label 'Christian'.

On a training day for catechists some years ago, we were all invited to find another person in the room and tell that person one quality about the people who made up our parish. Somewhat to my amusement I was told by the person who approached me that she very often found her fellow parishioners annoying! Those who attend church may well at times be annoying, but we're all still called to come together as 'church' to live out part of our faith journey and ultimately follow Christ's way. This is because, after all, we are the 'Body of Christ'.[78]

---

[78] *Lumen Gentium,* Paragraph 7.

*The Healing Touch*

# ~ *Chapter Six* ~

## The Healing Touch

A beautiful yet simple narrative explained how a young girl – something of a problem child and with special needs, created havoc every time she went to Mass with her family. Despite the exhaustive attempts of her mother, the child appeared to run riot and cause chaos every Sunday without fail. In fact her exploits included 'interrupting the homily with some loud and inappropriate remarks – skipping or tearing around the aisles – holding on to a collection basket, and fighting the usher for it.' After one particularly awful disruption, the priest asked, much to the mother's horror, to have a word with the girl. Against all the odds, the result of this conversation was an invitation for her to become an altar server.

This ministry became, beyond a doubt, her saving grace, as with a role and responsibility to undertake she became transformed – not only into a gracious and efficient altar server, but also an improved individual in her own right – both at home, school and at church. In fact, it would be no exaggeration to say that due to the timely intervention of the priest she had been healed in all the ways that matter most – healed behaviourally, healed in self-confidence, healed in self-worth, healed by empathy and understanding, and most importantly of all, healed with love. [79]

The beauty and essence of the story is quite remarkable from many perspectives. We can admire the insight of the priest as well as his generosity of spirit and his concern for his people. The response of the child is also remarkable, and we can read into this a message for each and every one of us. It would have been all too easy for the priest to have admonished the girl, and possibly her mother, for the appalling behaviour during Mass. Instead, he invites the child to undertake a responsible ministry, which could, let's be honest, have been a total disaster.

So why was it not a disaster? Like many of us, the child needed to be respected, appreciated and thereby healed. I have often heard it said by teachers that very disruptive children are the ones who are having difficulty understanding what is being taught. But when these children have gained some level of comprehension and their self-worth has been restored to some extent, then their behaviour shows a marked improvement. I am almost ashamed to admit to a childhood incident of

---

[79] *Faith Builder* – Hagan, Kane & O'Connell, p. 64.

a similar nature. My most dreaded lesson of the week was mental arithmetic, which was, beyond any doubt, a low point for me. Not only did I find the subject matter challenging, but I seriously suffered when 'marks out of twenty' had to be read out at the end of this agonising test, which allowed my classmates to see my poor performance and my shame.

One particular week I became so anxious at the thought of this ordeal that I pretended to be sick with stomach pains. After some time, the school rang my mother who was at work, and asked her to come and collect me, which she promptly did and brought me home. I was intensely relieved that my torture was to be postponed for a whole week but I felt terribly guilty for my deception. My mother soon became suspicious when she spotted that I wasn't really sick and when she challenged me I decided to be honest. I told her the truth and apologized for my deception. My mother wasn't particularly pleased by the turn of events, although quite sympathetic towards my miserable plight. She said that I should have confided in her sooner, and that difficult situations always have to be faced eventually. More importantly, she went on to say that no matter how badly I did in mental arithmetic she and my father would love me in exactly the same way they always had – unconditionally. And the situation had its benefits. Although my mental maths skills did not improve overnight, my fear, low self-esteem and worry certainly seemed to ease from that moment onwards. In other words I had been healed in love.

Both in the case of the disruptive young girl in the story and in the case of children in classroom situations, there's usually an improvement in their behaviour as they are healed. The healing which takes place is a healing of self-esteem, understanding and confidence.

### *Happy are the Healed*

In the Sermon on the Mount Jesus offers a list of Beatitudes [80] which basically set out the new Christian standards in a series of blessings which are given to the people. Despite controversy as to the origin of the extra Beatitudes in Matthew's version as well as reservations regarding the fourth one in Luke's account, there can be little doubt that they reveal Jesus's total care for his people. They were the basic rules for the salvation of mankind. Of course we understand today that when Jesus Christ died on the Cross he atoned for the whole of humankind and opened the way to eternal life. Yet, Jesus's manifesto of caring in the Beatitudes was a

---

[80] *Matthew* 5: 1 - 12 & *Luke* 6: 20 - 23.

loving act of healing his people. They were healed by his words in a new understanding of the Law of God – Jesus's Law of Love, similarly by means of his miracles, or signs, as John calls them in his Gospel testimony.

We can make a direct comparison between this and the words and actions of today's priest, who is, after all, God's servant and instrument on earth. In imitation of Christ, the priest blesses his people, visits the sick amongst his flock and attempts to heal those in his parish community. All achieved by his words of advice, his love of Christ and neighbour, and the absolution given from God through him, in the Sacrament of Reconciliation. Regarding the priest's healing ministry however, Henri Nouwen explains that:

> 'A minister is not a doctor whose primary task is to take away pain. Rather, he deepens the pain to a level where it can be shared. When someone comes with his loneliness to the minister, he can only expect that his loneliness will be understood and felt... This is because a shared pain is no longer paralyzing but mobilizing.'[81]

In other words, by taking a share of another person's pain, sympathizing with it, empathizing with

---

[81] *The Wounded Healer* – Henri Nouwen, pp. 92-93.

it, listening and becoming a part of it, we're eventually led into one of the first stages of healing help for the individual. What is more, every time a minister celebrates the Mass, the healing of Christ is freely given to every person who receives his Body and Blood in the Eucharist when Christ freely shares his great healing love with all:

'You can mend your broken life, and this broken world, because now, everything is possible. You have, in fact, all my power for compassion at your disposal – you only have to claim it. Heaven on earth lies open before you today, for the taking. But there is one condition – you must dare to believe it.'[82]

### *The Miraculous Christ*

Over and over again we come face to face with Christ the Healer in the Gospels. In every case the physical healing coincides with other forms of healing. It can be easily seen that social acceptance was often achieved as a result of Jesus's healing touch. When Jesus healed the leper, he actually touched him. This was astonishing because leprosy is so contagious and lepers were 'unclean'. Because Jesus so evidently shared the risk of

---

[82] *Prism of Love – God's Colours in Everyday Life –* Daniel O'Leary, p. 90.

disease, he not only healed the man but, as a result, gave him his life back in every possible way. Freed from the disease itself, which also meant a painful death, he was additionally freed from social exclusion from the community and their terrible fear of the disease. He was allowed to move back to his own people, move on with his life, and move nearer to God. Therefore like the girl in the story at the beginning of this chapter, he was socially healed, accepted and made whole again in many senses of the word.[83]

Similarly, in the healing of the crippled woman who had been bent double for many years, her posture was restored by the Lord, and she was able to stand upright again. However, she was also able to look up and forwards again – to move on in her life, to be part of her community and freed from only ever seeing the ground at her feet. She became upright once more – physically, spiritually and socially. As she found freedom from pain and discomfort, so she found both social freedom and spiritual freedom in the Lord.[84] In yet another perfect example of Christ's healing power, the blind man was healed at Bethsaida in two 'stages', which appears to be the exception rather than the rule when Jesus was

---

[83] *Mark* 1: 40 - 45.
[84] *Luke* 13: 10 - 13.

performing his miracles.[85] Patrick Coghlan is quite explicit as to why this occurred:

'Jesus doesn't make a mistake, or lack the power...
In performing this miracle, in the way he does, Jesus
is demonstrating yet more characteristics of the
kingdom; the first is patience and the second is the
progressive nature of God's revelation.'[86]

The blind man, as always, was physically healed. He could see again, and was spiritually healed, although the latter was a gradual spiritual awakening and understanding of the nature of the Lord. What is truly significant about both these and other accounts of Christ's healing are how they relate to each of us in our own lives over two thousand years later. In the miracle of sight restored, there will be those who would agree that age does indeed bring some wisdom and understanding, and often a more mature revelation of the importance of the Lord in our lives. Although we can hardly try to second-guess God, many of us have become more 'attuned' to his presence in later years. We've some appreciation of his ways, in a manner that was not evident when we were younger. This is very

---

[85] Mark 8: 22 - 26.
[86] The Fragrance of Jesus – Glimpsing the kingdom through his miracles, p. 59.

common, but requires us to move from selfishness and 'me first' imperatives and embrace selflessness, as taught by Christ and his Church. This understanding or revelation is very gradual. Our eyes can be slowly opened to the wonder of God, if we allow it, and will never be fully appreciated until the day we stand before him at the end of our time on earth. When Jesus healed the leprous male he actually soiled his hands as he reached out and touched him to affect his cure. How many of us, I wonder, show a comparable tenderness and commitment for those sick or in need?

At a time when AIDS became recognizable as a dreaded killer illness, especially in the Third World countries, and understanding of it was seriously incomplete, the late Princess Diana amazed and shocked the world by touching the hand of an AIDS victim. As a touch, gesture, smile, hug or kiss can generally make so much difference to people, Princess Diana's action was overwhelming in its significance. By that touch of the hand she was clearly showing 'I understand what you are going through. I care about you. I would like to help you. I am not afraid of contracting your sickness. I have socially placed myself alongside you. I have a connection with you.' Although unable to give physical healing to the AIDS victim, Princess Diana's action very closely mimics the actions of Christ. How many of us could have copied those actions, I wonder?

Both the woman in Luke's Gospel who's crippled and bent double and the leper are social outcasts, unwanted and unloved by their community for differing reasons. Jesus often cut through such barriers of social inequality, whether with women, prostitutes, tax collectors, lepers or the poor.

All are valued; all are to be included in the community and in the Kingdom of God. Yet today's society, although becoming ever more multi-cultural and even accepting differing sexual orientations, still has some distance to travel before the call of Jesus to all, whatever their origin, status, sex or condition of their personal lives, is universally accepted and discharged. Based on appearances alone, people are all too frequently shunned and excluded regardless of their individuality.

A friend of mine told me an interesting story in which he made a snap judgement, founded purely on the outward appearance of a fellow traveller when on a train journey to visit us. My friend was suffering from arthritis and had undergone operations for both an ankle and knee replacement. So carrying his luggage was something of an ordeal. Halfway through his journey he had to change trains and was struggling with his bags when he was suddenly approached by a young man offering to help. He would normally have been grateful for the offer, but was put off by the fellow's tattoos and many piercings. My friend thought he may be mugged rather than helped! However, much against his better judgement, he gave his suitcases over to his personal Good Samaritan and hoped for the best. Yet his fears turned out, in the event, to be totally unfounded. The young man, who was in fact courteous and polite, helped with his luggage, and indeed even carried it to the correct onward platform. Afterwards my friend confessed that he felt very ashamed of his judgemental attitude based solely on outward appearances and he clearly realized his mistake. Happily, this in turn led him to consider how he might react in similar situations in future.

Rejection for whatever reason inevitably results in pain, anger and sadness, but acceptance, liking, and even loving, results in inner healing as we, in turn, become imitators and ambassadors for Christ. To put it another way, 'Christ wants to touch and heal our world through us. In our families, in our workplaces, in our neighbourhoods, in our organizations, Christ wants to work through us.

'It is a great responsibility for we have the power to open the way of Christ to others or to shut him out.' [87] We're therefore left with a simple choice: we have the power to heal others in Christ in whatever way we can, or we can turn our back on this saving mission.

### The Time, The Place, The Restoration

As fragile humans all need to be healed in Christ and through Christ if we're to live life to the full. His healing love and power can only work through us and from within us. The finest example of this is, of course, during Mass and I still, on occasion, marvel at this experience. There have, without any doubt, been occasions when I have come to Mass in a state of mind which frankly, has not been ideal. I have come before Christ at the Mass at times annoyed, irritated, angry, sad or just plain 'out of sorts'. There have been times when I have been offended, hurt or annoyed with another person, and there have been times when I have been in church for the Holy Mass but my faith has not been at its best on that morning or day. Yet somehow a minor miracle is wrought within me, without my being aware of it or understanding how it happened. This is a miracle of transformation: in that whatever my state of mind when I entered the church, it seems to gradually

---

[87] *Living Baptism Daily* – Lawrence E. Mick, p. 97.

ebb away during the service. My anger, sadness, irritation or whatever may not be completely removed, but it has been significantly reduced, and I have myself been healed by the gentle peace of Christ through the medium of the Mass.

In a difficult and chaotic world it's surprising how well and how easily we are capable of healing one another. The power of a smile, a kind word or an act of friendliness, make a vast amount of difference to our own well-being and that of others. Warmth as opposed to coolness or even coldness immediately enhances that pleasure. As a catechist in the RCIA programme, warmth, joy and healing are common emotions which I witness at the sessions. The healing there can be experienced by any of those present, whether candidates, members of the community or the catechists themselves. When you hear another person reveal the same emotions, problems or feelings as yourself, it's a strangely healing experience. I've seen an incredible state of unity develop when this occurs.

Being informed, and made aware of another person's struggles in their daily lives, in situations like our own, as well as the daily challenges of our faith which we share, brings a measure of help and consolation in its own right. We may not be able to easily resolve these issues, but the simple sharing of them is both comforting and at times inspiring. Christ encourages us to live as a community, to love one another and to share our trials and tribulations, which in themselves lead to healing and recovery for us all – for you and for me.

Jesus healed physically, spiritually and mentally. Today we may seldom witness the physical miracles such as he wrought, even with the latest advances in medicine. However, it has become a common practice for those with illnesses or who are disabled to visit Lourdes in France which has become a place of pilgrimage, because of a number of 'miraculous' healings. In my own experience I have not yet known anyone to come back from Lourdes physically healed. However, I feel that there can be little doubt that the healing love of Jesus Christ produces healing of a different nature.

I know of a family who went on pilgrimage to Lourdes with their disabled child for whom the parents were his primary carers. By the time they actually embarked on the trip, the parents were burnt out and despairing of ever leading a relatively normal life again. When they returned from the pilgrimage, there can be little doubt that some transformation or healing had definitely taken place. The condition of the child appeared to be unchanged. However, the outlook of the parents was greatly altered. They returned with new hope, tolerance and optimism for the future. Moreover, they were able to cope in their daily task of caring for their child with renewed vigour and hope. A transformative change had taken place within them and this change clearly involved Jesus's healing power.

It makes little difference where or when we experience this incredible miracle or gift from God which we know as healing. The fact is that with open hearts and minds we're able to receive this great offering from our Lord, which as always, is freely given. However, in return, we're urged to pass on this gift of healing to others. We may be unable to heal them physically, but by following Christ's example we can bring about some measure of it during most of the days of our life. It's not difficult or arduous to do so, but a thoughtful action or word can often transform someone's world; who knows? As a consequence it's likely that they will soon be truly looking up, instead of looking down at the ground.

*That Lovin' Feelin'*

# ~ Chapter Seven ~

## Losing that Lovin' Feelin'

Every person, from the time that they reach an age of understanding, experiences an in-built 'search engine' which is permanently set to search for God; in other words a restless yearning for the Lord, which although difficult to explain is nonetheless ever-present and hard to ignore. But there are some people who attempt to ignore this hunger for God by using undesirable methods. Wilfully paying no attention to the call of the Lord and turning their back upon him is an example of this. In some cases however, the restless urging and longing for 'something unspecified' can lead, conversely, to the worship of other less wholesome activities and material things.

Alcohol and drug abuse, the compulsive acquisition of goods and the desire for notoriety could be labelled as being some of the contemporary 'false Gods' which frequently threaten and undermine individuals and society. In the Old Testament, God calls upon us not to worship any other Gods but himself. [88]   However, I must admit, there have been times when I have wondered whether this was an act of supremacy by God, who does, in fact, furthermore go on to say 'I… am a jealous God.' [89] Yet in my heart I believe that God says this because he is aware of the harm which we can inflict upon ourselves if we worship any 'idols' other than the Lord our God. On the very rare occasions that I  have seen some reality television shows, I have been surprised and quite shocked to observe the extent to which some people will publicly prostrate and humiliate themselves for a fleeting few minutes of 'fame', as their addiction to the 'God of stardom' is allowed to flourish.

Undeniably alcohol and drugs have more serious and far-reaching consequences for the person involved. Indeed the result of this can sometimes be a tragic loss of life. Yet in all these distressing examples, the underlying common factor is that no matter how intense the particular addiction is, the longing and searching remains utterly unsatisfied, because the cause of that yearning remains unfulfilled. Essentially, our hearts are restless until they rest in the Lord, [90] and only the Lord

---

[88] *Exodus* 20: 3.

[89] *Exodus* 20: 5.

[90] *St Augustine of Hippo,* Early Church Father and Doctor of the Church.

can completely satisfy our essential need. For those of us who recognize this restless longing as our search for God and acknowledge his open invitation and respond to it, our Christian journey through life will be marked with prayer, vocation, sacrifice, reconciliation, love, sympathy, care of neighbour, evangelization and many other Christian attributes. These attributes won't always naturally occur within us; very often we will have to work diligently to try to attain them. It's an acknowledged fact that the way of Christ is often arduous and, as his true disciples, we can struggle and suffer as we attempt to try to live out our own Christian beliefs. So, if we habitually wrestle and labour with the difficulties and the enormity of the task set before us by Jesus, the question is: does this become even more challenging if our life circumstances change and we encounter disaster, pain and sorrow?

### *Something Beautiful is Dying*

In 1965 the Righteous Brothers had a 'smash hit single' which was number one in the pop charts in both the United Kingdom and the United States of America entitled "You've lost that lovin' feelin'." While the lyrics clearly relate the story of a failing love affair, with one of the partners begging the other to reconsider their actions, rekindle their love and not damage their relationship, I think that the same concepts in this song could equally be applied to how God often feels about his human children. The Righteous Brothers wrote:

'If you would only love me like you used to do.
We had a love, a love, a love you don't find every day;
So don't, don't, don't let it slip away.'

I could easily imagine that these words could express exactly how God feels, when we're angry with him, reject him and turn away from him. For there can be little doubt that when life becomes tough, it can be very easy indeed to blame God for this and banish him from our lives, hearts and minds.

Many years ago I experienced a massive event that changed my life irrevocably and affected me in ways that I could never have visualised. Typically, the incident occurred at a time in my life when I couldn't have been happier. I had been married for about five years and we were both blissfully content in our marital life. We had recently moved to a lovely large Victorian house which we were enjoying renovating and making essentially 'ours'.

To complete our joy we had a beautiful two year old little boy whom we both adored. Out of a clear blue sky disaster struck one cold November afternoon and due to a plumbing fault there was a massive explosion in the house. The consequences were momentous. I suffered a major head injury and burns to both my legs. They were total agony and this meant that, once healed, I had to learn to walk again. However, this was as nothing compared to our little boy's injuries. He had a depressed fracture of the skull and burns to various parts of his body. Any mother will understand how I felt when I looked at my baby. My sadness and pain was overwhelming. I would rather have taken every one of his injuries into my own body. Then there was depression and finally anger that this should have happened at all. Added to which I was constantly seeking to understand exactly *why* this had occurred. Had I committed a sin and was this the punishment which I deserved? Had I made God angry?

Puzzled, bewildered and angry, with my life in tatters around me, I decided that if God could do this to me, or indeed even allow this to happen to me, then I didn't love God and I didn't want him in my life in any way whatsoever. In other words I was finished with the Lord once and for all. To return to the lyrics in the Righteous Brothers song: something beautiful died inside of me at that moment.

But the only problem was that I might have been finished with God but he certainly wasn't finished with me! Or to put it another way: I tried to take God out of me, but I couldn't take me out of God. So what did all this actually amount to? The reality was that for about four years, a time of great pain and suffering I might add, I completely cut myself off from the Lord. Prayer was obviously taboo, thinking about God likewise, and of course, when God tried to communicate with me, he came up against a brick wall or a torrent of rage directly aimed at him. The sad irony of this is that it was a time when I most needed the gentle abiding presence of Christ, to be with me, to comfort me, listen to me and walk with me. I realize now that Christ *was* still with me anyway, sharing my pain and suffering every day of that arduous and painful period of time. A time when we had to help our little boy regain his health and strength.

It would though, without a doubt, have helped me so much to have been able to turn to God if I'd only realized this. I would like to be able to say that eventually I received some sort of divine revelation that brought about a transformation and led to my reconciliation with the Lord. However, the truth of the matter is that one day I simply realized how lonely I felt without God in my life, and equally how much I missed being able to 'talk' to God in prayer, both formal and informal. In short, I simply missed the Lord. Possibly in hindsight, however, this *was* a divine revelation in itself. As I came to this realization, I suddenly felt an overwhelming need to pray; after all, it had been four years since I had last done so.

The situation felt really reminiscent of the circumstances which can occur when a serious argument has taken place. The two people involved can end up by not speaking to each other or acknowledging each other for some time. Eventually when the quarrel is resolved and the people reconciled, there can be such great joy in talking to that person again at last; in the sharing of news and views and the meeting of common ground. This feeling is even more highly accentuated where there is love between the two people concerned. And so it was that I eventually became reconciled with God after this long separation, although of course I was still saddened that I had broken our relationship in the first place.

A realistic subject for one of the great arguments against Christianity is regards pain and suffering. Indeed, the main thrust of the argument is often based along the lines of, "Where is your God when this earthquake/ this tsunami/ this landslide/ this accident/ this illness/ this early death and so on occurred?" This is not an easy question to answer – especially since God is not the real culprit. God has not created the world as a risk-free 'safe zone'. There are all sorts of natural events like eruptions, earthquakes and tsunamis. There are also man-made events due to greed and avarice, climate change, deforestation, landslides, war and pestilence. God is really not to blame in all this. In fact, quite the opposite holds true because God sent his only Son to show us the one and only truly effective way to get from birth to death without problems, trauma, wars and sickness. This is Christ's way of love, the way to 'have life to the full.' [91]

However, this teaching is for *us* to follow, but ironically, we so often don't and then we blunder from mistake to mistake. And so, when we're hurting, we need to remind ourselves that Christ suffered for the sake of all humanity and I have often found it completely mind-boggling that the Lord our God chose to redeem us in a fashion that was guaranteed to cause him maximum pain, rather than by a much easier 'opt out' method. Moreover, if we believe the teaching of our Lord, then our suffering has to have a purpose, with the additional certainty that love for another person will resound until the end of time. Despite any suffering

---

[91] *John* 10: 10.

that we may have endured in our earthly lives, this should help to console and reassure us. And we really do need all the consolation and reassurance on this issue that we can get!

I have also noticed that every moment of pain and suffering is usually followed by an act of consolation of some kind or another. When there's famine, the world sends aid, when there's flooding likewise. Where our personal tragedies prevail, friends and family who are filled with compassion and love draw closer to the one who's suffering, and very often new relationships are forged as a result. This could be said to be a model of 'God drawing us together into one family', as explained by William Barry in his theories on how God reacts to the horrors of our world. [92] As always, God always holds all things in perfect balance.

### *A Lifeline for the Drowning*

Sadly, I turned away and rejected God at a time when my need for him was most acute. My incomprehension, confusion and anger against the Lord were all present at this particular time. However, it will come as no surprise to learn that although some people can react in a similar fashion to the way I did when disaster or

---

[92] *Finding God in all Things* – William A. Barry, p. 58.

tragedy strikes personally; equally there are those who do not. Not only do they react differently, but they also find their faith a great consolation in circumstances such as these. A 'friend of a friend' experienced two cataclysmic disasters in quick succession. Her husband died and then her son was diagnosed as being terminally ill. On receiving the second lot of bad news, she insisted that if her son also died, she would never attend Mass again. Her son, sadly, did indeed die, but far from quitting the Mass, his mother found her faith revitalized, and a new closeness to the Lord came about as a result. This presence of the Lord, which for her became even more significant at a time when she most needed it, guided her, comforted her and brought her new hope for the future.

There's a useful exercise which I have given to a range of people at various times during the course of my work in catechetics. It consists of the drawing of a tracker line from birth to one's current age. People are then invited to fill in their significant life events at the appropriate age on the line, for example, starting school, getting married, commencing work, going to university and others. Not only are the major life events tracked, but also episodes which have a personal significance. These can vary from giving birth, illness, moving house or relocation, to the death of a person they were closely involved with. Those participating in the exercise are then asked to mark on their tracker graph the level of intimacy they felt during those times with the Lord; whether they felt closely bonded or more remote at these significant periods.

Of course, each and every one of us responds in a different way, at a different time and according to different circumstances. But interestingly, results generally indicated a trend of closeness to God both in our times of joy *and of pain*. I strongly believe that there's a critical reason for this. As rational human beings, we're constantly searching to fulfil our own basic needs as Maslow's hypothesis [93] clearly illustrates.

We need to feel comforted, reassured, rescued, loved and wanted at the most primal level. We've a consuming need to feel close to a being that unconditionally loves us, cares for us and will always be there for us – forever. Yet the only being who can fulfil our needs is, without doubt, God.

### *Blessed and Broken*

When we're at our most broken it seems that we're conversely at our most blessed. Our brokenness is an

---

[93] Maslow's hierarchy of needs.

integral part of our lives, a part which is uniquely ours whether we want it to be or not, and we're blessed at this time because Christ shares our brokenness – *every step of the way.* This is why I wept both tears of joy and tears of sorrow when I finally came back to Christ after my 'extended leave of absence' I wept tears of joy to be once more reunited into the life of Christ with all the blessings – mixed and otherwise, that this brings. My tears were also of sadness for the time that I had not only spent apart from him, but also for the realization that he had, in effect, been shut out from sharing in my own brokenness in that loving way which is unique to Christ. This is because he, in his turn, had been broken too.

This sympathetic sharing, participating and understanding by the one who welcomes those who are saddened or in pain, means that we're truly blessed when we receive it. This is a gift to be prized, one which is not to be taken lightly. Yet when we're *in extremis,* how many of us manage to not only recognize this gift, but appreciate it, value it and take comfort from it? Generally, as in my own case, we only come to identify and appreciate this at some point well after the event has taken place – sometimes even years later.

'Our life is full of brokenness – broken relationships, broken promises, broken expectations. How can we live that brokenness without becoming bitter and resentful except by returning again and again to God's faithful presence in our lives? Without this 'place' of return, our journey easily leads us to darkness and despair. But with this safe and solid home, we can keep renewing our faith, and keep trusting that the many setbacks of life move us forward to an always greater bond with the God of the covenant.' [94]

Nouwen's words clearly illuminate a forward path whereby our pain, anger and suffering can be turned around to gain us greater love and intimacy with God. Indeed, one wonders whether we would be able to endure our pain and continue our living, loving relationship with the Lord, without this process. This 'safe and solid home' which we call God welcomes us, comforts us and grieves with us and for us. Our human logic often means that we think of God as someone who can prevent any disaster, unhappiness or pain. And indeed, when we consider the miracles that Christ performed during his time with us, there may be some reasoning for this. Yet conversely, we're not at all sure of

---

[94] *The Heart of Henri Nouwen* – Henri Nouwen, p. 147.

exactly the 'power' Jesus possessed. There can be little doubt of his humanity which was concurrent with his divinity.

The manner of his early death and his own uncertainties before this, especially in the garden of Gethsemane, clearly indicate this. Surely then, it's feasible to believe in a God who will not overtly intervene in our world and yet who is, however, ready to understand, console and love us when we're hurt? It may even be that in our fragile state we become helpless children to be cared for and adored and so we then have an even more special place in the loving heart of God.

We're reminded that Christ spoke clearly of the need for us to be like little children, when he directed his disciples to remember that:

'Unless you change and become like little children you will never enter the kingdom of heaven.' [95]

When my own children are in pain or suffering, then I too become a sharer in that pain. My love for them blossoms and expands to an even greater extent than

---

[95] *Matthew* 18: 3.

that which I normally experience. I am sure that most parents feel the same.

## *United in Pain*

If we can understand that our brokenness – for whatever reason, can actually bring about a desirable state of closeness with God, and not an anger *against* him, then we're making great strides towards strengthening our human bond with his divinity. Surprisingly this is not as impossible as it may seem. We need only recall that Christ is present and dwelling in every single one of us and that Jesus is in the Father and the Father is in the Son also.[96] If we can apply ourselves to the truly mind-boggling idea that we, God the Father and Christ the Son are all uniquely and exquisitely entwined and interlinked, we can then begin to see how our anguish is shared, understood and identified with in a spiritual way.

'*The Shack*', a fictional Christian novel,[97] is about a man trying to come to terms with his grief over his daughter's abduction and murder. He experiences conversations with the Trinity, which give voice to this whole idea of divine empathy – 'you suffer, we suffer'.

---

[96] *John* 14: 11.
[97] *The Shack* – William P. Young.

Although I remain dubious about the theological dynamic of the story, I could not help but be moved by the image of Jesus closely accompanying the abducted child during her horrifying experiences and comforting her as her earthly life ceased. In the story, Young again appears to be reinforcing the view of a God who will not intervene in our lives like a spiritual puppet master, especially since he has given us free will, but will stand by us in our time of need with great tenderness, love and compassion.

And this is not all – our human condition that makes us all too susceptible to pain and sadness is a common denominator between each one of us. In other words, we can become united in our suffering, pain and grief. How many times do we express the opinion that situations can be better understood if we ourselves have experienced them first-hand?   Personally speaking, I know for a fact that I have stated this many times over the years. With suffering the same rule of thumb applies. We're drawn to those who have suffered in a similar way to ourselves. We seek their company because we feel that they will understand 'where we are coming from' and they will sympathize.

Dropping into a local hotel recently for a quick swim and a drink I became engaged in conversation with a lady who was staying there for a week's holiday. She was on a coach holiday with other ladies who were in the same situation as herself – they were all widows. It's no coincidence that holiday companies run these kinds of 'experiential' holidays. They understand the need of people who have shared the same sort of painful experiences to be together, as they share a common bond. They can support one another through their mutual awareness of certain situations. And so, while we're being comforted by God we're also being comforted by our own 'brothers and sisters'. These two factors are surely our great gift from God, but when we're in the eye of the storm of our pain, it can be virtually impossible for us to recognize this truth. Let's also not forget that the greater our love, the greater our pain and that 'where love is, there too is God.'[98]

## Time Well Spent

Since I started writing this work I have been involved in an accident. The general consensus of opinion seems to be amazement that I was not killed nor had life-threatening injuries. In the event I suffered from concussion, multiple bruising, cracked ribs and a broken leg. Certainly this was bad enough. Unsurprisingly I felt

---

[98] *'Ubi caritas et amor, Deus ibi est.'*

quite low in my spirits as I recovered from my injuries. Due to my broken leg I had a considerable amount of enforced inactivity and this was most decidedly not compatible with my personality, which demands 'action' most of the time. Also patience has never been one of my virtues either! I have to admit that my first thoughts were, 'Why has God let a second accident happen to me? Why should I have to suffer again?' I feel that many people would perhaps think along the same lines under these or similar circumstances. However, I quickly realized that enforced inactivity can bestow a huge amount of time for thought and prayer. And thought and prayer appeared to be exactly what I needed at this time.

I had been feeling quite disillusioned and unsettled by some aspects of my life prior to the car accident, and there can be little doubt that I had been giving God far less time in my busy schedule than he deserved. In fact I had slipped into the error of becoming so busy with church and other secular matters, that God – that divine being who deserves our love, worship and attention, had in fact, become neglected, and put on the 'back-burner'. My recovery time however, gave me ample opportunities to review this situation, come to terms with my mistakes, and try to rectify them.

Of course this can't happen overnight. I would even venture to suggest that were it to do so its authenticity could be suspect. And so, I made certain observations at this time. Firstly, despite realizing the importance of prayer and God in our lives, I had still allowed myself to slip back into the 'God on hold' situation which I had experienced earlier in my life. Secondly, I became aware of God's hand in these circumstances in a variety of ways. The love and concern of all my family and friends was completely overwhelming and uplifting. We can recognize the Lord in others when their love, compassion and care are so evident. Probably most interestingly was the fact that my tiredness, disillusionment and confusion with certain aspects of my life were able to be set aside during this time of rehabilitation.

Furthermore, the opportunity to examine, re-examine and formulate some conclusions as to how I had been feeling and what I had been experiencing was not to be wasted. In fact, my serious reflection and prayer on these matters appeared to me to be significant. Indeed, it even occurred to me that Jesus had given me some 'time out' in order to accomplish this very objective. Of even greater importance was the idea of channelling my energies into putting together an onward life plan, which could address my previous issues, yet let God guide me as he saw fit.

I truly believe that the Lord sees our struggles – even if we ourselves don't acknowledge them to him in prayer, and he eventually acts in our best interests. What that act will be, what it will consist of and what the consequences of it will be, no-one can say. What I am convinced of, nonetheless, is that when pain, suffering or disaster strike, we should turn to the Lord with confidence. We shouldn't attempt to extinguish him from our lives, as this is probably the time when our need for him will be greatest. We're given God's unconditional love, a gift which we can keep and nurture until the end of time. Only man himself can allow this to perish. My sincere prayer is that we never let this beautiful gift wither away and die.

# ~ *Chapter Eight* ~

## Denying the Self

Mastery of self, selfishness and self-indulgence is the principal challenge that Jesus demands of every Christian. It's epitomised in the famous story of Sir Philip Sydney [99] who was offered a glass of water when near to death but, pointing to a wounded soldier nearby said, "Let him have it – his necessity is far greater than mine."

---

[99] 1554 – 1586.

Few of us are as good at self-denial as this. But Christ knew that with his help and teachings, each of us can eventually become selfless instead of selfish and put the needs of others before our own.

But why is this so important? Because, to put it simply, it is the key to the creation of God's Kingdom on Earth. A self-less Christian is said to be 'exocentric' rather than 'egocentric'. It is they who display courage, gallantry, charity and a deep love of God's own people. Basically, they're usually the ones who get things done! They are the pioneers, explorers, builders, peace-keepers, lovers of justice and champions of the poor, hungry, sick and oppressed. Just take a look at all the benefits and progress we've gained from such people since Christ came to Earth. That's the real reason we needed Christ so much – without him we couldn't see any way out of our own daily survival and death.

The phrase 'self-denial' can be an evocative term which often conjures up the most dramatic images and can be associated with asceticism. Asceticism was, and is, practised by certain religious groups, including the Desert Fathers, who had an extremely austere lifestyle with only the basic necessities of everyday life. Common misconceptions of self-denial include the impression that it's *only* for those in religious orders;

clergy and religious sisters and brothers. Historically it involved actual bodily self-punishment such as the putting on of sackcloth or a hair-shirt and self-harm. However, nowadays, the reality is quite different. Simply put, one aspect of self-denial can be explained as follows:

'Say 'no' to your desires, and you will discover what your heart really desires'. [100]

So what does this actually mean? Certainly in refusing to give way to our own desires we're left with space for our hearts and souls to feel and yearn for a higher reality than that selfish one which is basically an immature survival instinct. Yet this remains only a small part of the entire picture, because in the rejection of our wants and desires – in our denial of self – we find our characters immeasurably changed for the good in ways we could never have imagined.

### The Lenten Approach

Lent is traditionally the Christian period of time for Christ's followers to put their spiritual 'house' in order by increased reflection and prayer, reconciliation and

[100] *The Impact of God – Soundings from St John of the Cross –* Iain Matthews, p. 44.

charitable good works, commonly referred to as 'prayer, fasting and almsgiving'. These are all praiseworthy spiritual exercises, which ultimately help to bring us closer to God. However, another common practice which often takes place during the Lenten period consists of 'giving something up for Lent'. This is when we deprive ourselves of something that we normally enjoy, such as abstaining from chocolate, smoking, alcohol or coffee, to name but a few.

Yet I question the wisdom and the motive behind these actions. In these examples, the only person who will benefit is the person who's actually renouncing these pleasures. For example, someone who gives up chocolate or cakes will lose weight and save money. The person who gives up cigarettes and alcohol will improve their health and save money and even the person who denies themselves coffee, benefits from cutting down on the amount of caffeine they consume.

In fact, I had a personal experience of giving up coffee for Lent myself a few years ago. I had had a real struggle at this particular Lent to decide exactly what to do without. Thankfully I don't smoke and I had already given up alcohol, cakes and chocolate in previous years. I could have repeated one of these but I felt that I wanted a new challenge. So after much brain-racking, I thought, "I've got it! I'll give up coffee for Lent." Yet this was not the best idea that I had ever had, as I am something of a coffee addict. Apparently I became grumpy, bad-tempered and frazzled as Lent progressed.

To be honest, the giving up of coffee for me was definitely not prayerful or reflective and I was far too preoccupied to think about giving the money I had saved to a worthy cause. I felt fed-up and made everyone around me fed-up too. In fact, on reflection there seemed to be little point to it. So in view of all this, I sometimes wonder how this Lenten discipline helps us. It goes without saying that if money saved was given to a charitable organization, or to someone in need, then this becomes viable, commendable and sustainable. However it's not uncommon to find that those involved in this particular Lenten merry-go-round, overlook donations in their enthusiasm for the actual undertaking and the eventual 'winner' is simply themselves. On the other hand, the intentions of those who subscribe to this yearly ritual are usually well-founded and of course, self-discipline is rarely wasted.

Self-denial reaps untold benefits even if our reasoning can be slightly flawed at times. Typically, when we diet either because we're overweight or for medical reasons, we experience a complex range of feelings, emotions and sensations. Primarily we feel hunger – especially at the beginning of a diet. We can also feel irritable and crave the foods that we most enjoy, but which are usually the ones guaranteed to pile on the pounds. Yet we also experience a sense of well-being and satisfaction in that we have taken an action, albeit an uncomfortable one, towards self-improvement, and this generally yields a noticeable 'feel good' factor. Similarly, when we stop smoking this has much the same effect. Again those unpleasant sensations of withdrawal are counterbalanced by a lightness of mind which derives from this type of discipline. The bottom line is this: in our self-denial we become cleansed in a variety of ways.

### *Self-cleansing – A Revitalizing Experience*

In our denial of those pleasures which we normally seek, we find ourselves transformed, cleansed and revitalized in ways which we had never formerly considered. Firstly, let's examine our own self-image; the view that we have of ourselves. A change in our own self-image and indeed in other people's perceptions of us doesn't occur by chance. Part of the way to true self-denial involves the stark reality of considering ourselves in depth, and being completely honest as we do so. Only by doing this can we really see ourselves as others do: warts and all.

For instance, it would be easy to think of oneself as a generous person when this may not, in fact, be the case. And so we're challenged to take a harsh reality check and deny any false ideas we may have about our best or most impressive attributes. This allows us to see our faults and failings in a more authentic and clearer light, which then allows us to move on to the next stage; that of trying to correct those self-same character flaws. It's unlikely that we can entirely eradicate those personal characteristics, but by denying ourselves the arrogance and conceit of a ridiculous and foolish self-image, we can more easily and permanently control those defects. Iain Matthews carries this argument even further by explaining that an undesirable self-image can almost be harmful for our well-being in our everyday thoughts, words and actions:

'The weariness of an over-demanding self-image,
the claustrophobia of being 'full of oneself'.'[101]

Simply put; the upshot of self-denial of this kind is straightforward. If we can eliminate or even reduce

---

[101] *The Impact of God – Soundings from St John of the Cross –* Iain Matthew, p. 47.

our faults and failings we're far closer to attaining the best version of ourselves that we can possibly be – the version that God intended us to be and to live.

Battling these negative or harmful personality traits is however, not for the faint-hearted. The old adage about leopards and spots contains more than a grain of truth. As humans we are the way we are, and the way we are is not always wholesome or attractive. Yet if we can grapple with these difficult aspects of ourselves, the rewards can far outweigh the discomforts of this inherent conflict.

### *Too Stubborn to Change?*

If we can accept that we need to deny our rosy view of ourselves, so as to recognize our faults, it's only then a short step to ask whether it's our own innate stubbornness which will prevent us from accomplishing this. To make matters even more critical, it may actually be that stubbornness is one of those inferior character traits which we already possess.

But, if we can be strong enough to gain control over our obstinacy, we have then, in effect, been able to deny ourselves the selfish luxury of surrendering to this useless characteristic, which can become an awful hang-up. It can prevent us from admitting that we're wrong. It can lead to arrogance and an unfounded belief that we have to be right. Therefore, we can understand that without this we gain humility and foresight and in so doing we move closer to God.

Many of us have a propensity to nurse a grudge against someone else for all sorts of reasons: possibly an argument, comment or action has brought this about. Sadly, whatever the underlying cause, we sometimes take pleasure in this type of situation. It frequently provides us with something to dwell on, feel sorry for ourselves over, or gives us the satisfaction of 'sticking the knife' into someone else. Yet in spite of this we have to be able to 'let go' of that grudge, forgive them and so deny ourselves the indulgence of such hostile emotions. When we can achieve this the outcome can become truly remarkable.

We've freed ourselves from the trap of anger and resentment and in so doing we move away from sin. We've mastered all these destructive emotions by the simple self-denial of our stubbornness. And we've achieved the freedom of spirit which can only be gained through perseverance, determination and a genuine love of the Lord which makes us long to act as he would have us act, namely to love others as we do ourselves.

Similarly, self-control plays an enormous part in the practice of self-denial and this should be recognized. Negative emotions, thoughts, desires and feelings are however, exceptionally difficult to conquer and to restrain.

Yet by exerting our self-control we can really do this, and in fact, only by controlling these types of desires can our lives become richer, happier and more fulfilled, the better to serve the Lord.

### Self-Abnegation – A Lifelong Practice

As we continue our faith journey, the words from St Patrick's breastplate can be an effective example for us to try to follow:

*Christ be beside me, Christ be before me,*
*Christ be behind me, King of my heart.*
*Christ be within me, Christ be below me,*
*Christ be above me, never to part.*[102]

However, this presents to every practising Christian who has an innermost desire for intimacy with Christ, a challenge and a set of tasks to perform in their

---

[102] A Christian hymn whose lyrics were thought to have been written by St Patrick.

lifetime, in an attempt to move towards 'the kingdom of God.'[103] One of the most common ways in which we should attempt to imitate Christ, is by the act of putting others and their interests before ourselves and our interests. The reason for this is simple: we live for Christ and not for ourselves. To go even further: if we live for Christ then we live for our neighbour and not for ourselves. In short, we must be prepared to deny ourselves in all the ways which matter most, and attempt to give to others in a never ending stream of self-abnegation, which means renouncing a little to gain a lot.

Using St Luke's Gospel as its source, Richard Daly goes on to explain the benefits of this type of self-sacrifice:

'Use what you have to enrich the lives of others and you will soon find your own cup running over with joy.' [104]

This whole idea of giving for the sake of others and then giving again and again and again is by no means a new concept. We can recall Jesus's words to the

---

[103] '....the kingdom of God is close at hand.' *Mark* 1: 15.
[104] *God's Little Book of Calm* – Richard Daly, taken from *Luke* 6: 38.

young man who asked what he must do to attain eternal life:

'If you wish to be perfect, go and sell what you own and give the money to the poor, and you will have treasure in heaven',[105] and indeed Jesus's 'appearance in our midst has made it undeniably clear that changing the human heart and changing human society are not separate tasks, but are as interconnected as the two beams of the Cross.'[106]

Self-denial, in the form of putting our brother or sister before ourselves, follows the law of love that Jesus sets out so clearly for us, but it also corresponds with the concept of self-cleansing. If we give to others by any means, then we will, in turn, experience our own transforming purification of mind and spirit. It really makes no difference whether our giving is at a personal level – to friends or family – or whether it involves the giving to charity in terms of time or money, the result remains the same: not only do we *feel* transformed, but eventually we will *be* transformed.

---

[105] *Matthew* 19: 16 - 22.
[106] *The Wounded Healer* – Henri Nouwen, p. 20.

### *Richer than Gold is the Love of My Lord*

And so it seems that self-denial is not merely one simple straightforward act that's set out in black and white with 'user friendly' rules for all to follow. On the contrary, it is multi-faceted, involves much soul-searching and a strict discipline which can rarely be relaxed. The young man in St Matthew's Gospel who so earnestly desired eternal life with the Lord but who 'went away sad, for he was a man of great wealth' [107] highlights the fact that riches, fame and notoriety don't always enhance our earthly lives and will play no conceivable part in our after-lives. We need only to look at those with celebrity status or abundant wealth, to realize this.

The twentieth and twenty-first centuries have been fairly littered with the tragic deaths of famous personalities who have suffered an appalling end, often due to their own self-destruction. Amy Winehouse, Whitney Houston, Janis Joplin and guitarist Paul Kossoff (from the former 1970's band '*Free*') were all the victims of drug addictions which ultimately cost them their lives, and '*Nirvana*' frontman Kurt Cobain tragically committed suicide. These are merely a few high-profile celebrity examples. The unfortunate truth

---

[107] *Matthew* 19: 16 - 22.

is that there are quite a lot of them whose lives have come to a tragic end by their own lifestyle choices.

And so we can clearly see that all too often we indulge our greed, whims and fancies to satisfy our desires. There are times, in fact, when this is quite overwhelming, and this is when we succumb, often to the detriment of ourselves and those who are nearest and dearest to us. Fame, fortune, and wealth may be a part of the celebrity lifestyle, but sadly happiness is not always a part of the deal. This is, of course, a generalization. Presumably there are many other aspects of the celebs' lives of which the public are completely unaware. Actually, we would do well to remember that such people have their own private lives and these may not always be happy ones despite their abundance of wealth and fame. Certainly we have to wonder why the need for 'artificial' boosts of joy or contentment and escapism – such as drugs – are needed in the first place. What we can observe though, is that for whatever reason, self-denial is absent and drug and alcohol abuse and even death is the sad outcome.

People who suddenly and unexpectedly acquire great wealth are also in grave danger of forgetting the value of self-denial. The National Lottery, football pools and  everlasting competitions, have made the prospect of overnight prosperity a dream which can, for a few, become a reality. Nevertheless, it's not unknown for the dream to turn sour and turn into a nightmare, as the temptation to self-indulge over and over again takes precedence because *this has then become entirely possible.* There are times when every one of us submits to some level of self-indulgence, and indeed, a 'little of what you fancy' can occasionally be wholesome, if we feel that it's genuinely deserved. On the other hand, wholesale self-indulgence often leads to various levels of destruction.

There are those who have won huge amounts of money, received a legacy or had a windfall and yet have become miserable due to begging letters, and whose friends and even family members have become jealous of their good fortune. The disastrous results which have followed have been well documented. There's an enormous problem with the undeserved acquisition of wealth of this type. This is that it leaves no margin for 'the winners' to renounce material gain anymore, and means that the option of self-denial is forever lost. This in turn can lead to all sorts of difficulties. How can we ever 'give something up' as a means of self-sacrifice for a time, if we have so much? Of course the answer to this would be to donate all, or some, of these assets to others who have need of them. Indeed, we're blessed with many rich philanthropists who frequently help others, often demanding anonymity or secrecy. However, I strongly suspect that like the rich young man in St Matthews Gospel, some of those in this position have not yet realized that 'wealth' can be found in so many other ways and this is not always just in monetary gain. For those of us who have the joy of the Gospel message as part of our lives, we know that the greatest riches are to be found in the Lord.

### *Turning the Spotlight on to the Lord*

Most of us spend our lives concentrating on what we need, desire or aspire to and then struggling to satisfy those self-imposed demands. In self-denial the reverse is true and we're freed to spend precious time with the Lord our God. We're all too aware of the demands made upon us by today's society, which generally maintains a frenzied 'rush, rush, rush' outlook, with not a moment to be spared. However, it's not only possible, but truly beneficial to break away from this type of treadmill and I should like to explain why and how this can be done.

If we can deny ourselves some of our more everyday pleasures such as shopping, watching the television, cutting down on the amount of time spent socializing and pursuing hobbies, or even reading a book, this will automatically give us some 'free' time.

There are obvious benefits to this. Firstly, by indulging ourselves less, we shall inevitably feel more wholesome and generally happier with ourselves. Secondly, we can then put this extra time to very good use: we can spend it with the Lord in reflection and prayer. However, I must add that I am by no means averse to enjoying the sort of social and relaxation pleasures which make such a difference to our lives! In practical terms I am simply suggesting that every so often it's good to give up or let go of something which we enjoy, because in so doing we will 'buy' ourselves a little quality time to devote to God.

After careful consideration then, we come to realize that self-denial is a really important part of our Christian living. When we attempt to follow Christ, both our outlook on life and our behaviour should actually change in a way that means that we're attempting to imitate him in every possible way. Unfortunately our own genetic instincts tend to counterbalance this. Indeed, it takes a very strong personality to deny our own character traits, no matter how horrible we think they are. Yet somehow we must try to do this if we're to follow the one who was 'the Way, the Truth and the Life'.[108] If we can deny

---

[108] *John* 14: 6.

ourselves the luxury of surrendering to bad behaviour such as hypocrisy, fault-finding, intolerance, impatience and censoriousness to name but a few, our hearts are spontaneously softened [109] and our outlook transformed.

Even more importantly, when our own deprivation can be turned to the benefit of someone else, then we're truly giving them something extraordinary. However, it's vital that we recognize that self-denial critically involves turning to the Lord and asking for his help with what can seem at first to be an impossible task.

We also must closely follow him and more importantly, do it *for* him. For without Christ's saving help we are nothing and can do nothing. Our life's work should be to live for him who died for us; he who made the greatest act of self-denial of all time.

'We receive Him in the 'inspiration' of secret love, and we give Him to others in the outgoing of our own charity. Our life in Christ is then a life both of receiving and of giving. We receive from God in

---

[109] 'I shall give you a new heart, and put a new spirit in you; I shall remove the heart of stone from your bodies and give you a heart of flesh instead.' *Ezekiel* 36: 26.

the Spirit, and in the same Spirit we return our love to God through our brothers.'[110]

And so, when we consider the notion of self-denial let us try to think about it in a pragmatic and level-headed way. Feel free to give something up for Lent by all means. Fast at this time or any other, and of course on actual Fast Days. Give away some of your income to those in need, both in this country and globally. Even wear a hair shirt if this appeals to you! But above all, remember that self-denial can be at its most effective in its simplest form. Denying ourselves the luxury of submitting to the basest of our feelings and desires can be far harder than giving up something for Lent. In fact when we give in to these it is without doubt an act of self-indulgence and a conscious choice, so managing to subdue these can be a wonderfully cleansing, sinless and refreshing experience. Putting our selfish desires aside and considering our brother and sister in Christ before ourselves is one of the most effective ways of denying the self. And all too often we're only able to achieve any of these by removing those 'blinkers', which prevent us from seeing the 'real us'. When we effectively deny the ego – our false self

---

[110] *New Seeds of Contemplation* p. 162 – Thomas Merton.

who tries to mislead us into doing selfish acts – this is an extremely difficult but rewarding act of self-denial.

In fact, self-denial can easily become a part of our lives and our natural behaviour, welcomed gladly by all. There's so much good work for us to do that's around us all of the time. The problem is that we often just don't realize it. Or we *don't want to realize it*. Yet it can revolutionise our own attitude, both towards ourselves and other people.

Furthermore, when we're able to give up some of life's pleasures – those that are both enjoyable and those that are bad for us – we're then in a far better position to help and support our 'neighbours'.

But even more importantly, we're able to give much more time, care and attention to the Lord. Jesus was the perfect 'suffering servant' [111] and the master of self-denial. May we live by his example.

---

[111] *Isaiah* 53.

# ~ *Chapter Nine* ~
## From Adversity to Positivity

Question: What do we actually mean by adversity? Answer: In essence, an unpleasant or unfavourable event or misfortune of some kind. Subsequent question: Have any of us suffered from this kind of adversity? Answer: Usually, a resounding 'yes'!

So you will know how difficult it is to escape from adversity, especially without help of any kind. When you were hungry, someone fed you; when you were homeless, someone gave you a room. When you were sick, someone healed you and when you are dying, someone will soothe your pain. It is they who do the work of Christ.

In a previous chapter the effects of hardship and disaster upon our spiritual lives was discussed. There was also an acknowledgment that as humans we're fairly divided in our reactions to these situations. Some of us turn to the Lord even more intensely at these difficult times, but others blame God for their misfortunes, and turn away from him at the very point in their lives when he is most needed. I know from personal experience that it's very easy to bemoan our fate – the hand which we have been dealt. I have been guilty of this many times during my lifetime. Yet ultimately we're left with simply two choices: to wallow and drown in our own self-pity, or to pick ourselves up, dust ourselves down and start all over again. A well-known exhortation on this is beautifully summed up by James Finlay as follows: 'We are called upon to live Christ's life. We are called into the desert to meet the demon within. We are called to face God alone in the night of our own solitude. We are called to die with Jesus, in order to live with him. We are asked to lose all, to be emptied out, in order to be filled with the very fullness of God.' [112]

---

[112] *Merton's Palace of Nowhere* – James Finlay, p. 17.

Certainly some of us are able to identify with Finlay as it would seem that this perspective can perhaps help us to understand the nature of our human suffering. Like many people, I have frequently suffered in my own lifetime and every time this occurs I am at pains to understand it, come to terms with it, and reap some benefit from it. Most of all I can usually be found trying to 'second-guess' God's underlying plan. And of course, this can only remain unknown, although St Paul's words to the Romans offer reasoning, reassurance and comfort:

'We know that by turning everything to their good, God co-operates with all those who love him.' [113]

This, of course offers comfort, but the really interesting aspect is how we deal with this kind of adversity and how we can try to transform it into a 'blessing in disguise.'

It's fascinating how, as rational beings, we're so often deeply contrary in our reasoning. When someone has fallen on hard times and is facing misfortune or even disaster, we consistently admire that person if they take a positive attitude, and try to overcome their adversity in any way they can. On the other hand, I think it would

---

[113] *Romans* 8: 28.

be fair to say that in similar circumstances, little sympathy is given by others to a person who complains and mopes and does little to improve their situation. All in all, trying to be positive and taking positive action can be really difficult and tough for many of us. So how can we achieve this?

## *Strength for the Journey*

Sadly, I had to recently attend the funeral of a friend. I think we all realize that despite celebrating a life, this can still be upsetting. However, on this occasion I was struck by the widower's calmness and grace during the event. When we had an opportunity to talk after the service, I asked him how he was coping following his much-loved wife's death. I found his reply deeply moving. He told me: "I'm alright. I'm coping. You see, it's amazing how the Lord gives us strength when we most need it."

At that moment I felt sympathy, affection and a genuine awareness deep within me, that something extremely profound had just been said. I recognized that even in the midst of our adversity God is not only with us, but is strengthening us, even though we may not realize it. I felt very close to God just then.

Turning the most adverse times in our lives into positive experiences can be really tough to achieve, but with God's help, as in all things, it's indeed 'do-able'. As I write this chapter I am still recovering from the car accident which I have already mentioned. My body is healing well but I am, in effect, virtually housebound as I wait for my broken leg to completely mend, to allow me to bear weight upon it so I can walk again. I have good days and bad days, because life can be frustrating as the result of an injury of this type. I can often be irritable, bored and impatient for my complete recovery. It would be so easy to become depressed and immediately after the accident I definitely felt low for a while. However, bearing in mind my watchword for life which is that 'something good comes out of everything', I have had plenty of time to come up with something positive which may come out of this. Consequently, I believe that I have now been given ample opportunity for some much-needed reflection about my life and the direction I would like it to take. Later on, I will have the opportunity to make important decisions. Furthermore, there will be a great deal of quiet time for prayer and reflection with the Lord and I have been given a time to rest – I was very tired before my accident.

A further positive thing is that I have received so many cards, gifts, flowers and visitors, which in itself is a true gift of love and friendship. My own self-knowledge has also increased, in that I now have an empathetic understanding of the huge difficulties that disabled people face on a daily basis. Although my own condition is only temporary, the problems of manoeuvring steps, inclines and uneven surfaces have really been brought home to me. As always, when we experience such a situation personally, we gain a deeper understanding of what it's like for others. Finally, I have been given some 'free' time to continue to write this book!

And so it's possible that we can unearth and discover some positive aspects in the adverse events that we experience. However, it's really important that we bear in mind that the strength for this positive attitude - our desire to remain undaunted - comes from the Lord. For God teaches us and inspires us, encourages us and fortifies us with an unexpected ability to cope, even when we think we're not coping at all! God also sends others to comfort and help us, to aid and support us in our difficulties, to make us laugh and to lend an ear or a caring shoulder for us to cry upon.

In a nutshell, God and his people on earth give us strength for the journey in the way that only they can. In fact, it's the people of God who rescue us from the most challenging adversity and despair when they genuinely, unconditionally and actively obey Christ's command to 'love your neighbour as yourself'.[114] It's their love and love of God which saves us when we cannot save ourselves.

> 'God is always in conscious relationship with each one of us as our creator, our sustainer, dear father or dear mother, our brother, our saviour, the spirit who dwells in our hearts.'[115]

### *Life is Just a Bowl of Cherries*

How often do we stop and think that life is good and precious and we're so blessed and lucky to be alive at all? I would guess that very few of us actually think this unless they hear of someone else's adversity or dilemma. In fact, in these circumstances we've a tendency to reconsider, and to 'put things into perspective'. Ordinarily though, we take our place on this earth very much for granted. We consider it our right to be here, and we don't question it for a moment.

---

[114] *Mark* 12: 31.
[115] *Finding God in all Things* – William A. Barry, p. 14.

This attitude is foolish, as our very lives are a huge gift from our creator and should never be wasted:

> 'We try to live in the real world in which all is gift. Nothing we have would be possible if we had not been created by God out of pure love.' [116]

When we therefore allow our adversity to become dominant and give our negativity free rein, we're not making the most of the incredible gift of our lives. We're not using our lives wisely and deriving as much pleasure from them as possible. Neither are we spreading that pleasure to others or living out our own God-given path or vocation in life.

It may be that some of us have become so adversely affected by life's ups and downs that it has become no longer possible to do this. In fact, it's almost impossible for someone who's clinically depressed to 'pull themselves together' or to adopt a positive attitude without professional help, medication and lots of practical, loving support. However, although it's a struggle for those who try to conquer their adversity, it's definitely a task which they may set themselves. One way of looking at this, would be to say that they owe it to the Lord to try and do this and moreover, they owe it

---

[116] *Finding God in all Things* – William A. Barry, p. 103.

to other people. This arises out of the fact that when we're negative, when we give up trying and wallow in our depression, this has a knock-on effect upon others. And these 'others' are usually our nearest and dearest.

Stephen Pattison in his work on Pastoral Care writes a chapter on the importance of this action. In this chapter he cites this account:

'A psychiatric hospital chaplain had been called to a ward to see a very depressed young woman who had been talking of committing suicide. She was worried about whether, if she took her own life, she would go to hell. He tried to reassure her of God's love and acceptance and eventually prayed with her and blessed her. He was shocked when at the end of the encounter the woman thanked him for coming and said she could now take her life with a clear conscience and no fear. He had completely failed to communicate to her the value of her continuing to live!' [117] There are many interesting points to note in this passage, and certainly Pattison points out the extreme value and gift of our lives and how vitally important it is not to lose sight of this. Depression is, of course, a serious medical condition which shouldn't be taken lightly and often requires medical intervention to treat it.

---

[117] *A Critique of Pastoral Care* – Stephen Pattison, p. 155.

Nonetheless, in this particular instance the woman involved does appear to be more concerned with her own well-being (will she go to heaven or hell?) rather than in the well-being of those she would leave behind and who would then presumably, be grieving for her. Again, no doubt the depression had a huge influence on her thoughts and actions at that time, but the fact remains that if she had placed her trust in God, in whom it appeared she believed, it's possible that she may have been able to turn her life around and make that life count in the way that God intended.

### Pray to God Sailor, but Row for the Shore

I first came across this saying in a children's book many years ago and even as a child I was struck by the perceptiveness of this statement. We make our entreaties to God and we ask for his aid over and over again, in the certain belief that he will supply it. On the other hand we are, I am sure, required to make at least some effort ourselves in resolving our difficulties.

In the frame of a mirror in my bedroom I have a small prayer card which has the following words inscribed upon it:

'Nothing will happen today that you and I cannot handle together.'

This prayer card is, in essence, proclaiming the same message as the 'Pray to God…' quotation. The critical word in my card is the word 'together' and indeed this word opens up our understanding of the essential co-operation required between God and mankind. God is always ready to listen to us, love us and on occasion grant our petitions, but we must be prepared to meet him halfway and contribute our part in it, whatever this may be.

When we become locked into a world where the present joyless situation has become all-consuming, we also become locked into a world of self-pity and incredibly self-pity can actually become addictive. It becomes progressively harder and harder to break out of this frame of mind.

In fact, it seems to captivate us as we feel miserable, misunderstood and alone with this huge burden of negativity. When this mind-set is at its most dominant, we then become unable to participate and co-operate with God in 'rowing for the shore'. And there's more: when adversity has us in its grip and we make little or no effort to overcome it, we become isolated in our misery, cut off from not only other people, but sometimes from God. This exacerbates our downward spiral as we increasingly lose heart and hope and become utterly convinced that there's nothing whatsoever to feel joyful about.

Perhaps most importantly of all; we're unable to contribute by thought, word or action to the well-being of other people, and this in its turn, contributes to blocking our relationship with the Lord. But why feel so bad when we could simply chose to feel better?

Our lives are full of challenges. Turning adversity to positivity is another challenge to be added to an already long list. Every time we make an attempt to co-operate with God and try to fulfil his hope for us, we're also trying to follow his ways; for God is faithful and he has proven in Jesus Christ that he keeps his promises. As weak and fallible human beings, all we can do, therefore, is to mimic Christ, and there's little doubt that we will often fail at times and probably fall far short of our goals.

However, trying to become positive and take constructive action in the face of our adversity is a key element towards living a more fulfilled life, a part of which is quite simply trusting in the Lord. How many times do *you* think God has thrown you a life-line and you've not caught it?

## *I will Give you Rest*

Self-help is of the absolute importance when attempting to transform adversity into positivity; the need for positive, determined thought and action. Conversely there are times when we should appreciate our need for grace and simply trust in the Lord and allow him or others to solve our troubles and hardships. A well-known expression used to describe handing over our worries and traumas to the Lord is to 'offer it up to God'. This can, I know, be much more difficult than it appears. The problem that we often have with this course of action is usually that our trust in the Lord is not as firmly rooted as we would like to believe it to be. If this were the case, we would surrender those anxieties to God, and then never give them another thought, because we would be one hundred per cent sure and confident that he would resolve them. The truth of the matter is that we continue to fret about whatever is troubling us, rather than wholly relying on God. Yet Jesus told us himself that our worries are in safe hands when we give them over to him:

'Come to me, all you who labour and are
overburdened, and I will give you rest. Shoulder my
yoke and learn from me, for I am gentle and humble
in heart, and you will find rest for your souls. Yes, my
yoke is easy and my burden light.' [118]

Alongside this, it's also helpful to remember the
words of St Ignatius of Loyola who said:

'Few souls understand what God would accomplish
in them if they were to abandon themselves
unreservedly to him and if they were to allow his
grace to mould them accordingly.'

While many of us would still feel uncomfortable
with the idea of offering up to God anything which
causes us anxiety or discomfort, there can be little
doubt of the benefits of this. Although some believers
feel that to 'offload' onto God our worries, annoyances
and pain could almost be considered irreverent and
should be dealt with entirely by ourselves. Placing
complete trust in Christ and allowing ourselves to let
his plan for us proceed, can only improve our spiritual
and human lives in the long term. Pope Benedict XVI in
his encyclical letter on Christian Hope, *Spe Salvi,* refers
to this idea of offering up our hardships to the Lord. It

---

[118] *Matthew* 11: 28 - 30.

further asks the question as to whether there are benefits in doing so. He concludes as follows:

> 'What does it mean to offer something up? Those who did so were convinced that they could insert these little annoyances into Christ's great "compassion" so that they somehow became part of the treasury of compassion so greatly needed by the human race. In this way, even the small inconveniences of daily life could acquire meaning and contribute to the economy of good and human love. Maybe we should consider whether it might be judicious to revive this practice ourselves.' [119]

We've been bestowed with human life and life in the Spirit and we've a loving responsibility to make the most of these wonderful and free gifts. All too often we ask ourselves what life is all about and the secular answer to that is that it is indefinable. The Christian response however, is that it's about living our life in Christ, which is also a life of love. What we also know, is that the great life-force of God is part of our lives, and that life is precious and should be treated as such.

Adversity enters the lives of each of us at some point and there are almost certainly those who have

---

[119] *Spe Salvi,* Encyclical Letter on Christian Hope, p. 41.

more adversity to contend with than others. Adversity is never easy to bear, whether we're lucky and only come face-to-face with it on a small scale, or whether our lives are dominated by it. Whichever the case may be, to bring joy to our own existence and those of others, to live life to the full, and to love, care and be compassionate towards others, we must attempt to transform our adversity into positivity.

It's only when we've regained our own strength that we can fulfil our mission to help others find hope and joy in the wonderful life Christ has gained for us. And we should never be discouraged, because our faith in God will give us the strength to achieve this – for ourselves and for others – as the words of St Peter tell us: 'Reverence the Lord Christ in your hearts, and always have your answer ready for people who ask you the reason for the hope that you all have.' [120]

---

[120] 1 *Peter* 3:15 - 16.

# ~ *Chapter Ten* ~
## All Things Bright and Beautiful

We often hear the word 'beauty' but many of us don't realize that we've actually done so. Traditional expressions such as 'Beauty is in the eye of the beholder', 'Beauty is only skin deep' and referring to something as 'a thing of beauty' are frequently heard and used. Yet beauty is *extraordinary* and ideally should be treated as such.

Beauty is all too often thought to refer to the outstanding good looks of a woman – or a man. The notion of being beautiful seems to be increasingly important to some of the youth of today. They are no doubt influenced by celebrities land-marking beauty and fashion trends, with manufacturers claiming spurious and often un-attainable benefits. Of course, physical beauty *should* be appreciated and admired, for in common with so many other traits, attributes and aptitudes, it's pure gift which we receive from God. Therefore it should be considered special and not in any way to be taken for granted. In fact, as in all good things which we're offered, it should be respected and, if at all possible, used to benefit others and not merely ourselves.

### Physical Beauty

The sight of a truly beautiful man or woman can actually be quite breath-taking. I have often wondered how that person might feel. Do they appreciate the great gift they have had bestowed upon them or do they take it for granted? We sometimes jump to the conclusion that physically beautiful people are arrogant and narcissistic in their outlook. However, we should remind ourselves that it's unfair to make this type of 'blanket judgement'.

Possibly when beautiful people *are* conceited, it has arisen as a result of the way in which that person is regarded and treated by others. I feel sure that we've all witnessed, at some time or another, a beautiful person having their adoring 'slaves', or fans and in the school environment the 'fittie' holds court. She (or he) becomes the most popular person in the school and the one that has the most potential 'dates' queuing up! Even books, television and films regularly portray these kinds of scenes. So if we bear this in mind, it's probably unsurprising that such people start adopting attitudes and poses which are diametrically the opposite of beautiful. In other words, we can sometimes contribute towards damaging someone, albeit by our own good intentions.

Humility is a very valuable quality and it can be difficult for anyone to remain humble if they are admired, feted and adored for most of the time. There are even times when we can be accused of 'spoiling' another person, often a child; and frequently this is due to our good or well-meant intentions. Whenever we constantly 'give in' to someone else, it's possible that they may eventually lose sight of all humility, then their ego that selfish integral part of them can easily become dominant.

In direct contrast, a physically beautiful person can seem to be unaware of their physical attributes. Their behaviour is, as a result, often modest and unassuming. When this does occur, the result can be a fine person. To be modest when constantly admired must be challenging and personally I admire anyone who can achieve this.

Mistakenly, we often have the idea that these gorgeous people only know, and are seen with, other gorgeous people. If this were the case, it would probably be extremely difficult for them to have any friends, as the truly beautiful seem fairly thin on the ground! Sadly, however, it's not unknown for a physically beautiful person, to befriend someone who's the opposite, merely in order to enhance their own good looks by comparison. But, it will come as no surprise to learn that this form of false friendship fails the test of time. Through lack of any real substance or genuine affection, it usually withers away and dies like an un-watered plant.

And so it is that we can employ the great gift of beauty either to our own selfish advantage or to bend others to our will, who are in awe of our beauty. Far better, though, to be for the *benefit* of others: to love and care for them in the manner of Jesus Christ who commanded his disciples *and us* to 'Love one another; just as I have loved you.' [121]

Celebrities often fall prey to the pressures of maintaining their beauty as they become older. They cannot bear the world to observe them as anything but young and glamorous. Many of us try to make the best of ourselves and this is understandable, but how far should we go? It has been well documented that surgical beauty techniques are now ever more popular, with thousands of pounds being paid for procedures such as face lifts, tummy tucks, breast enhancements and eye-bag removal and these are but a few. And people, especially women, follow the example of celebrities and commit to such procedures every day, sometimes with disastrous results. And yet, beauty can often be truly in the eye of the beholder.

As an example of this, take the case of a happily married couple who have been together for about thirty years and have always been faithful to one another. Then the wife makes a decision to have a face-lift and uses money from their joint savings to carry this out. Whether the surgery is successful or not, the fact is that she was already loved in her own right by her husband,

---

[121] *John* 13: 34.

in the way that God had made and formed her. The couple were slowly growing older and physically changing together and their relationship was a stable and loving one. The cosmetic procedure may help the woman's self-esteem or not. It may help or damage their marriage. It may enhance their lives or again, or it may not. In essence, although it is right and good that on these important occasions we make decisions *for* ourselves and *about* ourselves, we should always try to consider how other people may be affected.

In this example, the wife was already loved regardless of her changing outward appearance. Beauty is, after all, only skin deep.

### Spiritual Beauty

'God's numinous or sacred presence was meant to be discovered within the inner depths of our being' [122]

This statement from George Maloney skilfully captures the meaning or essence of our inner or spiritual beauty. Jesus Christ is an indwelling presence in every single person; a God who pervades every part of our very existence and our spiritual beauty resonates with the

---

[122] *Deep Calls To Deep* – A Christian Spirituality of the Heart – George A. Maloney, p. 16.

Holy Spirit. Unlike physical beauty, our spiritual beauty cannot be observed by the naked eye. Nonetheless, it's apparent in our words and actions every day. I have noticed that a man or a woman who's physically unattractive often possesses an innate beauty that shines from within. This beauty manifests itself in the manner in which they interact with others.

Publicity often headlines news items such as murder, rape and rioting and this can lead to a belief that many people are indifferent or even wicked. Sadly, there *will* always be a small number who actually are, although there's always the opportunity of repentance and reformation at some point in their lives, even if it's at the *end of their lives.*

The critical point is that there are a *huge* number of people in the world who are the very essence of kindness, generosity, humility, compassion and gentleness and they are easily spotted in their interactions with others. In other words the spirit of Christ is at work within these people; alive and active and helping them to practise the Lord's two great commandments. St Paul, when exhorting the Church in Galatia to be led by the Holy Spirit and not by self-indulgence, used the following words:

'What the Spirit brings is very different: love, joy, peace, patience, kindness, goodness, trustfulness, gentleness and self-control.'[123]

What is more; when the Spirit does indeed lead us, not only do these qualities become obvious, but our spiritual beauty becomes apparent also. Meister Eckhart wrote:

'For just as God is boundless in giving, so too the soul is boundless in receiving.'[124]

Meister Eckhart, was I believe, referring to the human soul's ability to soak up the love, care and compassion of God like a sponge, and we, of course, are born with the ability to do just that. However, just one word of warning: the soul is boundless in receiving from God *only if we allow it to do so.* God is sublimely generous with his gifts, his help and his love, but in turn, we must be open and receptive to receive them. In fact, Jesus himself makes this very point in the Parable of the Sower and the Seed. [125] We must have faith in the Lord and a desire to be in a relationship with him, or his generosity can be wasted if the recipient is unwilling or

---

[123] *The Letter of St Paul to the Galatians* 5: 22 - 23.
[124] *Sermons and Treatises* – Meister Eckhart, p. 22.
[125] *Matthew* 13: 18 - 23.

unable to receive it, or sublimely unaware of it. On the other hand, those who attempt to follow the path of our Lord Jesus Christ in faith and hope, and receive his boundless love and generosity, will enjoy a spiritual beauty that comes from deep within, and which will last them all the days of their life – on earth and eternally.

## *The Beauty of Nature*

'In the beginning God created the heavens and the earth.' [126]

The opening line of the first page of the Bible states in the clearest of crystal clear terms that God formed earth and heavens alike. As the account continues we learn that every specimen in nature that we take for granted and every animal, bird, reptile, fish and insect was made by God. *And so were we.*

Some time ago when I was at a workshop, the question was raised as to whether our appreciation of nature lessens as we grow older. Although I cannot speak for others, I personally find that my appreciation of the wonders of nature have actually intensified as I have gone through life. Often as I am out and about I am struck again by the absolute miracle of how

---

[126] *Genesis* 1: 1.

beautiful nature is and frequently when I am a car passenger, I can marvel again at a sunset, a cloud formation, or the splendours of the countryside and I feel aware of the hand of God who has created all this magnificence. In fact, at times this awareness of nature's beauty, and God's role as creator of it, is so powerful, and the scene that I am beholding so perfectly formed and exquisite, that I feel full of joy, and in that moment God seems very close. 'God moments' such as these are a rare and perfect treasure too and in that fleeting moment a singular, pure happiness uplifts me, so that perhaps for a few seconds, God, nature and I chime together in perfect accord, and become one in a relationship of Creator, nature and human. It's perfectly possible – albeit rare, to experience these fleeting flashes of pure, unadulterated joy, and they can occur at any time and in any place.

I was once told that when we experience this, we've been gently touched by the finger or hand of God. I don't know whether this is true or not, but it's an explanation which appears to be fitting. What is more, it seems that if this *is* the correct explanation, then the sensation of great joy which we can feel in the presence of nature's beauty is yet again God-related. Instead of being touched by the finger of God, we're instead touched by the natural beauty of the earth which God created. Yet the wonders of nature are the work of God, but not the nature of God himself. The simple fact of the matter is that the beauty in nature bestowed upon us by God, can be sometimes difficult to express in words. The sheer wonder and awe that God himself inspires can render mere words inadequate.

Gerard Manley Hopkins, English poet, Roman Catholic and Jesuit priest who often devised new words for use in his poems, used the same technique in 'Pied Beauty', which narrates the story of the splendour of the natural world. It's possible that the inadequacies of our language when referring to these wonders inspired him to invent new words, in an attempt to give voice to the magnificence which was all around him.

These words give value to the abundant work of the Creator:

*Glory be to God for dappled things –*
*For skies of couple-colour as a brindled cow;*
*For rose-moles all in stipple upon trout that swim;*
*Fresh-firecoal chestnut-falls; finches' wings;*
*Landscape plotted and pieced - fold, fallow, and plough;*
*And áll trádes, their gear and tackle and trim.*
*All things counter, original, spare, strange;*
*Whatever is fickle, freckled (who knows how?)*

*With swift, slow; sweet, sour; a-dazzle, dim;*
*He fathers-forth whose beauty is past change:*
*Praise him.* [127]

### The Beauty of The Trinity

'So when all things keep an inner silence in the soul, which has run its full course in the heavens, then there is that inward encounter in the soul, in which the Holy Trinity has formed itself and made a heaven and united itself.' [128]

The love that we receive from our God is infinite, and this in itself gives it an unparalleled beauty beyond compare. Wanting us to model ourselves on his ways, Jesus unrestrainedly and at length speaks of love, urging us to love our enemies, [129] love our neighbour; emphasizing [130] love one another 'as I have loved you' and emphasizing [131] also 'love the Lord your God with all your heart, soul and mind.' [132] Jesus's law of love possessed an innovative quality that was unknown in his

---

[127] *Pied Beauty* – G. M Hopkins, *Poems of G. M. Hopkins,* p. 69.
[128] *The essential sermons, commentaries, treatises and defences* – Meister Eckhart, p. 22.
[129] *Luke* 6: 27.
[130] *Luke* 10: 25 - 28.
[131] *John* 13: 34 - 35.
[132] *Matthew* 22: 37 - 38.

time and which both entranced and alienated him from others: 'there has never been anybody who has spoken like him.'[133] Yet this law of love was key to the very essence of Jesus Christ. His actions were based around and central to this beauty of love. His healings, his inclusion of those on the fringes of society: the poor, the sick, the sinners and women are all evidence of his law of love. His compassion, sympathy and empathy, and the gifts of himself in his crucifixion and Eucharist prove beyond doubt his love for us. Fundamentally, the actions and words of Jesus in his public ministry all show us the love that he bore for every human – Jew or Gentile, and the beauty of this has never been surpassed.

'Love is always patient and kind... Love does not come to an end.' *(St Paul)* [134]

God remains a mystery to us. However, if we apply ourselves to the Gospel message and heed the words of our Lord Jesus Christ, we're given, at least, some inkling as to the nature of God, who sent his only begotten son to redeem us. Jesus said:

---

[133] *John* 7: 46.
[134] 1 *Corinthians* 13: 4 - 8.

'If you know me, you know my Father too. From this moment you know him and have seen him'. [135]

Consequently, if we can see and feel the beauty of Jesus who gave love and *was* pure love, it naturally follows that God, who is part of Jesus, and vice versa, has this in common.

' "God is love, and he who abides in love abides in God, and God abides in him" (*1 John 4:16*) ... The Christian image of God.' [136]

So yet again we come face to face with the incontrovertible fact of the love of God, and in that great love we clearly find a source of great beauty. One of the most moving experiences in life can be to behold a mother looking at her new-born child for the first time. Her eyes and her expression reflect the huge love that she feels for this small being which she has carried in her womb for nine months, and her face is beautiful with that overwhelming love, which has come straight from her heart.

---

[135] *John* 14: 7.

[136] *Deus Caritas Est*, God is Love, Encyclical Letter of Pope Benedict XVI, 25th December 2005, Paragraph 1.

Similarly, falling in love is said to transform a person into someone of beauty, giving them an innermost glow; this is the power of love. So our God who is 'all love' must surely be great in beauty.

God, in his generosity, gave us the gift of the Holy Spirit and the purpose of this was to guide us through life and remove our fear of being alone, as the Spirit is our constant companion. Jesus reminded us that:

'...the Advocate, the Holy Spirit, whom the Father
will send in my name, will teach you everything and
remind you of all I have said to you.' [137]

During the course of our lives, we all, at some point or another, feel gratitude for help we've received from another person. The idea of help is, of course, wide-ranging; from a kindly word of advice, the giving of our time, to the donation of money where necessary. Yet in whatever method we've been helped, or indeed have helped others, we cannot avoid being affected by this. We feel warmed inside whether we're the recipient or giver, and the reason that we feel warmed is because we're either showing our care and concern for someone else, or we're in receipt of this. Very little in this life

---

[137] *John* 14: 26.

ever makes us feel quite as good as when we feel genuinely cared for, because alongside the caring comes love. An Advocate who constantly cares for us, leads us and teaches us, is a Holy Spirit of beauty; for caring produces love and we know that in love we find beauty.

In short, the Trinity still remains a mystery for us all. However, based on the words and actions of our Lord Jesus Christ, we're given a sense of unconditional love. A love so beautiful that we, in our turn, should try to give it to others.

'Do not dress up for show: doing up your hair, wearing gold bracelets and fine clothes; all this should be inside, in a person's heart, imperishable: the ornament of a sweet and gentle disposition – this is what is precious in the sight of God.' [138]

### The Beauty of the Mass

The Mass has often been described as the glue that holds and binds Catholics together. And it is no accident that this is so. Pope Benedict XVI writes of the Eucharist:

'The Lord meets us; men and women created in God's image and likeness, and becomes our

---

[138] 1 *Peter* 3: 3 - 5.

companion along the way. In this sacrament, the Lord truly becomes food for us, to satisfy our hunger for truth and freedom. Since only the truth can make us free, Christ becomes for us the food of truth.' [139]

Every time we receive Jesus under the appearance of bread and wine we receive the greatest and most beautiful gift that we *can* receive this side of Heaven. During one Sunday Mass I can remember vividly experiencing a feeling of the most pure, uplifting joy and well-being, as I participated in the responses. Of course, it's difficult to account for exactly what caused this, but I do remember that my mind was firmly fixed on Mass and I was not distracted. Perhaps simply the wonder of the Mass with Holy Communion as its high point, with Jesus truly present among his people who had gathered together in his name, was the primary reason for the deep experience which I had had. I hope to be always able to recall the wonder and beauty of that particular moment.

The beauty of the Mass is given to us in so many ways: in the great Eucharistic feast, in the liturgy of the Word, in the power of the Holy Spirit who comes down upon the priest and changes simple bread and wine into

---

[139] *Sacramentum Caritatis,* Post Synodal Exhortation on the Eucharist – Pope Benedict XVI, p.7.

the Body and Blood of Jesus Christ, and in the beauty of celebrating the Mass in communion with each other.

I never fail to be amazed by the unfailing beauty and power of God's Word. Even those passages which are so well-read, and so well-known to us, have the power to reach out and enable our discovery of a new meaning or nuance that we had hitherto not noticed. God's word is made available to every one of us, but we have to open our hearts and minds to listen to what is being addressed to us personally. Once we're able to do this, then the beauty of what we've been given becomes apparent. It's little wonder that scholars and theologians examine and re-examine the books of the Bible in a never-ending quest to discover all that God wishes us to understand. It's quite possible though, that we will never absorb even half of what God wants us to discover, but even a fraction of this would be exquisite.

The beautiful, holy Màss contains all that is noble, decent and good in our sinful world. There's our humility in recognizing and repenting for our sins and our praise of God in community worship. Our 'sign of peace' to others represents the peace and loving care for our neighbour that Jesus commanded us to give. Our mission at the end of Mass, to live our lives as witnesses and examples of Christ gives us plenty of opportunities to spread the Good News to others. Yet in the time and place where we receive Jesus, to do otherwise would surely be unimaginable.

If we're fortunate enough to be physically beautiful, may we remember that this is not just a lucky bonus, but a treasured gift which can be used for good, if only we've a mind to do so. In our care and concern for others, we're able to feast upon the great beauty of love, compassion and empathy which are ours for the taking; if we only choose to do so. Christ walks beside us and the Spirit is within us every step of our life and the beauty of this will always be with us, wherever we go and whatever we do.

We may be disabled, disfigured, disadvantaged, diseased or dying, yet the love and person of Jesus Christ is one of unimaginable beauty and will shine out in us. With such a gift, how can we not be beautiful in mind and spirit in return?

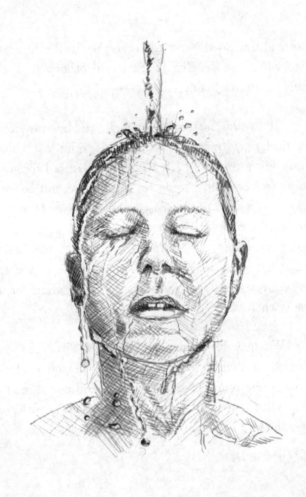

*Baptism – time for a change…*

# ~ *Chapter Eleven* ~
## A Change is as Good as a Rest

One of the most interesting and challenging situations for us to observe in life, is that of change in all its variety. Some changes in situations are welcome, others are forced upon us. There are changes in personality traits, changes of 'heart' and gradual unconscious changes, usually involving people or circumstances. Change occurs around us and also within us, and may be anticipated or entirely unexpected. Whatever the case may be, the fact remains that change in any one of its forms is an inescapable part of all our lives. How we, in turn, manage or even survive those changes and how they affect our secular and spiritual lives, is worth exploring.

In a world where change is often an inevitable and integral part of our lives, even if we're not always cosy or comfortable with it, the direct contrast with the Lord our God cannot be overlooked. We're led to believe that the self-same God who has been worshipped since time immemorial has always been, and will remain, forever unchanging:

'Make no mistake about this my dear brothers: it is all that is good, everything that is perfect, which is given us from above; it comes down from the Father of all light; with him there is no such thing as alteration, no shadow of a change.' [140]

We're called in so many ways to adapt, to change, to 'make the best' of situations, while God remains the one constant in all our lives. Furthermore, the word 'constant' has a double meaning: 'constant' in the sense that God is available to us always until the end of time, and 'constant' in the sense of invariable. Indeed, we spend all our earthly lives growing, changing and developing while our ageless God simply *is*.

In any marriage or partnership, love for the other person should ideally be an unconditional love which encompasses the other person's faults and failings, as well as their attributes. The reason for this is clear: we each have our own personal characteristics and another person's genuine love accepts these, 'warts and all'. In the same way our love for the Lord should be absolute and resolute; with no reason to try and change him. God is *unchanging* and the only people who should change are

---

[140] *The Letter of James* 1: 16-18.

ourselves, so we accept the challenge to 'follow thee more nearly' [141] every single day.

Human beings have a natural resistance to change and the main reason for this is because it makes us anxious. It's clear that change can be unsettling, scary and even frightening for many of us. Even in the most positive forms of change, this can still hold true. For example, a new job may be cause for celebration – especially in areas of high unemployment. Even so, the start of any new job can be unnerving and worrying. We often refer to our 'comfort zone', that place in all our lives where we feel most comfortable, and an occupation that we're familiar with, working with people with whom we're well acquainted, is indeed a comfort and cosy and rates 'low' on our personal 'stress-ometers'!

### *Clerical Shift*

Changes in our spiritual church life and rituals operate in a similar way. It is a well-known fact that a change of priest or pastor can affect the parish congregation

---

[141] Lyrics taken from *'Day by Day'* from the musical *Godspell*. (1971). Written by Stephen Schwartz, but its refrain follows a prayer ascribed to the 13th century English bishop, St Richard of Chichester.

deeply. Indeed, from the moment that this is announced, speculation, observation and anxieties begin. 'What will he be like?' is a common question, almost immediately followed by queries about how the new incumbent will run the parish. These questions often relate to  whether he will, actually change tasks, routines and the general running of his particular church, as well as how much is likely to remain *un*changed. Most of us dislike uncertainty, because with uncertainty comes anxiety. So our speculation could be said to be quite reasonable in these circumstances.

However, once the new incumbent is in place new considerations and attitudes may prevail.  Some people can feel strangely threatened in these circumstances, and begin to react in a number of unexpected ways. Some will accept any changes made, perhaps stoically, others will be forced to accept them, but reluctantly. Yet again, there will be others who will resist any form of changes and protest vociferously. There may even be those who try to take advantage of change to bolster their own standing within the community and these reactions can be really unsettling. However, it does call into question whether those who accept  changes do so because they are happy about them – and of course this will be the attitude of some easy-going people – or whether it's due to a common lethargy that cannot be dispelled. Sometimes, even a negative reaction to change – or indeed to anything – is better than no reaction at all!

In general, if change has to be enforced for whatever reason, the best method of doing this is to instigate it very gradually to give the people themselves the chance to take on 'ownership' of the changes and even contribute to the process. Sometimes, even the Holy Spirit can take a bit of time to work in the hearts and minds of the people!

### *Climatic Change*

The notion of 'moving on' as circumstances dictate is challenging. Yet change is all around us all the time. We may feel that there's little we can do to escape from it. We're advised that our earth; our world, is physically changing all the time due to global warming. The polar ice caps are melting, the ozone layer is gradually being destroyed, our seasons appear unpredictable and flooding and severe weather is rapidly becoming the norm. Most of us are disconcerted, disorientated and frightened by what we see and hear in this respect and often ask, 'Where will this all end?' International talks have taken place on the subject of climate change, often with little or no agreement being reached, leaving most of us as apprehensive onlookers.

We're advised so often to 'hand it all over to God and let him take care of our worries', and this advice is probably worthy of note. Our trust in God should, and could, be absolute if we would only be willing to allow it to be so. In the case of earthly climatic changes we're powerless to a certain extent and know we should turn to the Lord for our saving help. Yet, in practical terms, most of us cannot help but fret about matters over which we very often have no control. Yet historically mankind has had to contend with so many various and debilitating environmental conditions, including ice ages and natural disasters, and yet both humans and the earth invariably endure. In spite of this, how many of us, I wonder, ever stop and try to envisage how the Lord our God feels when he considers the way that man is seeking to destroy our wonderful earth, some of his animals upon it, and indeed man himself, which he, the Lord has created?

'In the beginning God created the heavens and the earth... God said 'Let there be light', and there was light... God called the vault heaven... God called the dry land 'earth' and the mass of waters 'seas'... The earth produced vegetation... God made two great lights and the stars… God created every kind of living creature with which the waters teem, and every kind of winged creature… God made every kind of wild beast, every kind of cattle, and every kind of land reptile… God created man in the image of himself, in the image of God he created him, male and female he created them… God saw all he had made, and indeed it was very good.' [142]

Some climate changes have undoubtedly been brought about by our errors in daily living, and indeed, humans and mistakes are synonymous with each other to some extent. Moreover, our consistent failures since the beginning of time have possibly exempted the Lord to our propensity, sadly not only to sin, but to make serious errors time and time again:

'Accursed be the soil because of you. With suffering shall you get your food from it every day of your life. It shall yield you brambles and thistles, and you shall eat wild plants. With sweat on your brow shall you eat your bread, until you return to the soil, as you were taken from it. For dust you are and to dust you shall return.' [143]

---

[142] *Genesis* 1-2.
[143] *The Fall, Genesis 3: 17-20.*

However, if our mistakes have caused change, then we must be prepared not only to rectify our mistakes, if at all possible, but to accept the accompanying change as best we can and try to turn the outcome of these changes into a positive experience.

## Constructive Change

Difficult as change may often be, its effects can sometimes be far-reaching and often advantageous. As adults we're able to perceive what children cannot – that after the disruption of change gradually comes the settling-in period followed by contentment – until the next major change takes place! One of the greatest and most far-reaching changes in the history of the Catholic Church was, without doubt, the advent of the Second Vatican Council:

'The most revolutionary Christian event since the Reformation.' [144]

It's hugely interesting to note that despite the resistance of the Roman Curia at that time, the Council was greeted with eagerness and enthusiasm by most people, who were clearly keen to welcome the winds of

---

[144] *Why the Catholic Church Needs Vatican III – T. P. O'Mahony,* p. 68.

change in the Church, which its sixteen documents would inevitably bring to light.

'Each of the 16 documents produced by the Council had its own importance to the particular sphere of church life it addressed.' [145]

The Second Vatican Council changed the face of the Catholic Church in many major respects. The event has obviously been well documented but the personal accounts of those who remember the experience are interesting. One and all appear to share a universal excitement and anticipation for forthcoming changes, and there appears to be no mention of concern about what the future may hold for the Church at large.

This emerges as an oddly diametric attitude to that which is normally evidenced when people are faced with change. Could this be accounted for by the fact that the Church needed to change so badly that *any* prospect of change would be welcome? Or was there a conviction from the very beginning of the Council that the changes would be beneficial? Or yet again, was the Spirit blowing where it will and preparing all for the changes to come with breathless anticipation? It's

---

[145] *Why the Catholic Church Needs Vatican III – T. P. O'Mahony* p. 69.

difficult to speculate why this was so, but it does give one cause to wonder if a miraculous transition in the attitude of people took effect at this time, and indeed, if this were to be the case, surely this could have been God related? I would go so far as to state that normally humans find change disconcerting, frightening and usually upsetting, and yet this certainly did not appear to be the case at the time of the Second Vatican Council. It's just possible that the observers and onlookers of that time could give us later Catholics a directive for the future in coping with changes within the Church. It's often a comfort for those of faith to see the hand of God in many a 'consecrated' endeavour which proceeds with little or no impediment.

### That Critical Transformation

We believe that God knows us through and through; all our virtues and all of our faults and failings and yet loves us regardless. We exist with the reassuring belief that this holds true; that we're loved because we're one of God's children – just as we humanly *are*. However, as always there's a price tag attached to this unconditional love that we receive at the hands of the Father. And it is this: we may be loved despite our many weaknesses and imperfections *but* we have to attempt to live our lives in a spirit of change, in which we must try to improve upon, if not eradicate, many of those individual flaws which we possess. Change is vital to help us to accomplish this task and changing ourselves can be the most challenging task of all. I have sometimes wondered why mankind was intrinsically infected with the ability to cause pain and suffering. If we examine our history, it's littered with man's cruelty, barbarism and duplicity over the centuries and our Saviour himself, while fulfilling his mission here on earth, cruelly suffered at the hands of mankind. If we pick up any Bible and start reading the Word beginning at Genesis, Chapter One, it's quite incredible that barely a page passes between the creation account and the first fall into sin. Our predilection for this would appear limitless. Yet the answer to this age-old predicament appears easily solved: we must change and change for the better.

The problem with this directive though is simple: to improve ourselves we must first be aware of and acknowledge our mistakes and sins. Only then can these be rectified and improved upon. And the problem with *this* is that many people don't believe they are at fault or have committed any sins. However, help, in its simplest form is always at hand. The easy answer to this is in the examination of conscience and in prayer. In prayer we're automatically changed anyway, and in that change we can perceive that we need to change so many other areas of our lives and our personalities. If we really dislike another person, or even hate them, then the answer is to pray for them too. Believe me; it's not possible to hate someone that you are praying for! So we've immediately initiated the process of altering ourselves for the better. As a result we do not hate that person anymore and we can start to see and believe that, even if they won't or can't change, *we can and must*.

By changing our own attitude towards someone else we're actually changing ourselves at one and the same time. St John the Baptist exhorted others to repent, to change their ways and his reasoning was clear. [146] We were to follow the path of righteousness which Christ would clearly illuminate for us, and this could only be achieved by the experience of our innermost personal renewal or *metanoia*. These sentiments are summarized by Father Richard Leonard:

'Often we have days when we regret our behaviour and wish we could do it all over again. This response is good if we learn from these feelings and change our behaviour… If we're unhappy, we should look at what we are doing and giving out, as much as what we are receiving or taking in. Both efforts create and

---

[146] *Matthew* 3: 1 - 2.

re-create us. And we are the lump sum of the choices we are making.' [147]

Our efforts and attempts to change may or may not be successful, and are largely dependent upon a number of differing factors, such as our character, our situation at the time; our life situation; our background; the amount of effort we apply to attempting to change; whether we're encouraged by others and a variety of other reasons which are probably highly individual. Yet, paradoxically, we often change without intending to or realizing it; in fact we can be completely unaware that this has taken place at all, until it's brought to our notice in one form or another. Interestingly, many of the previously stated factors which influence changes in us are also shared factors, which can bring about that unconscious change.

Today, there's a growing awareness of how past events and experiences influence our behaviour and actions. Indeed, the expression 'having a lot of baggage' is a commonly used term in this context. These types of subconscious changes can, however, be beneficial on the one hand but detrimental on the other. If, for example, our life experiences and our interaction with others is

---

[147] *Movies that Matter – Reading film through the lens of faith,* p.2 – Fr Richard Leonard, S.J.

rewarding and bears fruit, then it would be fair to say that we're nourished by these encounters, softened and imbued with a sense of well-being that we generally reciprocate. If, however, we've suffered at the hands of others, we may also have become hardened, angered and embittered. It can be so difficult to actually realize that we've changed at all, or that we've possibly altered in an unhealthy way. To have the strength to try and rectify this, is admirable and requires enormous courage. However, we should also recognize that; if we're given this gift of self-realization we should thank God for it, while at the same time praying for the strength to achieve our goal of self-improvement.

### *The Ultimate Moment of Change*

'Sacraments ritualize moments of change. Water, bread, wine, oil, light, rings, gestures, words and dress symbolize the changes they signify.' [148]

Every time we celebrate the sacraments we celebrate an enormous change which has taken place by the grace of God. Indeed, the old adage 'sacraments are an outward sign of an inward grace' clarifies this. However, what is relevant is the fact that this inward grace can only come

---

[148] *Movies that Matter – Reading film through the lens of faith, p. 94* – Fr Richard Leonard, S.J.

from the loving hand of God. Sacraments, we know, are the great gift which we, the Church, have received as a result of the bounty of Jesus Christ and we should try not to forget this. In baptism we're changed as we enter into a new life in Christ and as part of the Christian community, when all previous and original sin is wiped away. This is symbolized by the cleansing and life-giving action of the water, the strengthening with oil, the putting on of Christ with the white garment of purity and the flame of faith in the lighting of the candle.

Furthermore, the baptism of adults by total immersion is a powerful symbol of change – a high-impact sacrament of death and re-birth – now ritualized especially for infant baptisms. One of our deepest fears is that of drowning. Nobody would ever allow someone to hold them under water but when adults are baptised by total immersion, that's just what happens. When baptised in the name of Christ, each person emerges from the water – essentially saved from drowning by the hand of God – to start a new life as a child of God: purified and with a permanent gift of faith, having been changed for all eternity. Yet, although we recognize the symbolism in these actions, we ourselves at the time of our baptism are transformed and admitted to an everlasting life with Christ as we are 'Christ-ened'.

In a similar way we recognize change through the other sacraments. That innermost change which we desire, which God desires and which unites in perfect harmony, is ritualized in them. In confirmation we're transformed by the gift and graces of the Holy Spirit and can be led by the Spirit throughout our lives *if we allow this to happen* and bear fruit in us. In the sacrament of the anointing of the sick, the ill person is transmuted by the grace of God, spiritually or mentally, if not physically, and given that much needed strength to endure their pain and suffering. Priests are changed in their very essence and being by the sacrament of Holy Orders, by God's power working within them. Similarly in marriage, the bride and groom mutually give each other God's blessing and transforming love and express their consent before the whole Church. This will help to strengthen and sustain their human partnership.

When we're reconciled with God in the sacrament of reconciliation, commonly known as 'confession', we're forgiven and our sins are wiped away as we are given pardon and peace. We are, of course, immediately forgiven for those sins as soon as we're sorry for them, but in this sacrament we feel as though we've been given a hug by Jesus himself, even if not immediately forgiven by the rest of our community, who cannot help but be affected by our errors and transgressions. How could we not help but be changed and softened in the face of such forgiveness and love? Our burdens simply roll away as we're freed from our guilt and fortified so we don't sin again; thus helping the change in us to be permanent!

### *Changing Through the Years*

One of the greatest changes and gifts that we abundantly receive from God is the ability to change with the passing of time. Pain, sorrow and grief may sometimes remain our human crosses to be borne, (we may think) until the end of time. But we know that Christ himself will be with us also until this time, to accompany us through the pain and suffering which he, in his humanity, has already shared with us.

A prime example can be observed in the death of a loved one – whether they be friend or close family. Grief is without a shadow of a doubt debilitating, self-absorbing and personality-shattering. When we're consumed with grief this process appears to embrace and completely encompass our lives in a way in which many of us could never have previously imagined. Our grief becomes a garment which some of us are unable to shed and the depth of our grief is absolute, although strangely, our abhorrence of it is undeniable. Despite all this, there is light in our darkness, because after a time the grief becomes more bearable, and our ability to cope with it is improved. Indeed, bereavement counsellors suggest that six years is roughly the amount of time needed to get over the loss of a loved one. Therefore, as the flow of time goes on, so the process of recovery is more evident. Although we suffer and grieve as we were warned by Christ that we would, we've also been granted the great gift of time healing our hearts, souls and therefore our lives, which helps provide a coping mechanism for all.

The passing of time also often alters our version of events in our minds. Holidays which were once thought of as being a disaster can be viewed with equanimity and affection, highly embarrassing moments can be thought of with amusement, and traumas are often diminished in our minds. Only the passing of time can bring about the change of feelings such as those described, and indeed, these are just a few of the more obvious examples.

The expression 'time is a great healer' is a valid one, but this gift of emotional and heart healing, due to time passing, is usually something that is completely out of our orbit and control. God alone has given us this truly wonderful phenomenon, and it can be a source of comfort for all those who seek to change from any current uncomfortable or upsetting situation and leave it behind them.

Many of us are frightened by the process of change and by what these changes may bring in our lives. However, God's gift of free will has enabled humanity to change in many ways.

Indeed, God brings about a very special change every time during the consecration at Mass. Therefore we can safely assume that God wishes us to change when necessary, to try and accept it and to endeavour to understand and come to terms with it, in its many forms. We know we shall continue to struggle with this; our human minds generally find this a worrying and challenging concept and one which we continue to resist. Yet change is all around and a critical dimension of our lives.

Sir Winston Churchill [149] reminded us that:

'To improve is to change; to be perfect is to change often' and the following words by Reinhold Niebuhr [150]

---

[149] November 30th 1874 - January 24th 1965.
[150] June 21, 1892 - June 1, 1971.

capture every sentiment that has been expressed in this chapter into one short sentence of beauty:

'God grant me the serenity to accept the things I cannot change, the courage to change the things I can, and the wisdom to know the difference.'

May we, therefore, all find in our lives that serenity, courage and wisdom which is so fundamental for change and essential for fullness of life. [151]

---

[151] 'Fullness of life' based upon Jesus's words: 'I have come so that they may have life and have it to the full.' *John* 10: 10.

## ~ *Chapter Twelve* ~

# Trying to Escape the Inescapable

There are so many delights to be found in life, many of which come to us as a pure gift from God. Even those which are manufactured or man-made have often been created through man's ingenuity, which itself is the direct result of God's providence.  On the other hand, we know that there are some aspects of life which are clearly less enjoyable, but nevertheless have to be endured and tackled with the help of the Lord and of others. Sometimes these unpleasant experiences can strike us when we're least expecting them. Maybe an accident, a sudden illness or a traumatic event, which can leave us almost 'winded' with shock. Alternatively, there are those times when we can foresee a difficult event beforehand.

For example, we all know that at the end of our earthly lives we will depart this world. Greek mythology tells the story of Sisyphus who actually managed to cheat death not once, but incredibly twice. But his triumph was short-lived as he was eventually punished by being banished to the very lowest regions of the Underworld – presumably the equivalent of Hell, or maybe Hell itself. We, as mortals however, are unable to cheat death and cannot extend our earthly lives for ever. Many people have a natural fear of their demise, yet the idea of continuing to live in a world where all family and friends are long departed and life, science and technology are then light years on, can be a really daunting and scary thought.

Many of us foster the hope that we will live to a 'ripe old age' and then gently slip away. Each of us is familiar with the idea that the cycle of life remorselessly turns round and round. When life is snatched from people at an early age we're often indignant, and feel that that person has somehow been unfairly treated. Even in old age, fear of death can become quite acute as the imminence of it gradually kicks in. Some time ago, an old lady of my acquaintance who was one hundred and eight years old died – eventually! Although very sound-minded, at the end of her extremely long life, she was bed-ridden and no longer enjoying it. In fact she quite frequently said that she couldn't understand why she was still around!

There are, however, those 'who are afraid to think of their approaching death, or who think of it in fear and trembling',[152] for it is unknown and difficult to envisage. It has been documented that when faced with the prospect of death, our human minds and bodies rebel, fight and cling on to the very last vestiges of life - to the bitter end. We've a natural desire to prolong our lives and live them to their natural conclusion, as God wills. Indeed, there have been many arguments for and against the use of medical intervention, in the preserving and extending of human life. The reason for our fear is fairly obvious – we're frightened of something beyond our control, which few of us understand and which is outside the experience of many.

---

[152] *Reaching Out* – Henri Nouwen, p. 139.

Of course, the main reason for the growth of Christianity was that after the death and resurrection of Jesus Christ, we had the promise of eternal life, which to this day, gives so many Christians comfort and hope. The Good News of the resurrection was really Good News for us all – all of mankind. Because once we've mastered the fear of death, we can do (and indeed, have done) great things for God, mankind and the salvation of souls.

Some of us, though, may wonder whether we're worthy to be given such a reward, considering our life on earth. How successful have we been in imitating Christ, and are we fit to be in his wonderful presence until the end of time? This is purely a matter for our own consciences, yet these questions have often led to 'death-bed' confessions. We may perhaps, be scornful of this, considering that the confession was perhaps made because death was at hand and the prospect of being withheld eternal life was terrifying. We could further infer that there's no genuine repentance at all and the confession was merely a means to get into Heaven. But even if the motives are not entirely pure, there has been a clear recognition of sin and forgiveness sought, and an irrevocable step taken closer to Christ. Who are we then to make a judgement or to question that person's motives?

## Death Comes as the End *

Our own mortality is inevitable but most of us avoid this thought, pushing it to the far recesses of our mind. But when the death of a loved one or maybe even an acquaintance occurs, the thought of death reluctantly makes its way to the forefront of our minds, and we're reminded of our own human frailty. Even in a society that has adopted a free-wheeling attitude to such issues as gender identity, teenage pregnancy, and gay marriage, death still remains an uncomfortable subject for discussion. Managing the topic can be quite difficult for many people, especially as generally they don't know what to say to someone who has recently been bereaved. There's little doubt that most of us are uneasy in these situations. How often have we heard the expression 'it makes you realize how lucky you are', or alternatively, 'it puts everything else into perspective'? Both of these statements are, of course true, yet at some point we ourselves will be facing a trial of this nature.

Anyone who has been bereaved usually requires support, care and a listening ear, while they try to come to terms with what has taken place, and with the strong emotions they are feeling at that time. Grief, anger,

---

* *'Death Comes as the End'* is also the title of an historical mystery novel by Agatha Christie (1944).

loneliness, shock, and sometimes a sense of betrayal, are all common symptoms for a bereaved person. Family and friends usually rally round in most cases, except when someone has literally no-one to help them, but after a time, there's an expectancy the person should be 'pulling through and moving on'.

To recover from the pain, shock, and emotional trauma, takes a long time and well-meaning people who avoid a bereaved person for fear of saying the wrong thing, or simply don't know what to say at all, are not really to be blamed. We should though, try to understand that the person who has suffered a loss may really need to talk about how they feel.

### Sharing our Frailty

We generally try to conceal any vulnerability and weakness for fear that others may see them as faults, and think that our character is weak. Conversely, in our very weakness can sometimes be found our strength. Christ didn't seem to be very strong at the time of his arrest; he was scourged at the pillar, jeered at, stripped and finally suffered the agony of his crucifixion. However, his power lay in the fact that he came to us as suffering servant, one who suffered agony so that he, as God, could experience our human mental and physical agony. In fact, he drew strength from his Father's great love. In the same way, when we allow others to witness our mental weakness and vulnerability, we've laid aside our everyday 'mask' and have revealed the true person which is hidden in the depths of our heart and soul. To allow others 'in' and to allow them to see our inner person is, in essence, a courageous action, as we are then defenceless, at the mercy of other people with our guard firmly laid down. In so doing, we're making ourselves as much of a target as Christ himself did for our sakes. Yet by exposing this softer, more susceptible side of our nature we can often bring about surprises.

Some time ago, the storyline of the soap opera *Coronation Street* focused on the terminal illness of one of the most popular characters and over ten million viewers tuned in to watch her on-screen death. Some may have been ghoulishly fascinated, but I think for most viewers the raw emotions as vulnerability and fear were revealed, held the British public in thrall and sympathy.

Why were the viewers so moved by what they had seen? The answer is partly because they could identify with this televised trauma, having lived through something similar themselves, but also because the storyline allowed the actors to show those emotions which we generally choose to hide. When we do allow others to see this side of our characters, we immediately, due to our frailty and humility, become a softer, gentler, more attractive and lovable person and in this we can make a direct comparison with the Lord. In his humility, as one who came to serve, and in his frailty and suffering we can see the great love of God. God allows us to be ourselves, if only *we* can allow ourselves to do likewise. There's a reason that we're moved by another person's vulnerability. God so created us that we're able to soften, empathize, and comfort anyone who's brave enough to expose their pain to us.

### *A Light at the End of the Tunnel.*

This common phrase used to describe the passing from trauma to peace, chaos to normality and adversity to joy, is also an expression often applied to those who are recovering from a severe illness or those who have been bereaved for some time: 'You can see a light at the end of the tunnel now'. The use of this phrase is interesting as connotations of 'dark' always imply fear, death, illness and an ending, whereas light brings to mind hope, joy and new beginnings.

Witnesses to near-death experiences have often described a bright light at the end of a long tunnel, the implication being that they were nearing the presence of the Lord, in a transition from mortal to eternal life. Therefore, we can probably assume that this 'light at the end of the tunnel' which we draw upon in everyday language, holds, in some form or another, the saving grace of our Lord Jesus Christ.

Christ is universally known as the light of the world and he who has taken us from the darkness and into his own wonderful light. In fact, every time we light a candle in Christ's name, we can be sure that we can connect with his light, he who is keeping the flame of our faith as alive today as it has always been. St Matthew reminds us that:

'The people that lived in darkness has seen a great light; on those who dwell in the land and shadow of death a light has dawned.' [153]

In our doubts, our uncertainties and our fears about death, we need to be reminded that there's a light for us to dwell upon, and not darkness, for in the 'shadow of death a light has dawned.'[154] Jesus is that light and he himself says that:

---

[153] *Matthew* 4: 16.
[154] *Matthew* 4: 16.

'I am the light of the world; anyone who follows me will not be walking in the dark; he will have the light of life.' [155]

Christians of great faith approach the end of their lives in the confidence that they will be going to God and to life everlasting. My own aunt was one such person. Terminally ill, she confidently informed my mother that she was not in the least bit afraid. She would be going to a far better place than the one she was in now. Her faith was absolute; her total trust and belief in the Lord one hundred per cent.

When I explained all this to a priest, I very much enjoyed his response. He said: 'Having a faith that is so strong it overcomes our fear of death is wonderful. I also truly believe that I will live until the end of time with God, but that's not to say I wouldn't be a little bit anxious about it all.

It's a bit like starting a new job really... You can be confident that you will be good at the job and master everything you are required to do, but it's still nerve-wracking and a bit worrying when you actually start, on the first day!'

---

[155] *John* 8: 12.

*There's no Escape, so Face the Fear*

Each of us will depart this life at some point, but for some of us the fear of our demise can become cripplingly debilitating. Susan Jeffers poses the question:

'What is it for you? ... We fear beginnings; we fear endings ... We fear dying.' [156] She goes on to explain that we can overcome our fear of *anything*, even dying and can 'move from a place of pain, paralysis and depression (feelings that often accompany fear) to one of power, energy and excitement.' [157]

We can learn a lot from Ms Jeffers. Firstly, our fear of dying should never be allowed to overrule our daily lives. Life is precious and God has given life to us all. We should live our lives to the full, bearing fruit and making our lives a personal achievement of our time on earth.

To be blighted by fear is to prevent us from gaining the full measure of the life with which we've been graced. Furthermore, Daniel O'Leary explains that Jeffers recognizes that our fear can often bring about a

---

[156] *Feel the Fear and do it Anyway!* – Susan Jeffers, p. 2.
[157] *Feel the Fear and do it Anyway!* – Susan Jeffers, p. 2.

new closeness with God. He says that: 'While fear can clearly diminish and even destroy our joy and freedom, it can also be a hidden grace. It's only when we are afraid – at the moment of our fear – that we can take a unique step forward into a new, personal freedom, into another stage of growing towards God.' [158]

If we consider the two statements to be true, then the sum total of their combination is fascinating. To clarify: we can be frightened of dying, despite the fact that our death will bring us so much closer to God than we can ever be in our early lives. Yet in our very fear of death, we're actually becoming closer and growing towards God anyway! And so it is that God seizes every opportunity to turn our negative feelings and emotions into a positive, life restoring, loving act.

This will ultimately result in an ever-growing closeness with our heavenly Father. We should try to face our fear and believe in the promises which were given to us by Jesus Christ, but if we're unable to overcome it, then we should take some consolation and appreciate that God understands our fear anyway and uses this weakness in us to draw us inexorably closer to him.

---

[158] *Prism of Love* – Daniel O'Leary, p. 61.

## *An Ending or New Beginning for One and All*

Christ suggests on more than one occasion, that at some undisclosed point in the future, mankind will be forced to face the 'end-times.'

The readings for the beginning of Advent each year particularly highlight this theme, with predictions of pain, fear and bewilderment as all are called to justice, as the Son of Man re-enters our world:

'There will be signs in the sun and moon and stars; on earth nations in agony, bewildered by the clamour of the ocean and its waves; men dying of fear as they await what menaces the world, for the powers of heaven will be shaken.' [159]

In the similar confusion and misunderstanding experienced by the disciples when Jesus tried to explain many things to them, we too are unsure of what exactly Jesus is referring to, in both the phrase given above and also in others:

'Immediately after the distress of those days the sun will be darkened, the moon will lose its brightness, the stars will fall from the sky and the powers of

---

[159] *Luke* 21: 25 - 27.

heaven will be shaken. And then the sign of the Son of Man will appear in heaven; then too all the peoples of the earth will beat their breasts.' [160]

St Mark's Gospel gives a similar account [161] and the Second Letter of St Peter and the First Letter of St Paul to the Thessalonians give further testimony to the end times which have been foretold:

'We must be careful to remember that during the last days there are bound to be people who are scornful, the kind who always please themselves what they do... The present sky and earth are destined for fire, and are only being reserved until Judgement day so that all sinners may be destroyed.' [162]

'You will not be expecting us to write anything to you, brothers, about 'times and seasons', since you know very well that the day of the Lord is going to come like a thief in the night. It's when people are saying, 'How quiet and peaceful it is' that the worst suddenly happens, as suddenly as labour pains come

---

[160] *Matthew* 24: 29 - 30.
[161] *Mark* 13: 24 - 37.
[162] 2 *Peter* 3: 3 - 7.

on a pregnant woman, and there will be no way for anybody to evade it.' [163]

The idea of the end of our world as we know it, when we're all called to account for our lives, our actions, and our behaviour, as Christ re-joins humanity, will supposedly shake the foundations of our world to the core. Even theologians can only hazard a guess as to what the future holds. Yet we can be certain that we must try to do our utmost to prepare ourselves for this moment in the world's history. We should establish a life-plan that's in accordance with the Father's wishes and tallies with that specified by Jesus.

We can only be sure that we must take this advice unreservedly:

'Stay awake, because you do not know when the master of the house is coming, evening, midnight, cockcrow, dawn; if he comes unexpectedly, he must not find you asleep. And what I say to you I say to all: "Stay awake!"' [164]

Anthony Spencer, in William Paul Young's *Crossroads,* is given a unique opportunity for conversion

---

[163] *1 Thessalonians* 5: 1 - 4.
[164] *Mark* 13: 35 - 37.

of the soul, as he experiences the Trinitarian presence while in a deep coma. When informed that he is 'lying in a room at OHSU' (hospital) and that he was 'approaching the event of physical death' [165] he is understandably horrified. But due to God's redeeming love and grace, he is able to realize the errors in his life, genuinely repent of them and devise a selfless gesture, (gifting his own opportunity of healing, recovery and life to another), in an action which reflects Christ's own on Calvary.

While at an enjoyable fictional level the story holds entertainment value, the message is however, very clear. We must live our lives as if every day were our last, because eventually in the future, this will indeed be the case and all the pain, hurt and wrong-doing that we've accumulated over the years will be unresolved.

Tony Spencer was given a unique opportunity for amendment while he was in a coma. We though, should remember to examine and re-examine our words and actions constantly and live each day as if it were our last. For Tony Spencer's situation was fictitious and could not happen in reality – or could it?!

---

[165] *Crossroads* – William Paul Young, p. 82.

*Stay Strong, be Courageous, take Heart!*

Death marks the end of our physical life and how this death comes about varies from person to person; old age, illness or accident. None of us knows which of these it will be until it actually occurs, but most of us hope for a quick, painless release from our earthly lives. Many of us are frightened of what is to come, and most of us have a dread of any physical suffering which might accompany the approach of death. There's no easy solution to these worries, and each and every one of us must confront these thoughts and feelings in our own personal way.

As an example, a down-to-earth acquaintance of mine, when referring to the death of her spouse, said, 'If you are a couple and you've been together or married for many years, it's obvious that at some point one of you will die, and the other be left on their own. It's just a question of which of you will 'go' first!' This is certainly one coping mechanism, but this method would probably not suit everyone. In short, whether we worry about the prospect of our own earthly demise or the death of those we love around us, or not, death is inevitable and we cannot change the fact that it will certainly occur.

Nonetheless, *The Catechism of the Catholic Church* reminds us that:

> 'The Christian meaning of death is revealed in the light of the *Paschal mystery* of the death and Resurrection of Christ in whom resides our only hope. The Christian who dies in Christ Jesus is "away from the body and at home with the Lord."' [166]

Christ's sacrifice on Calvary earned for us eternal life and this fact needs to remain ingrained in our hearts, minds and lives. Theologian Thomas Groome further corroborates the Church's doctrine with 'cautious optimism', but in reference to the promise of eternal life, he remains, although cautious, positive:

> 'Yet, let's not be naïve about ourselves. We can and too often do choose sin and evil, hatred and destruction. Plus, all of us get sick and will die – the ultimate counter to naïve optimism about our existence. As the same psalmist also wrote, people "resemble the beasts that perish" *(Psalm 49:12)*. But over against the realities of sin and death, Christian faith claims that Jesus has conquered sin and made death go backward, not into the abyss but opening

---

[166] *The Catechism of the Catholic Church,* Paragraph 1681.

into new life. A cautious optimism seems in order.' [167]

Fear remains one of the hardest things in life to overcome. But alongside that fear, we're given joy and happiness and love. God gave us his only Son to bring these into our lives, so let us live our lives to the full and always remember that Christ promised us eternal life. And God doesn't break his promises:

Please God, help us be strong, courageous, take heart, and be optimistic about our eternal life with you.

---

[167] *What makes us Catholic* – Thomas Groome, p. 48.

*The Fullness of Life*

# ~ *Chapter Thirteen* ~

## The Fullness of Life

Most women will have experienced the thrill of looking at the ultrasound scan of their unborn baby in the womb, of having its heartbeat pointed out to them, seeing its tiny arms, legs and head and watching its movements on the screen. A photograph is even provided for the proud parents-to-be! The sight is awesome, precious and a moment to savour. Although most of us usually take life for granted, it is in reality an enormous gift. Usually it is not until our own lives are threatened in some way – by accident 'near-miss', serious illness, or hearing about the death of someone we know or love, that we take the great gift of life seriously and appreciate again its intrinsic value.

After the birth of my first child at 1.30 in the morning, I was so excited, awed and overwhelmed by the event, that although very tired, I was totally unable to sleep for the rest of that night. I kept re-living the whole experience for hours afterwards, and even though I had had a good idea of what to expect, the actual event was quite simply incredible. The fact that my husband and I, by the grace of God, had given life to this tiny being, which I had delivered early that morning, seemed to me to be completely mind-blowing.

Every time we bring new life into the world it's an absolute miracle. Usually, parents love their children unconditionally. In fact, it 'goes with the territory', except in those terrible cases which we often hear about from time to time in the media. Sadly, when my closest friend was dying of cancer, her mother told me during a conversation, that if she could swap places with her daughter, she would gladly do so. Of course, this can never be possible and is, furthermore, not the will of God. However, the fact remains that a parent's love for their child is generally all-consuming and unquench-able.

New life is so undeniably precious, and such a great gift, that it gives huge credibility to the Catholic Church's vehement opposition to abortion. Never-theless, as in so many areas of life, some situations regarding abortion are not easily definable or quantifiable. As an example, a woman who had been raped and then found consequently that she was pregnant, would be faced with a dilemma. She could then either be genuinely opposed to giving birth to the baby of her attacker, and feel that the subsequent child would always be a reminder of its father, or take the view that something good has come from this terrible experience. This of course, would be the new life of the child. Furthermore, she may also feel that the child in the womb did not deserve to die, because of an event that was not its fault and out of its control.

There are no easy answers or solutions to such questions; it would to some extent depend upon the nature and circumstances of the particular woman. In a different situation, a pregnant woman may still not want to keep her baby, and the reasons for this may be just as complex and painful. Therefore we should try to reserve judgement wherever possible because only the Lord can discern it. Whether we agree with abortion or not, whether we can sympathize with the circumstances surrounding this difficult decision, or not, the fact remains that all life is God-given and precious; a huge gift from God himself, which therefore should be afforded respect, love and care.

The Catechism of the Catholic Church emphasizes that:

'Human life must be respected and protected absolutely from the moment of conception. From the first moment of his existence, a human being must be recognized as having the rights of a person –

among which are the inviolable right of every
innocent being to life.' [168]

In recent years abortions have escalated at an
alarming rate and we cannot help but wonder about the
pain and suffering that these would-be-mothers
undergo, having reached such a difficult decision.
However, the removal of life is against God's will and
our Catholic doctrine. It's a worrying concept for all the
faithful to grapple with. Liz Dodd illustrates this in *The
Tablet* when she quotes The Archbishop of Southwark,
Peter Smith as saying: 'Over time we have seen the
gradual erosion of the moral significance of this
profound decision and the re-framing of it as a simple
medical procedure' and he went on to express that:

> 'Many people, while not necessarily agreeing with
> the Church's opposition to abortion are 'deeply
> troubled by the current situation where we have
> 200,000 abortions a year.' [169]

---

[168] *Catechism of the Catholic Church,* Paragraph 2270.
[169] *The Tablet* – 8th February 2014.

## *Jesus as Life-Restoring Healer*

Whether or not we agree with or have empathy towards women who undergo abortion, we do know that Christ, the giver of new life, constantly led the way in a crusade to bring life to all. His miracles often involved not only restoring life to people but giving them also true fullness of life and hope in him. In St Matthew's Gospel we read of double life-restoring miracles, virtually back-to-back:

'While he was speaking to them, up came one of the officials, who bowed low in front of him and said, 'My daughter has just died, but come and lay your hand on her and her life will be saved.' Jesus rose and, with his disciples, followed him. Then from behind him came a woman who had suffered from a haemorrhage for twelve years, and she touched the fringe of his cloak, for she said to herself, 'If I can only touch his cloak I shall be well again.' Jesus turned round and saw her; and he said to her, 'Courage, my daughter, your faith has restored you to health.' And from that moment the woman was well again.

When Jesus reached the official's house and saw the flute players, with the crowd making a commotion, he said, 'Get out of here; the little girl is not dead, she is asleep.' And they laughed at him. But when the people had been turned out he went inside and took the little girl by the hand; and she stood up.' [170]

In the second miracle: that of the official's daughter, we recognize Jesus as life-restoring healer, as the child is released from death and returned to life. We're unsure of her age as she is referred to as a 'little girl' in St Matthew's Gospel. However, in St Mark's Gospel, where the same story is retold with only slight variations, we're given the age of the child as twelve years.[171] This is interesting, as customarily, in Jewish society at that time, young girls were betrothed at the age of approximately thirteen years, (as was Mary, the Mother of God). This early betrothal had a purpose: that these girls could then realize the best of their child-bearing years. Not only was this the case, but life expectancy was far less than that we experience today. So when Jesus restored life to this twelve year old, there was every possibility that she would then be betrothed within a few months, and possibly bear a child herself, within a year or two. Hence, we recognize Christ as the liberator of life in a twofold way; restoring life to the 'little girl' and in so doing enabling her to pass on the gift of life by producing children of her own.

---

[170] *Matthew* 9: 18 - 26.
[171] The miracle is also recounted in *Luke* 8: 40 - 56.

In all three synoptic Gospels, we read about the haemorrhaging woman who's miraculously cured merely by touching the hem of Jesus's robes. [172] Again we see Jesus portrayed as one who heals the body and spirit of a person of great faith. However, we're told that the woman has been suffering haemorrhages for a number of years and no cure has been found for her. It's not clear from the Scripture passage exactly what part of the body the haemorrhage came from, but I think that we can probably assume that it was not life-threatening, as she is out and about in the crowds surrounding Jesus. It's entirely possible that the blood loss refers to a menstrual disorder, which today would be corrected by a small routine operation. If we assume then, that this was the illness that she was suffering from, it follows that her ability to reproduce would be severely impaired. In fact, she may not have been able to have children at all. And so we begin to see that by curing her of this complaint, it's likely that she would be able to start a family of her own and in so doing, we yet again recognize Christ as giver of new life.

### *The Sanctity of Human Life*

Despite the fact that the demand for abortions has increased year on year, the prognosis on the sanctity of

---

[172] *Matthew* 9: 20 - 22, *Mark* 5: 25 - 34 & *Luke* 8: 43 - 48.

human life is not all doom and gloom. We only have to turn on the television to see advertising campaigns asking us to make donations towards various causes around the world, where people are needlessly dying. The continuing food shortage in Africa is a good example of this. Shelters for the homeless, soup kitchens and adoption and foster-care organizations, are all part of a scheme to preserve human life, and afford it the dignity it deserves. Hospitals and modern-day medicines are designed to heal the sick, and prolong life for as long as is humanly and humanely possible. It should be noted that we're also dependent upon *each other* to sustain life to the full, and in so doing we once again witness God working in co-operation with man.

God himself gave us the commandment 'You shall not kill' in the Decalogue in the Bible, [173] and Jesus reinforces this message in the Sermon on the Mount, when he forcibly reminds the crowds of God's words. [174] We're called to love one another, and when doing so, it's then a natural progression that we nurture and cherish each other's lives. Miraculously, as we strive to maintain life in others, *so we are given a renewal of life of our own.* Our spiritual lives are revitalized and filled with the life-giving spirit of our Lord Jesus Christ. He holds all life

---

[173] *Exodus* 20: 13.
[174] *Matthew* 5: 21.

dear to him and has given that life to us in the first place. Additionally, in God's redeeming work, we see another example of where in our giving we're also receiving. Whether our life-giving actions are pre-planned to help others, or whether they are a spur-of-the-moment deed to prolong another's life, the net result remains the same: a life has been saved and extended, and new depth of life in the Spirit given to the one who brought this about. Furthermore, it's by God's grace that we're enabled and empowered to perform this type of action in the first place. Timothy Radcliffe enlarges on this point when he says that:

> 'Jesus ... is utterly in every act, incarnate in the deed. He is fully in what he does. Christ in us makes all our actions ours. 'The just man justices; keeps grace: that keeps all his goings graces'. For us such spontaneity is the fruit of a deep travail, of rebirth... Deep spontaneity characteristic of holy people who do not simply react, superficially, but rather respond immediately from the depths of their being, from the heart.' [175]

We recognize that, by according life the sanctity it deserves, we're not only following Christ's example,

---

[175] *What is the point of being a Christian?* – Timothy Radcliffe, p. 44.

but are allowing ourselves to become closer to him. We can then allow him into our hearts and lives, and we increase in holiness as we do so. In the beautiful yet almost teasing narrative between Jesus and the Samaritan woman at the well, Jesus speaks of drinking 'the water that I shall give and never be[ing] thirsty again' because, he goes on to add, 'the water that I shall give will turn into a spring inside ... welling up to eternal life.' [176] We can admit this living water, which we hear Jesus referring to, into our own lives every single day, by recognizing life in the Spirit. Through Jesus Christ it will continue for all eternity. We can learn to recognize it in others and in so doing help them to recognize it and receive it themselves.

In fact, Jesus reiterates this message again in St John's Gospel when he cries out that: 'If any man is thirsty, let him come to me! Let the man come and drink who believes in me!' As Scripture says, 'From his breast shall flow fountains of living water. He was speaking of the Spirit which those who believed in him were to receive.' [177]

In this speech we also hear Jesus quoting sacred scripture to lend an authenticity to his words, as he is

---

[176] *John* 4: 13 - 14.
[177] *John* 7: 37 - 39.

well aware of how much authority was given to such sacred scripture by the Jews of that time. The Scribes and Pharisees particularly placed the utmost importance upon it. When Jesus uses scripture to highlight and give emphasis to his words, we can be assured that they are of vital importance. We further recognize his frequent use of fruits of the earth or nature in his analogies. In other words, we hear Jesus giving an important truth set out in terms to which we can easily relate, and this is because he desperately *wants* all to comprehend it. And he wants everyone to comprehend it because if we are to receive life in the Spirit, then we must receive Jesus, and to be open to receive Jesus, we must treat our physical and spiritual lives with reverence.

### *The Very Life of the Lord*

In the encyclical *Evangelium Vitae* Pope St John Paul II writes that: 'The Gospel of life is at the heart of Jesus's message... When he presents the heart of his redemptive mission, Jesus says: "I came that they may have life, and have it abundantly." *(John 10: 10)*. In truth, he is referring to that 'new' and 'eternal' life which consists in communion with the Father, to which every person is freely called in the Son by the power of the sanctifying Spirit. It's precisely in this 'life' that all the aspects and stages of human life achieve their full significance...[178] As the Second Vatican Council teaches: Christ 'perfected revelation by fulfilling it through his whole work of making himself present and manifesting himself; through his words and deeds, his signs and wonders, but especially through his death and glorious Resurrection from the dead and final sending of the Spirit of truth. Moreover, he confirmed with divine testimony what revelation proclaimed: that God is with us to free us from the darkness of sin and death, and to raise us up to life eternal.' [179]

God in the incarnation sent his only son so that we may live forever, and have new life after death in Christ Jesus or, as St Paul puts it to the residents of Corinth:

> 'We are not all going to die, but we shall all be changed. This will be instantaneous, in the twinkling of an eye, when the last trumpet sounds...Death is swallowed up in victory. Death where is *your* victory? *Death where is your sting?* Now the sting of death is sin, and sin gets its power

---

[178] Encyclical letter of Blessed (St) Pope John Paul II, *Evangelium Vitae,* Paragraph 1.
[179] Encyclical letter of Blessed (St) Pope John Paul II, *Evangelium Vitae,* Paragraph 29.

from the Law. So let us thank God for giving us the victory through our Lord Jesus Christ.' [180]

By our baptism we become sharers in the life of Christ and the life of his church, and by allowing our hearts to receive Christ we can continue to live in and within him. Every time we partake in the Eucharist, we fully share in his life, death and resurrection, as we're given a taste of the new life that Christ promises will be ours, after our physical life has ended.

'When we die, in a sense that is it. The story that can be told of us is concluded… But there's more: in Christ, the whole of our life story, from birth to death, is taken up into God's life. This brief human life in all its particularity is embraced by God and opened to the infinite. All that we have done and been will be gathered up into God… Even our failures and sins find some sort of meaning.' [181]

This perspective given by Timothy Radcliffe, who also draws upon the wisdom of Julian of Norwich, explores the idea of eternal life with the Lord at an even deeper and more fascinating level. He suggests

---

[180] 1 *Corinthians* 15: 51, 54 - 57.
[181] *What is the point of being a Christian?* – Timothy Radcliffe, pp. 86/87.

that not only will we reside with the Father for all eternity, but that all our life experiences will be utilized, not wasted; even those which we ourselves wouldn't recognize as particularly useful. Personally, I find these words deeply comforting. It would seem that all the times during my life when there has been despair, pain and mistakes won't have been in vain. In fact, the new life which is to follow will encompass these in a positive way. However, we must have faith and trust in Christ, as we have no understanding of how this will happen.

### *Love Brings Life*

The union between man and woman can result in new human life, but love in itself can also bring new life. When a mother smiles down at her child, or two people in love look at each other their faces are alight with the love that shines within them and which transforms their life into one of love. In our difficult and troubled times, relationships rupture and hurt follows, as we stray from the sanctity of life, love and marriage, as Jim McManus indicates: 'Men and women have to struggle to make the sincere gift of self to one another. John Paul [182] said: 'The human body in its masculinity and femininity has

---

[182] Refers to Pope St John Paul II.

almost lost the power of expressing this love in which the human person becomes a gift.' [183]

Divorce rates have increased, marriages seem fewer, and numbers of single parent families are steadily rising. However, our salvation history makes it evident that we are God's chosen people, and for God's chosen people there's always hope and purpose. In each other we can find transforming love, and in Christ Jesus we can be doubly assured of this. When we share our love for each other, our love for the Lord (and his for us) transforms us and makes us whole. For the Lord not only loves us, he is totally *in love* with us.

'As a doe longs for running streams, So longs my soul for you, my God. My soul thirsts for God, the God of life; when shall I go to see the face of God…?

'Then I shall go to the altar of God, to the God of my joy, I shall rejoice, I shall praise you on the harp, my God' [184]

[183] *I am my body* – Jim McManus, p. 90.
[184] *Psalm* 42 - 43.

*Who do we Think we Are?*

# ~ *Chapter Fourteen* ~
## Who do we Think we Are?

The previous chapters of this book have attempted in some measure to explore various areas of our lives and how they are affected by our relationship with God. Although we can be unaware of it, most of us yearn for God, 'like a doe longs for running streams.' [184] We long for a personal relationship with Christ and to recognize and know the Holy Spirit working in our lives. Pope Francis in his Apostolic Exhortation *Evangelii Gaudium* writes:

> 'I invite all Christians everywhere, at this very moment, to a renewed personal encounter with Jesus Christ.' [185]

As a complex people we often encounter difficulties in trying to bring this about, but it seems fair to say that unless we understand ourselves, we have little hope of trying to understand and learn about the Lord and about others. The anonymous author of the *Cloud of Unknowing* makes the point that:

---

[185] *Evangelii Gaudium* – The Joy of the Gospel, Paragraph 3.

'For of all other creatures and their works, yea and of the works of God's self, may a man through grace have full head of knowing and well he can think of them.'[186]

['A man may, by grace, have the fullness of knowledge of all other creatures and their works, yes, and of the works of God's own self, and he is well able to reflect on them.'][187]

This quotation from this famous piece of medieval mysticism is interesting because when taken at face value, the author appears to be of the opinion that man is quite knowledgeable about his fellow creatures and God. On closer examination, in fact, it expresses the view that on the contrary, man actually knows very little about either of these. The key word on the first line is *may* have knowledge of other creatures and with regards to the Lord, we're only familiar with the 'works' of God; those actions which are apparent to mankind, such as the creative action of God. In general terms, most of us find it difficult to understand other people because essentially we're multi-faceted, complex

---

[186] *The Cloud of Unknowing* – Anonymous, p. 14.
[187] Taken from *The Cloud of Unknowing*, different edition and editor.

individuals. As a consequence, we often find it difficult to understand and know our own selves.

### *Learning to Love Ourselves*

In recent years, the contemporary phrase 'How can you love someone else if you don't love yourself?' has become popular. Hand-in-hand with this expression is a similar one: 'Feeling comfortable in your own skin'. But what exactly does this mean? Quite simply it means to be at peace with oneself, happy with the way our life is being lived and the actions we're taking. Loving oneself is really an extension of this state of being, with the added assurance of being happy, lovable and loved. We may strive to be independent, yet most of us love to be loved and need to be needed. To put it another way, Fowler writes regarding ourselves:

> 'It is a matter of becoming aware of self as self, and this means in relation to, and with the help of, the responses of others.' [188]

For many of us, the inability to love ourselves is only the beginning of the problem. A surprising number of us don't really understand ourselves either. As an example, we can so often hear people exclaim 'I don't

---

[188] *Faith development and pastoral care* – J. Fowler, p. 56.

really know why I did that!' or use a similar expression. In matters of the heart; in our relationships, we all too often behave in a way which we afterwards wonder at, and which can irretrievably damage a particular relationship. In fact, we're often surprised at how we react under certain circumstances, particularly in adverse ones or 'when push comes to shove'. In other words, we often give voice to words and use actions, which in retrospect puzzle us and make us wonder why we've said or done those things. While this appears to be a part of everyday life, we should really attempt to resolve these issues, by learning to love and understand ourselves.

In a previous chapter the fact that many of us are dissatisfied with our physical appearance was discussed and in this we can often be our own worst critics. Certainly in our younger years our outward appearance is of huge importance to us. Peer pressure in schools and the awakening of sexual attraction with the start of sexual relationships, contributes towards the desire to be acceptably appealing or alluring. Yet as we advance through our lives, our own personal priorities seem to change. Outward physical appearances often become less important. Happily, many of us will have found a partner to share our lives with by this time, and hopefully the maturity of the union will help us realize that each one is happy with the other just as they physically are. With advancing years we're forced to face the fact that unless we undergo cosmetic surgery of the 'nip and tuck' variety, we cannot hope to regain the appearance of our lost youth, and that younger men and women are now the ones who are more physically attractive than ourselves.

Although this may be a rather gloomy outlook, it is however, realistic. Yet with this mind-set comes a softening, a freedom from the angst which so often accompanies our younger years, when we're preoccupied with how we appear. With this attitude comes peace and acceptance, and alongside this comes a part of our learning to love ourselves – at least physically.

### *Looking all Right but Feeling all Wrong*

Strange as it may sound, I have also met people who don't like their own dispositions either. Every case is different and a generalization is, of course, difficult, but there are usually a set of common factors where this applies. Sometimes people dislike their own personality make-up due to a past incident involving other people. Fowler explains how we're inevitably shaped in relation to others:

'There is no selfhood that is not formed in relation to others and to the culture of shared social meaning and institutions.' [189]

A person's view of themselves can be affected when they feel they've committed some error or sin which has remained unresolved and this can easily become a negative perception. Resolution with the person or persons involved, prayer and the Sacrament of Reconciliation would make a huge difference in these situations. By the grace of God, that person would then be able to discard their own feeling of self-dislike and self-pain, and be able to enjoy life again as they recover their self-esteem and self-worth. Often after a series of unfortunate events a person may feel that they 'can't get anything right', and because of this belief they can become bogged down in self-recrimination, which inevitably leads to self-deprecation. In this we see a model for Fowler's definition. Personality traits could also be held responsible for someone disliking themselves; for example, a person who suffers from shyness, could well find that this interferes negatively with their interactions with others, particularly socially. As a consequence of this, they eventually come to dislike, if not themselves, but very often this *aspect* of

---

[189] *Faith development and pastoral care* – J. Fowler, p. 55.

themselves. On the subject of personality traits, sadly there are those who view the world through a negative lens and this negativity can even extend to their view of their own selves. Basically, through their own lack of positivity, people such as this perceive themselves in the most negative way possible, they feel unlovable and very often misunderstood. Naturally this explanation only scratches the surface of why some people do not, or cannot, love themselves as every person and situation is unique and quite complex.

We can like or dislike our physical exterior and the same goes for our spiritual and mental interior. Unfortunately however, we can come across people who have no liking for themselves either internally or externally. Why is the word 'unfortunately' used in this context and why therefore, should we be content with our physical appearances and our own unique personalities?

### *The Face of Christ*

It could be argued that if we've no desire to love ourselves, then why should we have to? It's our own *self* that's involved; our body, our mind, our heart and our own soul, and therefore completely separate from any other person. You might also add that it's no one else's business but the person themselves! This does seem a reasonable argument in the first instance. However, there are huge flaws in it as you will see:

If we cannot love our own self, it *does* affect others. It shapes our behaviour, our worldview, and also has a knock-on effect on the social and relationship aspects of our lives. Even more importantly, God created each and every one of us, along with the world, the universe and everything in it. He gave us our outward appearances and although these are not perfect for most of us, we often have at least some redeeming features! God made us in his own image and likeness [190] as we're told in the Bible, and therefore if we're made in the likeness of God, who are we to complain about our appearance? We know that God loves us.

This is explained to us repeatedly in the Bible and in the very action of Christ's incarnation, suffering, death and resurrection. As a consequence of this, if we're so loved by the Lord then how could we not love ourselves? As we've been blessed with this great love from the God who formed us, and given the ability to love others also, it becomes almost an affront to God and a rejection of God's love therefore, if we refuse to love ourselves to the same extent.

---

[190] *Genesis* 1:27.

Sister Helen Prejean fully understood the concept of being able to love oneself and to then be able to pass that love on to others. In her last conversation with convicted murderer Patrick Sonnier, before he was put to death by electrocution she said:

'I want the last thing you see in this world to be a face of love. Look at me... I will be the face of Christ for you. I will be the face of love for you.'

In this remarkable statement Sister Helen is expressing many thoughts and emotions. She is demonstrably trying to give Sonnier the love and comfort that he so desperately needs at that moment, but in so doing she is articulating a love that many would have found difficult to put into words.

No doubt the grace of the Holy Spirit prompted her to express such simple words of love, but the fact remains, that as Christ is present in each one of us, and God is unconditional love, then we should be able to love our neighbour and to love ourselves.

When Sr Helen says 'I will be the face of Christ for you' she identifies Christ within herself and alongside this his love for her, Sonnier and every other single person.

## The Subjective Face

We know that many of us assume a 'public face' or mask which we use to protect ourselves from hurt, ridicule and embarrassment. It has become a self-defence mechanism and as such is quite effective, as it usually helps keep our self-esteem intact. On the other hand, when hiding behind a façade, how can others know us as we really are? Sometimes the free exposition of our flaws and fragility can actually present us in a better light; a more truthful, human, realistic light, where our flaws are revealed with honesty and humility, which generally appeals to others.

Christ in his humanity was apprehensive about the fate which he knew was to be his, but he was not afraid to express this: 'Father,' he said, 'if you are willing, take this cup away from me.' [191]

Yet again we hear the anguished Christ who's unsure of his Father's intentions, expressing his feelings for all to hear: 'My God, My God, why have you deserted me?' [192]

---

[191] *Luke* 22: 42.
[192] *Matthew* 27: 46.

Christ may have been unsure and afraid of his fate, but he was not frightened to express those feelings, and allow others to see both his humanity and his vulnerability.

> 'We are rarely told about how much Jesus learned from his shadow side – from the outrage, the anger, the temptations, the doubts that plagued his life. In the dark light of his desert temptations we see one of his many faces. In his encounters with the women in his life, we see many more. To Mary and Martha he revealed the face of his need for human intimacy. On his day of anger in the temple, he showed the world his face of outrage... His face of despair stares at us from the Cross.' [193]

The problem that we have to accept is that if we continually wear the 'mask' and hide our true selves, then we're also at risk of concealing the Christ who dwells within us.

### A Blueprint for Ourselves

While it can sometimes take quite a while to get to know and recognize the authentic person that's at the core of ourselves, there are a few basic concepts that we

---

[193] *Prism of Love* – Daniel O'Leary, p. 12.

should acknowledge and apply to guide us in our quest. Firstly, in any given situation we should try to analyse how we're feeling about things, question whether we're being reasonable in our analysis, and then try to be true to ourselves in the outcome. Often, if we don't follow this line of reasoning we can 'chop and change' in our dealings with others and this can sometimes lead to hypocrisy – a wholly undesirable trait. We should certainly not try to be what we think other people would like us to be. We're a unique blueprint of ourselves; we were formed this way in the womb and that's our God-given inheritance.

In addition, we really need to put our beliefs into practice. We should attempt to live out our faith every day of our lives. But these are other beliefs that we hold which can be important to each of us as well. We're not required to have a campaigning 'soapbox' mentality, but the quiet determination and assurance of a person who sticks to their own particular values can be admirable.

Likewise, we should become familiar with those elements in our lives which help bring out the best in us. For some people creativity can achieve this, for others, caring for people, and yet again others may function at their optimum level in an academic context. It actually matters very little which of these examples and countless others, best suit us. What is important is that when we find our own calling or pursuit we will grow and change for the better. We will inevitably blossom in those circumstances which suit us best and in so doing we will then become far closer to the perfect blueprint of ourselves that we were designed to be.

Recognition of when and where we feel 'most alive' is also critical. These times and places may perhaps be simple and mundane, such as being with our children, partner, husband or wife or our families. It could be when we're at work or when we're at Mass or in prayer. Wherever it is, we can be sure that Christ is with us at those times, for God always aspires to bring out the best in us.

If we're able to recognize this time of 'feeling alive' and being close to Christ, then we should be able to maximize those occasions and actively seek them. When we can do so we're definitely making progress and should be glad!

Identifying our own moods, what makes us feel good and conversely what does not, is a helpful tool in learning about our characters. Better still, learning to change those feelings and moods can make all the difference to our quality of life. It's so easy to slide into negativity, but once we begin to consider all the positive features of our lives, our frame of mind cannot help but change. The frequently used adage 'live, laugh, love' definitely contains a measure of truth. We're required to live our lives to the full, turn tears into laughter and to love and *be* loved.

So important are these commands that we could almost add these to the Beatitudes that Christ gave to us. And the reason they are important is because if we live our lives to the full, following the ways of Jesus, loving others and allowing ourselves to be loved, then we will feel joy in our lives and will be able to pass on that joy to others. Daniel O'Leary explains on a personal note how negativity can never bear fruit:

'All this negative thinking is only damaging my own peace of mind. If I don't stop this now I'll make myself even more unhappy and I'll be impossible to live with…. So I began to think about all the good things in my life…. What is happening to me is a growing awareness of the choices I have about how I live and feel each day… So, God is good. Enjoy today…. It is up to you.' [194]

---

[194] *Prism of Love* – Daniel O'Leary, p. 16.

## *Character Flaws or Self Indulgence*

As we learn to understand our own characters – and remember; to do this we must be totally honest with ourselves – we can also learn to discern whether we act in a certain way because it's in our nature, or whether we're just allowing ourselves the selfish luxury of becoming undisciplined. When it's natural it could be said to be a fundamental part of our personality and is therefore unavoidable for us to react in certain ways. Interestingly, whichever the reason, it's a good idea to try and reflect upon whether our actions and reactions are a positive or negative experience.

Obviously, if we decide that they are positive, all well and good. If, however, we feel that they are negative, then our thoughts should turn to the how, what and why, of the situation. Self-discipline is vital; without it we allow our emotions and actions to go on the rampage unchecked, and once this takes place both other people and ourselves can suffer. After all, are you the slave of your emotions or the master of them? Who's the boss around here?!

At times we can feel unsure of who we are, where we're going, what we need, feel and believe. Yet critically, and in direct opposition to this, God always remains the same and is the one constant in our lives that we can be sure of. We don't understand God, nor are we meant to, but we *can* learn to understand ourselves. No matter how pessimistic we feel about ourselves, we should remember that we should not be, because Christ is present in each one of us.

Not only this, but despite our faults we've been made in God's image, called by name and given a meaning to our lives through God's healing power and love. If we desire to live lives that thrive on love, and benefit in the full sharing of God's grace, there's little to remember.

It's simply that when we learn to know and love ourselves, we learn to know and love Christ who is always present within us.

# ~ Chapter Fifteen ~

## 'I Was a Stranger and You made Me Welcome' [195]

The word hospitality originates from a Latin word and means 'love of strangers' and this is often commended in the Bible. Nowadays however, the word carries a different connotation, which is the provision of

---

[195] *Matthew* 25: 35.

refreshment and accommodation to friends, family and acquaintances, for just a while.

Christ extends his invitation to 'come and see' [196] where he lives, which has a twofold interpretation. On one level he wants us to recognize that he lives within each and every one of us, and on another level there's the invitation to come to know and follow him. We understand that the disciples responded to the hospitality that was offered to them by Jesus, as they left everything and followed him to an unknown destination and destiny. As Jesus offered his hospitality to those disciples and moreover, accepted and even sought out hospitality from others, ('Zacchaeus ... I must stay at your house today.'[197]), so we're expected to do the same.

While it's anticipated that we will do likewise, this doesn't just mean inviting our friends around for coffee and cake, or for dinner! However there's absolutely nothing wrong with this kind of hospitality. As humans we naturally interact with other people, form friendships and relationships and these sort of social occasions will always help to reinforce this. Indeed, it's a privilege to be invited to another person's home and

---

[196] *John* 1: 39.
[197] *Luke* 19: 6.

to share in their surroundings and accept their refreshment, because when we do so we're sharing in a part of their lives. We also need to recognize that there's a certain intimacy about inviting other people into our homes and to share our meals. When we do this, we are in fact, growing in our imitation of Christ:

'Each time we meet someone, we are called to see, hear and touch them with the love and wisdom of Christ. To see Him in the stranger, to hear Him, to go to Him and to touch Him we need to be vessels filled by His presence, allowing him to show God's unending love to and through us.' [198]

Jesus instructed all of us to make the stranger welcome. At some time or another, many of us have encountered a situation where we were in unfamiliar circumstances with no acquaintances or friends nearby to chat to, be with, or support us. This is a lonely feeling. When someone then comes to our aid, and strikes up a conversation with us, it's a great relief.

Naturally, we're usually glad to be included in an event, social or otherwise. Few of us enjoy feeling 'left out' or unwelcome. But do remember this caveat: by all

---

[198] *Life Journey* – Mary Fleeson, p. 126
(Quoting St Teresa of Avila).

means, make the stranger welcome in any way possible, but don't forget that there could be people with whom we're *already acquainted* who also need to be made to feel welcome. To clarify: there are many people who are socially on the fringes – who are 'looking in' – people who are often lonely, or shy, and long to be included.

However, for one reason or another they feel that the offer to be included must come from another person or source. In my experience people of this nature need to be cared for, welcomed and made to feel at ease, no less than an actual stranger. Be ready to spot anyone who falls in this category and be prepared to help them by showing your generosity of spirit and your warmth of heart. It will be worth it.

### Fostering Hospitality

When we provide a welcome and love to others, we dispense hospitality, whether we realize it or not. For those people who find social interaction easy, offering hospitality is quite natural for them. But those who don't mix so easily can find it a much more challenging task. Nevertheless, God recognizes those with this difficulty and yet despite it, with his help, they still manage to be loving, caring, friendly and welcoming.

When we recall the Beatitudes we can easily apply some of them to the ideal of hospitality:

> 'Happy the gentle: they shall have the earth for their heritage... Happy the merciful: they shall have mercy shown them. Happy the pure in heart: they shall see God. Happy the peacemakers: they shall be called sons of God.' [199]

Scholars have shown that the Beatitudes are packed with a wealth of meaning and interpretation which have not dimmed through the ages, but it would seem that they are entirely relevant to the matter of hospitality. Those who are gentle, merciful and pure will be able to find it in their hearts to offer hospitality, of whatever nature, to other people. Those who are called to be peacemakers would naturally find the idea of warmth, generosity and friendliness a prerequisite for generating that peace and maintaining it.

Furthermore, Christ tells us in the Beatitudes that God recognizes all these traits and actions and rewards those who achieve them, whether they find it an easy or arduous task. In fact the more difficult the task, the more God appreciates our personal struggle and effort to accomplish it.

---

[199] *Matthew* 5: 5 - 9.

Altruism is not always easily achieved and selfless hospitality is no exception. The characteristics of it can be far-reaching and fairly numerous and while at one end of the spectrum, there's the simple act of entertaining our friends in the comfort of our own home, at the other end, there's offering shelter to those who are in need of it. This can even include the fostering and adoption of children.

Many adults, who are unable to have children of their own, turn to these as a means of forming their own family, so that they can fulfil their vocation of parenthood. However, to adopt a child and provide them with a family home and more importantly, allow such children to become fully part of their adoptive parents' lives, calls for altruistic qualities of love, understanding, patience, generosity and caring – all those special characteristics which Christ advocated for mankind.

This extended type of hospitality is not for an evening, a week, a month, or just for a long stay, it's for life. Even when the child in question has reached an age to leave home, the parents should still maintain their love and a duty of care. This way they are always readily 'on hand' in every significant way; in love, support, by supplying a home again should it become necessary and often financially! In other words, an adoptive parent should have all the same attributes which a natural mother and father supply. Yet all this starts with the opening of a real or metaphorical door to those who have no family to provide for them.

In fact, the child fostering initiative can possibly be even more challenging than the adoptive one. Children who are to be adopted, and those who are to be fostered, often come with emotional 'baggage'. They can come from broken homes where both they and their natural parents have suffered trauma. This can often have a profound effect upon these children, and enormous quantities of patience, sympathy, love and understanding are needed by adoptive and foster parents alike. It's safe to say that the care of these children is not for the faint-hearted.

However, as always when we strive to be unselfish and carry out an action in the name of Christ, the rewards can be deeply satisfying. Many adoptive and foster parents would agree that when giving these children life-changing hospitality, they themselves are fortified to help them flourish and grow into decent young people, who are fit to go out into the world. Furthermore, the love that was given to them is usually returned with dividends.

There are many commendations for hospitality in the Bible and St Paul in particular, stresses its significance:

> 'Remember always to welcome strangers', [200] and 'You should make hospitality your special care', [201] and from the First Letter of Peter: 'Welcome each other into your houses without grumbling', are but a few of the more obvious examples. [202] Arthur Patzia points out that although Samaritan encounters in the Bible were often negative, due to their abhorrence of the Jews, and vice versa, even here we can recognize hospitality in the following meeting:

> 'The Samaritan women's report about her encounter with Jesus at Jacob's well *(John 4: 1 - 42)* led 'many Samaritans' to believe in Jesus *(John 4: 39)* and even to invite him to stay longer in their territory.' [203]

The fact that the Samaritans pressed Jesus to remain for a longer period of time on their land is in

---

[200] *Hebrews* 13: 2.

[201] *Romans* 12: 13.

[20] 1 *Peter* 4: 9.

[203] *The Emergence of the Church* – Arthur Patzia, p. 26.

itself miraculous, as Samaritans and Jews generally avoided each other like the plague!

In the book of Genesis, early in the Bible, we meet Abraham and his wife Sarah. They were meeting, greeting and immediately offering refreshment to three strangers who passed their way. There appears to be not the least hesitation on the part of Abraham to do this, and he and his wife who 'were old, well on in years', were rewarded by God with a son, Isaac. [204] This Scriptural reference is merely a thumb-nail sketch and just one of the numerous examples of hospitality to be found, but what is of special note is the great value that's placed upon it.

If we now fast-forward a couple of thousand years, we can find another extraordinary and life-changing example of hospitality. *The Monastery*, when made for BBC2 television in 2005, [205] was filmed at Worth Abbey which threw open its doors and offered a haven of peace, respite and silence for a group of five volunteer laymen. They were keen to experience monastic life first-hand. Undoubtedly the atmosphere of the Abbey, the frequent calls to prayer, the Mass and the silence itself were hugely contributory factors to the effect that

---

[204] *Genesis* 18: 1 - 15, 21: 1 - 3.
[205] *The Monastery*, first broadcast on BBC 2, 10th May 2005.

this experience had upon them. However, if the invitation to stay at Worth hadn't come about in the first place, these men would never have been able to experience the silence and peace, as well as the grace of God in their lives.

### To Share is to Love

The Eucharist is sublimely unique. All are invited to come to the table of the Lord and partake of Christ's precious body and blood. The Mass is correctly referred to as celebration and sacrifice but is rarely referred to in the context of abundant hospitality. Yet this can in no way be denied. At the holy Mass we're invited to the Lord's table, *just as we are* – 'warts and all', to become as one with the risen Lord, to be united with him in that deepest and most profound encounter; by sharing his Body and Blood. Unlike our own offerings of welcome and sharing, the Mass offers us the unique opportunity to go to Christ and become a part of him in this way. Incredibly, we need have no fear that this great gift of hospitality will be withheld. We can be assured that it's available at every celebration of the Mass.

We know that in the early church, hospitality played a vitally important part in spreading the word of the Gospel message. Christ's followers met regularly at each other's houses for 'the communal *service of prayer*... an occasion for saying the Lord's Prayer together, for interpreting sacred texts, for recalling the words of Jesus and studying his life in the light of the Old Testament.' Likewise, 'the communal eschatological *meal* of the community was celebrated, probably often in association with the simple service of prayer, in memory of the meals shared with Jesus and particularly his last supper.'[206]

Certainly if these early followers of Christ hadn't offered their own dwellings for the type of meetings Küng refers to, and which, in essence, were the forerunners of today's Mass, one wonders if Christianity would have expanded and spread throughout the world as quickly as it did? St Justin Martyr describes the first celebration of the Mass in his First Apology in this way:

'On the day called Sunday, all who live in cities or in the country gather together to one place, and the memoirs of the apostles or the writings of the prophets are read, as long as time permits; then, when the reader has ceased, the president verbally instructs, and exhorts to the imitation of these good things. Then we all rise together and pray, and, as we before said, when our prayer is ended, bread and

---

[206] *The Church* – Hans Küng, pp. 109 - 110.

wine and water are brought, and the president in like
manner offers prayers and thanksgivings, according
to his ability, and the people assent, saying Amen;
and there is a distribution to each, and a
participating of that over which thanks have been
given, and to those who are absent a portion is sent
by the deacons.' [207]

It's significant that in the celebrating of this early
version of the Mass the worshippers had to come
together in a communal setting, which realistically
meant using their own homes. By making others
welcome and offering their houses to one another in
this manner, they were, in fact, following the precepts
of the Lord by the very execution of this action. Even
today 'house' Masses, as they are so-called, are not
uncommon.

There are a number of reasons for these.
Typically the householder may be housebound or again
it may be part of a special occasion. A priest, a table,
wine and wafers are basically all that's needed to
celebrate the Mass, plus a venue. It actually matters
little where that venue is, but it must be an agreed
gathering place for all to come together to participate in

---

[207] *First Apology of St Justin Martyr,* second century AD to the
Roman Emperor, Antoninus Pius.

the Mass. A house Mass, therefore, fulfils these conditions and enables the host to share their home with others and for them to respond to this invitation.

### *Give and Receive*

All things in life are held in balance, so that those who have given freely receive in return, as a consequence of this. Not only that but, they often receive in abundance. Hospitable 'giving' is no exception to this rule.

This means there's a flip side to giving of considerable worth. In other words, we must not only *give* our hospitality but also be prepared to *receive* it, as and when circumstances allow. In this we can draw a parallel with forgiveness.

We must be prepared to forgive others when we've been wronged by them, but we must also be capable of being forgiven ourselves. In the same way, if we're able to offer our hospitality in whatever form, then we must also allow others to offer it to us and we must be open to receiving it. Jesus reminds us of this as follows:

'The Lord appointed seventy-two others and sent them ahead of him, in pairs, to all the towns and places he himself was to visit. He said to them, "Stay in the same house, taking what food and drink they have to offer, for the labourer deserves his wages... Whenever you go into a town where they make you welcome, eat what is set before you."' [208]

My aunt had a large family of seven children and as they grew older, their partners, wives, husbands and their children were also incorporated into the family. However, she was well known in the neighbourhood for her generous, hospitable nature.

She would decide to have, what she termed a 'bake-up' – an enormous amount of cakes and pastries baked by herself and her daughters and which were given to friends and neighbours. Furthermore, undaunted by her own large brood, there was always a spare bed, (bed-settee or even simply the settee!) to be given to anyone who was in need of one.

There was a notable occasion when my mother was visiting her sister and she remarked on an elderly man who was sitting quietly in an armchair. 'Who's he?' my mother asked, somewhat mystified. 'Oh, that's Bert,' my aunt replied casually, 'He'd got nowhere to stay, and so I said he could stay here for a while until he

---

[208] *Luke* 10: 1 - 2, 7 - 9.

got himself sorted out.' Bert remained at my aunt's house for over two years until he 'sorted himself out'! In this we can see a similarity and parallel to the excerpt from St Luke's Gospel of the sending out of the missionary disciples. There's an extending and acceptance of hospitality. These two combined aspects make up the whole action.

### *Opening the Door, Opening the Heart*

There will always be people who complain of the lack of caring, compassion and help in society. However, in times of catastrophe the opposite usually holds true. During the devastation of former wars, people found themselves without their possessions and homes. It was incredible how under these circumstances those who were more fortunate, gave away their own belongings to help others, and furthermore, provided shelter to those who had been made homeless.

The offer was extended and the recipients glad to receive it. In recent years we've seen huge amounts of flooding across the United Kingdom with many homes underwater and uninhabitable. Encouragingly, we've again witnessed the help provided to those unable to live in their own homes. Invitations were received and gladly accepted, and when we witness this kind of hospitality, we're witnessing the Gospel message in action.

Floods, tsunamis, earthquakes, wars and other disasters bring about an extension of warmth, love, caring and welcome from most of us. As God's people living on earth, some of us are, at times, strangely reluctant to extend the hand of welcome to those who arc in need of it until they are *in extremis,* but when this does occur we're able to witness Christ working within them. The reluctance could possibly arise from the fact that we've become fearful, cautious individuals who anxiously cling to our property and possessions, and who very often view others with suspicion.

This unfortunate situation is sad but true and of course, inhabits many people. In contrast, Christ extends an offer of hospitality to all of us for the whole of our lives, indeed for all time. We've the assurance of knowing that his arms are extended in welcome and in him we can make our home. There can be no greater offer of hospitality than this. Equally, Jesus hopes for a place in our own hearts and lives. Those who love him will comply. He says:

'Look, I am standing at the door, knocking. If any one of you hears me calling and opens the door, I will come in to share his meal.' [209]

Sharing, caring, fostering, adopting, loving and welcoming, all encompass and help to describe aspects of hospitality. Christ revealed them to us; now it is up to all of us not only to invite our friends to our homes but also to 'remember always to welcome strangers.' [210] Our Lord Jesus Christ, who's *no* stranger to us, should always be given the greatest welcome and invited to stay in the warmest place of all – our own hearts.

---

[209] *Revelation* 3: 20.
[210] *Letter to the Hebrews* 13: 2.

*The Safe House of God*

# ~ *Chapter Sixteen* ~
## A Safe Haven of Peace

Images of protection, peace, security, shelter, anchor, sanctuary and refuge are conjured up by the expression 'safe haven'. No doubt there are probably many other adjectives that could apply. As part of our daily living, each of us has our own safe haven which naturally differs from person to person. For most of us, our refuge is our own home, the place to which we return, to relax and be ourselves without any pretensions. It's also where love is present; between husbands and wives or partners and between mother and father and children. It's a place of family love and care – or it should be. The notion of refuge is allied to that of hospitality, which we looked at in some detail in the last chapter, but it's really not the same.

The Oxford English Dictionary defines refuge as 'shelter from danger or trouble' and also as 'a safe place', which obviously suggests a different meaning to the 'love of strangers' which defines hospitality. And yet there's an obvious link. Those who seek refuge, for whatever reason, are sometimes offered sanctuary by others, even when those 'others' have little knowledge of them. More importantly, this gesture is often made with love. Typically, those who are fleeing war, persecution and political disruption, commonly known as refugees, fit the profile of those seeking a safe haven. Forced to flee, at a moment's notice, leaving behind their homes and most of their possessions, they are obliged to leave their own country to seek a refuge and safety in another. Whether this is due to the world's economic climate, or to war and persecution, there are differences of opinion as to whether these people should be welcomed, tolerated or even returned to their native lands as soon as possible. In Great Britain this has become a matter of some concern due to the size and capacity of the island that we British call home. However, we should consider that if we ourselves had to flee to a place of refuge in fear of our lives and those of our families, would we not appreciate it if we were offered shelter and made welcome?

It can be a real challenge when we're called upon to be understanding and compassionate about circumstances which we've not personally experienced. Even more so if we cannot *feel* the anguish and worry that they create. However, we're called to be sypathetic and if we find this difficult then we must keep on trying to be more caring. For some people it can actually take a lifetime to show even the least care for others, but we shouldn't be discouraged and we shouldn't abandon our efforts, either.

In terms of refugees, perhaps we should remember how God views his people. Rick Warren reminds us:

'God is a global God. He has always cared about the entire world. "*God so loved the world…*" From the beginning he has wanted family members from every nation he created.' [211]

God did indeed create every race and nation, all peoples of the Earth. However, it could be argued that in Jesus's dialogue with the Canaanite woman, he states that he 'was sent only to the lost sheep of Israel', and not to the rest of mankind. However, he thankfully appeared to quickly change his mind! [212]

The *Catechism of the Catholic Church* unequiv-ocally states that:

'The unity of the human family, embracing people who enjoy equal natural dignity, implies a *universal common good*. This good calls for an organization of

---

[211] *The Purpose-driven life* – Rick Warren, p. 300.
[212] *Matthew 15: 21 - 28.*

the community of nations able to "provide for the different needs of men; this will involve the sphere of social life to which belong questions of food, hygiene, education... And certain situations arising here and there, as for example... alleviating the miseries of refugees dispersed throughout the world, and assisting migrants and their families.'" [213]

In fact, we're told in the New Testament that Mary, Joseph and the infant Jesus were refugees themselves when they fled into Egypt, after Joseph dreamt that Herod would search for Jesus; intent upon killing him. They actually remained there until after the death of Herod, when they deemed it safe to return to their own native land. [214]

Therefore, Jesus himself was a refugee as an infant, and yet again in a manner of speaking, when he was led by the Spirit into the wilderness for forty days and forty nights, where he underwent Satan's temptation experience. [215] To summarize: Jesus himself was no stranger to being a refugee. He had lived it and he cares for those who endured it.

---

[213] *Catechism of the Catholic Church,* Paragraph 1911.
[214] *Matthew* 2: 13 - 15.
[215] *Matthew* 4: 1 - 11.

### Christ – the Aid of Refugees

Looking at this subtitle: 'Christ – the aid of refugees', we could consider the following quotation. Adapted, perhaps from those given in the Last Judgement in St Matthew's Gospel, I may suggest: 'Lord, when did we see you a refugee and make you welcome?'

Our first reaction to this may well be doubt. When did the disciples see Jesus as a refugee? Yet ultimately his 'new' way of teaching caused him to become an outcast on the 'wrong' side of the Law. What is more, Christ repeatedly came to the aid of 'refugees' or outcasts as we discover over and over again in the Gospels. When Christ healed the ten lepers, his action immediately allowed them to leave the place of refuge where they had been staying and return to their own community. They had been exiled from their own district in fear of contagion. [216]

Of course, we read practically the same narrative in St Mark's Gospel, where a single leper is healed and then sent to re-join his own people, when he is told, 'Go and show yourself to the priest.' The action of presenting himself to the priest would have counted as proof of his cure and cleanliness. It would have been the

---

[216] *Luke* 17: 11 - 15.

gateway to resumption of his former lifestyle with no further need of his place of refuge. [217]

In fact the sense of refuge plays a part in many of the miracles that Jesus performed. When evil spirits are driven out by him, they are forced from *their* place of refuge which they've imposed on their victim. In so doing that person is made whole again and cleansed, as always, physically and spiritually. [218] Additionally, in the miracle of Jesus casting out a legion of demons into a herd of pigs, there's a 'double whammy' in terms of refuge. Yet again, unclean spirits had taken refuge in these men's bodies, and the men, in their turn, had been forced to seek refuge in the tombs, as they were 'creatures so fierce that no one could pass that way.' [219]

On a similar theme, Jesus feeds the five thousand. In this encounter, we're made aware of a multitude of people, who have travelled to seek the sanctuary of Christ, who then proceeds to offer them refuge on two levels.

---

[217] *Mark* 1: 40 - 44.
[218] *Mark* 1: 23 - 27, *Matthew* 15: 21 - 28, *Mark* 7: 24 - 30, *Matthew* 17: 14 - 20, *Mark* 9: 14 - 29, *Luke* 9: 37 - 43. *Matthew* 12: 22 - 23, *Luke* 11: 14 - 23.
[219] *Matthew* 8: 28 - 33. Also *Mark* 5: 1 - 20 & *Luke* 8: 26 - 39.

On one level there's the refuge of the person of Christ himself, while on another level there's the physical refuge of the place they find themselves in, as they sought Jesus. Yet this place initially offered no source of nourishment, so Jesus then fulfils their solace by providing them with both a spiritual and physical refuge.

He satisfies their physiological hunger with bread and fish and their spiritual hunger with his loving presence and words. [220] There are various other examples of Jesus offering safety and refuge. One of these is the calming of the storm, where Jesus creates a haven of peace and calm for his disciples, during a tempest. [221] However, to list every example is superfluous. What is important is that we appreciate the Christ who aided refugees, the Christ who completely transformed their lives with love and compassion. Therefore, we ourselves are called to do likewise.

### Physical Refuge

Most of us will seek a place of safety and refuge at some point during our lives. Some of us will be driven to that place more often than others and there are those of us who will return there again and again. We could possibly add that even Jesus had a place of refuge after his ascension into heaven, as 'Jesus was seated at God's right hand.' [222]

Most of us can, if we wish, physically remove ourselves from any given situation that we're

---

[220] *Matthew* 14: 13 - 21, *Mark* 6: 30 - 44, *Luke* 9: 10 - 17, *John* 6: 1 - 15.
[221] *Matthew* 8: 23 - 27, *Mark* 4: 35 - 41, *Luke* 8: 22 - 25.
[222] *Jesus – An historical and theological investigation –* Jonathan Knight, p. 198.

uncomfortable with, or feel endangered by. However, the placing of ourselves in a safe environment takes us into a further dimension altogether. That's not to say that seeking refuge and taking 'some time out' is unacceptable. On the contrary, it can be most beneficial, as it allows us a time of peace and quiet, reflection and safety. But safe places can vary enormously and will depend upon individual circumstances. Generally speaking, these fall broadly into the categories of the home; being with family or friends; going to a safe place or 'shelter'; taking a trip, journey or holiday; attending the Mass or going on retreat.

The idea of home as refuge has already been mentioned and it's familiar to most people. In fact, when our homes are intruded upon or violated in any way, most of us feel intense distress, because the place which is valued as being a personal place of safety has been invaded and tarnished. Indeed, when people's homes are burgled, it's not unusual for the occupants to move house soon afterwards. This is partly due to the fact that the shelter and protection of home is held as sacrosanct by most people, and after a break-in, their safety and security is felt to have been violated.

Interestingly, the other places of refuge which have

been mentioned, all exist outside of the home – in fact, they take the person *out* of their home. Various shelters or refuges are a recognized sanctuary for the homeless, battered women, refugees and for various other groups. They are well known as safe places of temporary asylum for those in need.

Staying with friends or relatives or choosing to take a trip also provides a means for leaving the home and finding sanctuary, both with others and in different surroundings or a new location. A change of scene can be surprisingly effective as both a form of escapism and a means of shelter. A word of warning however: although refuge can be a powerful tool for a temporary reprieve from a given situation, eventually that situation has to be confronted and resolved. Generally the person will have to return to their home and resume their lifestyle, at some time in the future.

The final two forms of refuge are slightly different in nature. When we attend Mass we're there for many reasons. We desire an encounter with Jesus Christ in the Eucharist, we listen to the Word of God, we're with our community, we worship the Lord, we celebrate, pray, ask for forgiveness for our sins, sing, try to take out the Gospel message to others, and finally take refuge in a building which is God's house.

We know Christ will be present, because he told us that, 'where two or three meet in my name, I shall be there with them.' [223]

When entering into the spirit of a retreat there are certain similarities with entering into the Mass. On retreat we hope to have a personal encounter with the Lord, we read the word of the Lord; we often worship the Lord and we pray, reflect and often seek the Lord's forgiveness. In summary, we seek out the Lord in this place of refuge; a place where we can be quiet, at peace, feel safe in his presence and take the time to get to know him over and over again.

### Spiritual and Mental Refuge

Physical and spiritual refuge are generally interconnected and experienced at one and the same time. When indulging in spiritual and/or mental refuge we often conduct our lives in the same way, but spiritually we've retreated to a safe place where we feel comforted and at ease. Nevertheless, we do need to be a little careful, because sometimes certain forms of mental refuge can, in fact, lead to problems such as depression, difficulties with social interaction or even becoming reclusive to the point of agoraphobia.

[223] *Matthew* 18 - 20.

Retreating into ourselves without any kind of help from friends, family or professionals can, at times, be a serious mistake and should be regarded with caution. However in contrast, spiritual refuge, in which we turn to Christ, has unsurprisingly, a far more positive effect upon our mental and spiritual well-being. Christ the comforter is 'my refuge, my fortress, my God in whom I trust',[224] and as such, is the one constant in life of which we can be sure. Naturally, there are non-believers who would fiercely disagree with the perspective that Christ is the only other certainty in life, apart from death. Kendall explains this perspective as follows:

'In the single most outrageous claim he ever uttered, Jesus announced, "I am the way, and the truth and the life. No one comes to the Father except through me." Out of all the incredible statements by Jesus, this exorbitant assertion has the greatest tendency to outrage people. Many consider it arrogant, intolerant and politically incorrect.'[225]

Sadly, man-made self-help props such as alcohol and drugs provide a form of retreat and refuge for far too many people in society at this present time. This kind of refuge is fleeting and temporary and wholly

---

[224] *Psalm* 91: 2 - 3.
[225] *Out of the comfort zone* – R. T. Kendall, p. 221.

unreliable. The results can be disastrous and dangerous and the reasons for this are obvious. Here are negative, destructive forces which contradict all that's good and positive in life. They can never replace the loving grace of God. In stark contrast to this, refuge in the Lord exerts a positive influence in our lives. The guidelines of Christ are all constructive, with an emphasis on helping others, not ourselves.

In other words, by seeking God as your safe haven you will find a place of unselfishness, positivity and joy. Christ's law of love can, without a doubt, be extremely difficult to follow at times, for example in his command to love our enemies,[226] but it can only result in a purer heart and a more steadfast relationship with God – if only we can master it! Positivity instead of negativity, selflessness instead of selfishness, prayer instead of any kind of man-made indulgence: these are the ingredients of Christ's recipe for a haven of peace.

### Refuge or Confrontation?

In God we find our only true refuge. Nevertheless, to play devil's advocate and look at the opposite of this, there are times when sanctuary is not always offered by

---

[226] *Luke* 6: 27 - 35.

the Lord. Kendall reminds us of this fact when he states that:

> 'Being outside your comfort zone is not fun. You are uneasy. You yearn for the familiar. You want what will make you feel good – naturally… God almost always requires his servants to move outside their comfort zone… God isn't safe. But he's good. We must never forget this when outside our comfort zone but in God's will.' [227]

How many of us have experienced this, I wonder? We know that God's 'way' can make us uneasy and uncomfortable and we usually have to remind ourselves that the rewards are great, to help us allay the discomfort that this so often brings. It could be said that being outside of our comfort zone is the reverse of being in a state of refuge, and without doubt, a state of refuge is a far more desirable place for us to be!

We know that God has chosen the most unlikely heroes through the ages to help his people and proclaim his word, and most of them have protested loudly at his choice. This is often because they didn't want to leave their place of safety or their comfort zone and put themselves in a difficult or potentially harmful

---

[227] *Out of the comfort zone* – R. T. Kendall, pp. 42 - 43.

situation. Yet God is always persistent and always correct in his assumptions. Difficult as many of these unsung heroes may have found their task and reluctant though they were, they definitely 'delivered the goods' and were accordingly rewarded for their pains. Interestingly, Pope Francis appears to echo some of these views in his Apostolic Exhortation *Evangelii Gaudium:*

'People who compose the body of Christ – you and I – are exhorted to go out into the world, sharing the gospel message with joy, and if in so doing we have to withdraw from our comfort zone; our refuge, then so be it!'

'One of the more serious temptations which stifles boldness and zeal is a defeatism which turns us into querulous and disillusioned pessimists "sourpusses".... While painfully aware of our own frailties, we have to march on without giving in.' [228]

'The Church must be a place of mercy freely given, where everyone can feel welcomed, loved, forgiven, and encouraged to live the good life of the Gospel.' [229]

---

[228] *Evangelii Gaudium,* Paragraph 85.
[229] *Evangelii Gaudium,* Paragraph 188.

'Ideas disconnected from realities give rise to ineffectual forms of idealism and nominalism, capable at most of classifying and defining, but certainly not calling to action.' [230]

These quotations merely give us a flavour of the message which the Pope is trying to pass on. In fact, it could almost be said that we're being given a metaphorical kick up the backside. We're being told to get out into the marketplace and live our lives as joyous followers of Christ, because in so doing we can then begin living out the Gospel message.

### The Safe House of God

God asks that we constantly keep moving forwards in our faith, learning, growing and trying not to be afraid to move away from our personal safety net, into the uncharted waters of discovering him and helping others to do likewise. Yet God does provide us with a refugee's safety net, for he is the one being in whom we need have no pretence, need not explain, need not fear and who's always there. Even when we've sinned, then realized our mistakes and asked to be forgiven, he is ready and willing to love and forgive us.

---

[230] *Evangelii Gaudium,* Paragraph 232.

Most people have a place of refuge with their parents, even when they are adults themselves. We instinctively feel that parents can provide answers, will love us, protect us and care for us and we need never be afraid to ask for any of these. We can always be at our ease with them. Therefore, if our natural inclination is to feel this way about our own mothers and fathers, then it stands to reason that our father in Heaven will have these same qualities in even greater abundance; in essence with unconditional love. If we can turn to God wholeheartedly and ask for his help and protection, we can be sure of a favourable response.

When we rely on God as our refuge and he provides it, this is by no means the end of the story. As always God tries to use us to promote love and joy throughout the world. Therefore when we're given the gift of God's refuge, he asks that we find it in our hearts to do the same for other people, so that we provide them with a point of reference for refuge, whenever they should need it.

Make no mistake. People instinctively know who they can trust, who's genuinely concerned about them, who will be their friend and who will love and help them when they need it. In the same way, we can be sure that others will get a sense of who may provide them with care and refuge if it became necessary. Yet if we ourselves are enabled to provide this, then it has probably been given to us through the grace of our Lord Jesus Christ, who's always working for our good on earth despite all the world's troubles:

'In today's Bethlehem, still ravaged by fear and violence, we can still meet the God who has made human tears his own and still works ceaselessly for his purpose of peace and rejoicing...' [231]

It is in *this* God where we find our own safe haven of peace.

---

[231] *Choose life – Christmas and Easter sermons in Canterbury Cathedral* – Rowan Williams, p. 54.

# ~ *Chapter Seventeen* ~
## Cleanse Me from My Sin [232]

When as a child I misbehaved, my father would produce one of his favourite sayings. This particular one was: 'Your sins will find you out!' I was never quite sure how seriously he meant this, but the fact remains that it made quite an impression upon me. In fact, I would go as far as to say that as a child I was very much in awe of this perspective. This being the

---

[232] Taken from *Psalm* 51.

case, I would usually confess to whatever it was that I had done wrong, although not necessarily straightaway! The point was though, that I was utterly convinced that any misdemeanour would soon come to light anyway! I suppose you could say that I had been taught that if we do wrong, it's far better to face up to it, confess to it and get it over and done with, because lies and subterfuge only make any situation worse. Whether we believe that we will actually be found out or not, the fact is that every one of us is guilty of wrongdoing at some time or another, because sinning is horribly easy to do.

The commonly used phrase: 'That covers a multitude of sins', may be interpreted literally. It means that there are a multitude of ways in which we can sin each and every day. You see, sin comes in many shapes and sizes; tiny little sins, medium and moderate ones and whopping huge sins. The Catholic Church refers to the first as venial and the last one as mortal and it's a fairly well-known fact that venial or small to moderate sins are quite commonplace.

However, do we realize that they are *so* common that we can easily commit this type of sin ten, twenty, thirty times a day, and on a bad day even more times than this? Christ told his disciples and the gathered crowds in a long narrative, that they 'must therefore be perfect just as your heavenly father is perfect', [233] but of course, it would be impossible for us humans to achieve this pinnacle of perfection.

When my children were growing up, I set them goals as they progressed through school, took exams and went on to further education and careers. I told them to always aim high because if they aim for the top, the summit, and their aim falls short, they can then always be content with a lower standard. But if they aim for that lower level to start with, then their ultimate achievement may be very low indeed. In a similar way, God directed us towards aiming for that ultimate goal of perfection, in the hope that when we fail, as we surely must, our failures won't be as great as they might otherwise have been. I am sure that Christ knew that we could never achieve perfection. If we were able to do this, then we would be God-like ourselves, as only the Lord God is perfect.

### Count to Ten

In a moment of true revelation about the nature of Jesus, Simon Peter begs him, 'Leave me, Lord; I am a

---

[233] *Matthew* 5: 48.

sinful man.' [234] We don't know the nature of Simon Peter's sins, but by recognizing Jesus as Messiah, there's an insight that he is unworthy even to be in the Lord's presence due to his own sinful state. The crux of the problem for Simon Peter and indeed for all of us today, is that for most of the time we've sinned almost before we realize that we've done so. Our unkind thoughts and words, our 'little white lies', our boasting, intolerance, lack of sympathy, laziness, grumpiness and bad temper all count as sins. We might justify these to ourselves by saying, 'I'm having a bad day, no wonder I'm irritable!' or, 'It was only a tiny lie ... it was for the best.' or alternatively, "How was I to know that he/she wanted some help? They only had to ask!"

These are just a few of the most obvious and frequent examples of those little venial sins, which are so easy to commit and which we can equally simply rationalize – or try to. In fact, there are some people who wouldn't consider that such words and actions actually merited the title of sin at all. They would probably believe them to be an integral part of life – 'something which we all do from time to time.' However, according to Jesus's teaching, these *are* sins and as such are unacceptable and should be eradicated.

---

[234] *Luke* 5: 8.

Yet all too often we've sinned without even being aware of it; we've made a statement, told a lie, or merely said something without seriously considering the implications of it, let alone making the decision to omit it altogether. A well-known tool to help those who have a tendency to lose their temper is the old favourite of counting to ten before replying. This buys that hot-tempered person a few precious seconds as a cooling-off period. It also allows them time to consider what they are going to say next! It would not be unreasonable then, to apply the same rule of thumb when trying to avoid those persistent everyday sins.

If we can slow ourselves down a bit in our speech and actions, and try to consider the consequences first, maybe we could soon eliminate some of those annoying venial sins that we all seem prone to. Yet sometimes our minds can seem to be out of our control. It can be extremely challenging to discipline the mind, which at times seems to want to go merrily hurtling along in its own sweet way, like an unstoppable train. But we do need to take control if we want to avoid certain disasters. Unkind thoughts and words, irritability, boasting, lies and bad temper can all slip out through a lack of mental discipline. So, with patience, practice and determination we can go some way towards achieving the goal of self-restraint.

Earlier in this book, there was a discussion on how we can 'think' ourselves into a certain frame of mind. We can control how we feel about certain people and situations if we try hard enough. The wonder of this is that if we exert positivity into our feelings about someone we dislike, for example, and make an effort to appear friendly and actually try to like them, we can eventually genuinely find that our feelings have altered. We then sincerely come to like that person and enjoy their company. In other words, they've 'grown on us'. Similarly, the same can be said for channelling our mind against venial sins; especially those sins where we act before we think. It's not easy, but by continually striving for self-control and, more importantly thinking of others, we can in some measure achieve this.

Another great tool to help us is to focus on the Lord. The following type of questions can prove useful: 'What would God want of me?'; 'Would Christ approve of this particular thought?'; Would Christ be happy if I said what I really feel and want to say?' It's also helpful to be attentive to the Word of the Lord. This can take place at Mass or in our own private observances. When we're really listening to God's word there is little space and time left in our minds and hearts for sinful thoughts. These, as we know, can easily lead to sinful words and actions. Rick Warren simplifies this as follows:

'Spiritually, your mind is your most vulnerable organ. To reduce temptation, keep your mind occupied with God's word and other good thoughts. You defeat bad thoughts by thinking of something better.' [235]

Described in this way, the advice almost appears obvious. In fact so obvious that we probably wonder why we hadn't thought this way before. However, situations easily overtake us before we've thought about using any kind of preventative action.

Therefore, in view of this, it's a good idea to try Warren's approach where possible, but perhaps count to ten to buy some extra time first and before we become victims of circumstance.

### *A Sense of Sin*

'When a man or woman has no sense of inward sin, they predictably have no objectivity about themselves. They are utterly blind to their own

---

[235] *The purpose-driven life* – Rick Warren, p. 211.

minds, their assumptions and motives; they become un-teachable.' [236]

Kendall's statement may be quite difficult for some people to believe. I for one have always assumed that each and every one of us was born with a conscience; it comes as part of our human package. Our conscience is a marvellous God-given device. It keeps us on our toes, jumps in to remind us when we're going wrong and prompts us to do right. However, during one catechetical session we discussed the Sacrament of Reconciliation, our sins and our need to be forgiven.

All appeared to be going well until someone in the group said that they would be at a loss to know what to say to a priest in Confession. Thinking this was a problem with the actual 'nuts and bolts' of the Sacrament, or possibly a misunderstanding as to what a confession roughly consisted of, this was then all explained in some detail.

However, astonishingly, we were informed that this person had absolutely no idea when they had done something wrong. They therefore wouldn't know if they needed to say sorry to God, or if they needed to go to Confession. I explained about conscience but was met

[236] *Out of the comfort zone* – R. T. Kendall, p. 189.

with an utterly blank look. Apparently this person was at a loss to understand or know what conscience was or meant. Whether they truly were without conscience, or whether, as seems more likely, they managed to block out their voice of conscience I don't know. Significantly though, I then realized that a sense of sin may be totally lacking in some people. Indeed, psychiatrists have identified a number of seriously ill psychopaths with no sense of guilt or remorse at all.

For most of us though, our conscience nudges and pricks us most uncomfortably when we've done wrong. God whispers in our ear that we must put the wrong right. Yet may it be possible that, in common with our appendix or tonsils which perform very little function in the human body, some people's consciences might not be functioning? Put another way: unless we're committed to keeping fit, most of us have muscles that are not used to their full extent, and they lie flabby and idle through lack of exercise.

For some of us our consciences may be in a similar condition – unused and unfit for purpose. Our body muscles if unused will then become painful when they are exercised. Is it possible that in a similar way the conscience has a painful and rude awakening when it's eventually put to use? Is this uncomfortable for the person involved? In short, do we have to labour to use our conscience, or does it work entirely naturally? It's fairly safe to say that some people have more active consciences than others. This could be purely because their genetic make-up has defined them this way, or it could be that they are committing more sins and therefore it has to work all the harder! I would imagine that to suppress or ignore one's conscience must, in fact, be quite hard work and is something that needs constant attention. The important fact to recognize is that unless we use our conscience, allow it to work and nurture it, as we might exercise our muscles, it can become dulled and unresponsive. When this happens we will have no awareness that we're in a state of sin and that we need to be sorry both to God and to others.

'When we refuse to take the personal risk of admitting our failures and turning away from our wrongdoing – when we keep all that bottled up inside – it slowly eats away at us like rust devouring an old car.' [237]

Kendall's rather magnificent analogy makes our position absolutely clear: we must listen to our

display a firm purpose of amendment and not attempt

---

[237] *Out of the comfort zone* – R. T. Kendall, p. 247.

to hide from the fact that we are sinners. God knows we've sinned anyway and is saddened, but is also eagerly awaiting our admission of guilt and our repentance. As rust can destroy a car, we too can we be seriously harmed and destroyed by a failure to acknowledge our sins.

## Sin of Omission

In today's world people are often accused of lethargy, indolence or indifference to many aspects of their lives. Even practising Christians have suffered in a similar way by not attending church every week. Sometimes they've not bothered to pray regularly, lacked concern for others and failed to teach their children about God. Sadly, we can discern indifference in so many attitudes toward aspects of our lives. A priest remarked to me some years ago that he could essentially cope with the sinfulness of people, but what he found more difficult to deal with was their indifference. In some instances, indifference can become a sin in its own right. When we show a lack of concern for our neighbour because we 'can't be bothered', or when a friend, companion or family member is ill and we fail to care for them or visit them because we can't summon up the energy, this is actually a form of sin. Yet again, when we hurt someone, whether intentionally or otherwise, and we don't make the effort to seek them out and apologize for our words and actions, this again is an act of sin. They are the sins of omission. Through lack of effort and being unable to take the time and the trouble we've therefore, fallen into error. Although we're fallible humans we need to be bothered about others and we need to care for others. We know that we often sin by an action. Conversely, we can easily sin in the opposite way; by a complete *lack* of action; by not putting ourselves forward in the care of others. The Rt Rev'd Rowan Williams, former Archbishop of Canterbury (2002 - 2012), gives an example of the sin of omission:

> 'One of the worst effects of this culture… is what it does to those who are obviously dependent – the elderly, those with physical or psychological challenges and disabilities, and, of course, children. We send out the message that, if you're not standing on your own two feet and if you need regular support, you're an anomaly.' [238]

The elderly, those with disabilities and children, all suffer from a fragility of some sort and therefore they rely on others for help and caring. When we fail to fulfil our duty of care through lethargy, we've sinned in just

---

[238] *Choose life – Christmas and Easter sermons in Canterbury Cathedral* – Rowan Williams, p. 73.

as great a measure as we would have if we made a conscious decision to entirely withhold our aid.

## *Iniquitous Diversions*

As I mentioned earlier, our minds have a habit of 'doing their own thing', of going off on a tangent which is usually unbidden and often when we least desire it. During a lecture, during Mass or prayer, we know we can easily become distracted and start thinking about other matters instead of that which we *should* be concentrating on, at that specific time.

We already know that likely times for this to occur are in prayer and during the course of Mass and we realize that we have to work hard to try to overcome this. Nonetheless, there's another form of distraction which some of us can fall prey to during the Mass. At every celebration of Mass there will be a number of people engaged in ministries of some kind, such as welcomers, readers, musicians and choristers, ushers, offering collectors, those bringing up the gifts and Extraordinary Ministers of the Eucharist.

The Second Vatican Council changed the Catholic Church irrevocably and charged the laity with being able to fulfil these roles and ministries, enabling them to participate more fully in the life of the Church. This, we know, has always been greatly welcomed and acclaimed as a major innovative step in the Church's history. It has completely changed lay participation since that time. Yet on the other hand, as with any great initiative, it's not entirely perfect. The problem is that readers, choristers and cantors can easily become distracted from the content of the Mass.

Frankly, I can endorse this from my own personal experience. I don't mean this to happen, but inevitably I can soon slip into a lack of concentration. When I'm singing with the choir, there's a natural absorption with the music and the lyrics. I and other choir members are desperately trying to 'get it right' when we sing. Also, nervousness plays its part. Most of us become anxious when we stand alone before an assembly and 'perform' in some way. When we're under pressure like this, we're naturally distracted.

Finally, there's the 'rehearsal' aspect. I know I am not alone in mentally running through the reading or the psalm before I actually go to the *ambo* (lectern) and deliver it. However, if I am concentrating on this, I suddenly realize that I've missed a significant part of the Mass. It's probably fair to say that these roles provide more of a distraction than some other ministerial duties, but every one carries an element of distraction by its very nature. Even if we're only diverted for the minimum amount of time while waiting for our cue to get up and do something, we may be missing a vital part of the Mass. This is due to the fact that *every* component of the Mass is crucial to us and we need to be able to listen and absorb all of it as best we can. That's not to say that some words or phrases won't strike us more than others, this is natural and normal, but we need to have our ears, minds and hearts open and receptive throughout the entire celebration. Therefore it follows that when we're totally focussed on our ministry or role during the Mass, it may be to the detriment of our benefiting from what is taking place.

The question is: could this then be classed as a sin? Without a doubt this is a difficult question to answer, and in many ways probably too close to call. But we do need to bear in mind that although it's right and good that we always try to do our best, in whatever ministry we've been given, we must be on our guard against vanity creeping into the execution of our role. However, if we remember that everything we do is for Jesus Christ, then this shouldn't be an issue. And if we can keep this in mind, it should automatically follow that Christ (and not ourselves) is at the centre of our lives at all times. Therefore the answer to this question is obvious: when we're distracted and thinking only of our own ministry during the Mass, whose part is the most important – our own – or that of Christ our Lord?

## The Closeness of Transgressions

In her book 'A Journey into God', Delia Smith gives an interesting reflection. She feels that if we've built up a relationship with someone and come to love that person, then it's possible that we won't betray them; we won't sin against them. She goes on to say 'It won't be virtuous to keep true to the relationship, simply natural. This is what God asks of each of us, that we enter a relationship of trust in which we quite naturally grow in faithfulness.'[239] There can be little doubt that when we consider the words and actions of Jesus during his time with us, we're subsequently given a responsibility to enter into a relationship of love and trust with others and with Christ himself.

However, I would question Delia's statement regarding betrayal of the person or persons that you love. Unfortunately, while admiring her philosophy, the fact remains that there are vast numbers of people who betray their wife, husband or partner every day. One only has to consider the amount of divorces and single

---

[239] *A Journey into God* – Delia Smith, p. 101.

parent families there are at this time, or tune into one of the many reality shows on T.V. to be made brutally aware of these facts. It's difficult to say whether these situations are more common now because people have less regard for morality than they used to have, or whether they truly don't realize that these type of situations are actually sinful.

However, the fact remains that this occurs all too frequently, and most of us are mere bystanders who can only offer support when needed, as opposed to taking on the role of judge and jury. And if we do pass judgement, it's not beyond the realms of possibility that the person involved will sin again in a moment of despair or anger. This will probably be because they are already in a fragile state because sin is eroding and causes our innermost soul to become brittle and in need of treatment. So all in all, we must leave the judgement to the Lord, although if we remember the account of the 'Woman taken in Adultery' [240] it's probably unlikely that the Lord, in his great mercy, would condemn anyway.

Even if we do accept the fact that we would probably not harm or sin against a person that we love, unfortunately this doesn't account for all those people

---

[240] *John* 8: 1 - 11.

we know who we do *not* love. For most of us there must surely be a great number of people of our acquaintance, who, if plotted on a scale would range from those we heartily dislike at one end, to those we feel fondness for at the other. So, from one end of the scale to the other, we could not apply the word 'love' to many of these types of relationships. If we apply Delia's philosophy therefore, in that we wouldn't sin against a person that we love, this probably implies that we could therefore hurt or sin against someone that we do *not* love. It stands to reason then, that if there's a high proportion of people whom we associate with that fall into this category, the chances of us sinning against one or more of these would be quite high. We should bear this in mind. Just because we're not tied into a close relationship with someone, doesn't give us the right to harm them in any way.

### *No Blame Attached*

We're all sinners. Even Pope Francis surprised the world by describing himself as one! [241] Yet we've been awarded a bright ray of hope for all time, in that Jesus ate with the tax collectors and sinners and told them that: 'It is not the healthy who need the doctor, but the

---

[241] In an interview in September 2013.

sick. I did not come to call the virtuous, but sinners.' [242] In the passage which relates the story of the woman taken in adultery, [243] we recognize Christ's abundant mercy as he offers no condemnation for the woman, who in the context of that time would have been guilty of committing a heinous crime. Actually, she doesn't even say sorry for her offence, but we still witness the merciful and forgiving Christ. This outlook is echoed in the parable of the prodigal son, where the father forgives his son for his behaviour, before the son even has a chance to offer an apology. So it is with God. We sin and yet we're forgiven, not seven times but seventy-seven times. [244]

Nevertheless, we must try to curb our sinful ways, as we've been given a life and a purpose, for as Warren reminds us:

'Every human activity, except sin,
can be done for God's pleasure'. [245]

There can be no pleasure in sin. In fact your sins can harm you more than any disease or trauma. They

---

[242] *Mark* 2: 16 - 17.

[243] *John* 8: 1 - 11.

[244] *Matthew* 18: 22.

[245] *The purpose-driven life* – Rick Warren, p. 74.

can eat away at your sensitive soul and destroy you and your whole life. For the victim, they may never be able to forgive or forget and for the perpetrator they may drift into low self-esteem and be unable to face up to what they've done. But Pope Francis, in this Year of Mercy (2016), recognized that deep inside they are good, loving people whose lives have been spoilt and tarnished often just by chance and circumstances. But they can soon be cleansed and cured and brought back to the fullness and joy of life thanks to the great mercy and forgiveness of God.

All anyone needs to do is take a simple step through the 'Door of Mercy' and reach out to Christ for help. We may already know someone whose shame and sorrow has beaten them down. Maybe a drug addict or a felon, an alcoholic or an abuser, someone who still mourns for the baby they had aborted or indeed a soldier who cannot even tell his own wife of the horrors perpetrated in wartime. The mercy of God can sweep this all away if we just help them take the first tiny step towards the peace of mind, the joy and succour freely offered by Christ in the body of his Church and the Sacraments. So we can all utter the same heartfelt prayer together: "Lord, cleanse me from my sin."

# ~ *Chapter Eighteen* ~
## Born Free

Although we may not always acknowledge it, our freedom is a basic human right and immensely precious to us. In fact, so highly is it prized that the punishment for many crimes is to deny us that liberty. This of course, is the role of prisons. Freedom enters into so many parts of our daily lives and in so many ways and means that it would be impossible to set out all of them. Furthermore, in the western world we're blessed with an excess of freedom which we often take for granted. Although we're bound to follow society's rules so we can live in harmony with one another, we're granted freedom of speech, and we're also free to make our own life choices, find our life partners and are free to come and go as we please. We're fond of exclaiming, 'It's a free country!', and so it is, because in Britain, as in many other countries, we have a democracy; a level playing field where all opinions have worth and we can freely express them.

Most of us find the notion of being deprived of our liberty completely appalling. Often the elderly, who have become housebound, suffer when their personal freedoms become fewer. To have to remain in one building, which then basically becomes a prison, for no good reason whatsoever except for loss of mobility due to poor health, is not only irritating but frustrating and intolerable too. This can be worse for elderly people who have formerly enjoyed fairly active lifestyles.

### Follow at Will

In Graham Greene's *The Power and the Glory* we meet the little 'whisky' priest whose freedom is inexorably drawing to a close, during a period of religious persecution. Hounded like a fox during the hunt, he flees from village to village in Southern Mexico, fearful for his life and realizing that capture will bring certain death. However, the fact remains that as he is caught and shot, he is ultimately freed from the chains that bind him to life, so enabling him to be with his heavenly

Father. Despite his own self-loathing, he still brings his compassion and more importantly God, to those who are most in need, saying: 'I can put God into a man's mouth... And I can give him God's pardon...' [246] Today, we can learn so much from Greene's fictional cleric; so like us – humanly flawed, running for his life, his freedom hanging by a thread, only to be totally lost as he is captured. Nonetheless he manages to arise triumphantly as a figure of hope for the future. Despite his all too human failings, his belief in God is absolute and as a follower of Christ he carries his own cross in very desperate circumstances. The dream he experiences, which significantly occurs just before he awakens on the morning of his execution, triumphantly confirms his absolute faith:

> 'He dreamed he was sitting at a café table in front of the high altar of the cathedral. About six dishes were spread before him and he was eating hungrily. There was a smell of incense and an odd sense of elation. The dishes – like all food in dreams – did not taste of much, but he had a sense that when he had finished them, he would have the best dish of all.' [247]

---

[246] *The Power and the Glory* – Graham Greene, p. 195.
[247] *The Power and the Glory* – Graham Greene, p. 209.

He was prohibited from *openly* professing and celebrating his faith, due to the anti-clerical purge in Southern Mexico at that time, but he still preserved the freedom of his own firm personal belief in the Lord. His conviction that he had to do his best to carry out the Father's wishes, albeit in a flawed way, remained with him until the end. On the contrary, even though our own lives may be restricted in some of our ambitions and desires, we're totally free to follow the way of Christ, to profess it, to believe in it and to live it. Pope Benedict XVI reinforces this message when he explains that:

> 'The Beatitudes express the meaning of discipleship. They become more concrete and real the more completely the disciple dedicates himself to service in the way that is illustrated for us in the life of St Paul. What the Beatitudes mean cannot be expressed in purely theoretical terms; it is proclaimed in the life and suffering, and in the mysterious joy, of the disciple who gives himself over completely to following the Lord.'[248]

In fact for St Paul, other saints and martyrs, the little 'whisky' priest and for us today, a sweet freedom is

---

[248] *Jesus of Nazareth* – Joseph Ratzinger (Pope Benedict XVI), p. 73.

attained when we live for Christ and for others, and not for ourselves. In fact, when we let our selfish ego take control and become self-serving, then we soon become trapped and imprisoned spiritually and mentally in a truly harmful way of life.

The only method of escape from this prison of egocentricity of our own making, is to try to live our lives by asking what Christ would say or do, and then act upon this. We have, of course, been given Mary the mother of God as our perfect example to follow. She faithfully served her son all the time that he was with her and her every action was directed, not at herself but towards Jesus. If we can imitate Mary's methods, then our souls will become free, in the service of God.

### Assured Independence

One of the most important life choices which we make is whether to believe in the Lord or not. We're perfectly at liberty to refuse God's invitation to believe in him, follow his ways and hope in the resurrection. On the other hand we can fully embrace all of these. Yet again in Mary we can see the perfect model. She received an invitation from God, *and she had the right to accept it or refuse it*. God did not demand that Mary be obedient to his will, thereby allowing her no choice in the matter.

Rather he asked her if she would become the mother of Christ. In terms of today's phraseology it was a 'closed-ended' question in that it only required a 'yes' or 'no' response, but it was most definitely an 'open-ended' one in that Mary was freely allowed to choose her own option. In this we've some insight into the nature of the Lord. We're not cajoled or forced, just gently invited.

So often people bemoan the fact that suffering takes place in the world, and the usual question is raised over why God has not prevented it. The answer lies in the idea of free will with a reminder that many catastrophes are actually man-made. It appears that the human side of our nature wants to 'have our cake and eat it', in that we want God to intercede for us in our moments of distress, but we still want him to allow us to have free will when making our own life decisions, (good or bad) – and ironically this includes whether we turn to him or not.

Free to choose, Mary made her decision which, with the advantage of hindsight, looks like a 'no-brainer'. However, for Mary at that time, the choice was far from easy, and her decision has provided us with a pure and loving example for all time. She has shown us how to live our life in the Spirit.

In short, the Catholic Church maintains that:

'God created man a rational being, conferring on him the dignity of a person who can initiate and control his own actions. 'God willed that man should be "left in the hand of his own counsel", so that he might of his own accord seek his creator and freely attain his full and blessed perfection by cleaving to him." [249]

### Reality Check: Free People or Prisoners of our own Making?

God doesn't control us like a giant puppet master pulling our strings. However, for some people this can inevitably lead to issues of morality. Simply put, problems may just arise because we're free to make our own choices in life – however foolish they may be. It's inevitable therefore that some of these choices may not be particularly brilliant or even beneficial to us. To take this a step further, some of these poor choices may actually result in our becoming the prisoners of certain vices.

We've already acknowledged that our lapses into sin are all too frequent, and can occur so easily, that we often don't even realize that we've sinned at all. On the other hand, sin needs to be taken seriously; the

---

[249] *Catechism of the Catholic Church* – Paragraph 1730.

accumulation of even tiny sins can burden us, harden us and separate us from the Lord. When we find ourselves in this state of being, we've virtually become prisoners of these sins. And so it is that unless we can recognize where we've gone wrong and try to rectify things, it can then become more and more difficult to escape from the bonds of sin of our own making. In this case, only we ourselves can achieve this freedom and only then with the help and grace of Christ.

In fact the Church reminds us that 'the grace of Christ is not in the slightest way a rival of our freedom when this freedom accords with the sense of the true and the good that God has put in the human heart.... The more receptive we are to the promptings of grace, the more we grow in inner freedom and confidence during trials, such as those we face in the pressures and constraints of our world.' [250] Basically, we've been allocated free will, but this doesn't mean that the Father is not there to guide and lead us whenever we have the need of him. To simplify; when we make good and true life choices we're affirmed in this by the grace of God. This brings about that most desirable inner freedom and grace, which in its turn, supports us when we have most need of him in our lives.

---

[250] *Catechism of the Catholic Church* – Paragraph 1742.

Alongside our sin usually lies our guilt. As we're such creatures of habit, most of us repeat the same actions over and over again. We sin repeatedly – and what is more, the sin is usually the same kind of sin. Generally most of us then feel guilty about whatever it is that we've done wrong. To feel guilt is normal and a healthy sign that our conscience and the Lord are working well within us. However, an excess of guilt is not always good for us. It has a tendency to clog up our thought processes and impair our relationship with God. Furthermore, guilt issues need to be resolved sooner rather than later.

In the same way that we need to be able to love ourselves, we also need to be able to listen to our consciences, feel guilty, make the necessary reparation and *move on*. If we're unable to follow this process whereby the wrong has been righted and the guilt satisfactorily channelled and then eliminated, we can easily end up trapped in the prison of our own guilt. On the other hand, if we can bring this process to a swift conclusion, we can soon regain our own natural freedom of mind and spirit, which released from guilt will be able to move closer to God again.

As humans we've a terrible habit of tying ourselves up in fear, pain or emotion. God intended us to be free to love him and live out our lives in harmony. Yet strangely, we seem to have a natural inclination to become prisoners of our own making. Inexplicably, we often become addicted to many things in life; some more serious than others.

Drugs, alcohol and crime are serious addictions, but there are a number of others which can, just as easily, restrict our natural freedom. Drugs and alcohol can not only ruin someone's life, and the lives of those they are closest to, but can completely deprive that person of their liberty. When life revolves around where the next drink or fix is coming from, the addicted person is no longer free to live their life in an ordinary way, and everyday essentials become irrelevant. There's so much pain attached to this type of addiction and so little joy to be derived from it. Other addictions can restrict freedom too. Being addicted to gambling, shopping, lying, gossiping, sex, television or even eating, can be physically, spiritually and mentally damaging.

With all of these addictions, we're no longer free to make our own choices because our lives have become stuck in these bad habits. We need to be where they are taking place; we think about them and indulge in them constantly. We're in the grip of an obsession and with any obsession our freedom of choice is limited or even totally eradicated. Help is, of course, available to sufferers, but that alone is an indication of how many people are addicts and also what a serious issue this now is. Drug and alcohol rehabilitation, Alcoholics Anonymous and various counselling schemes are all designed to help deal with, and eventually alleviate problems of this nature.

### *Free to Change*

A human being, who cannot live out his or her life in the free fashion prescribed by God, becomes inhibited and inevitably when we're restricted in this way, we become more distant from the Lord. In fact, as we know, Christ's healing miracles restored bodily health, but always alongside this was a healing of mind, spirit and social status as well. The outcome of this combined healing was freedom; free to live, free to love, free to believe, free to be happy.

Even so, we can lose all of our sense of freedom in our lives. Many of us value our lifestyles and actually have no desire to change them, especially as change can be difficult for most people. However, there are some people who actively dislike the way they are living their lives, but seem powerless to initiate any type of change. Battered women and men are perhaps a good example of this. These people live their lives in fear and their physical injuries and scars give tangible evidence of this. They detest their lives, but appear strangely unable or unwilling to step outside of their destructive relationships and start afresh. They are trapped in both a relationship and a lifestyle which is anathema to them. They may fear change more than they fear the violence and abuse and so seem totally unable to escape and regain their freedom.

Even those of us who do live contented, wholesome lives, can sometimes feel 'stuck in a rut'. In moderation, trialling new experiences can be good for us; it can bring us new interests, new friends and allow us to step outside of our comfort zone and embrace the freedom of a new challenge. The greatest new experience we can have is to turn to Christ and savour the freedom of spirit which we then experience and the wonderful gifts which await us.

Irrevocably linked to our lifestyle is our behaviour. It will probably come as no surprise to learn that behaviour and actions can easily become repetitive. They become a way of life. Naturally, if our actions and behaviour are desirable and produce good results, then I would suggest carrying on in the same way – and be glad! On the other hand, if we fall into the trap of bad behaviour and immoral actions, then we must seriously take stock of ourselves. We'll see that we need to change for the better and as soon as possible.

Some time ago I made several new friends with whom I shared various interests and acquaintances. My daughter was not particularly impressed with this new circle as she maintained that they were often gossipy and malicious. Admittedly I took little notice at the time, but after a while I began to appreciate what she meant. However, I was totally unprepared for what she said to me one day. She informed me that I too was becoming like these people. Unwittingly I was starting to imitate their behaviour. I was absolutely devastated when she said this to me, but on reflection I realized that there was more than a grain of truth in it. The problem had taken place without my even realizing it, as my behaviour began to mirror theirs. I became aware that I had become entrenched in gossiping and character assassination of others.

You see, my mind had become tangled up in all this, which meant that it was no longer free to concentrate on other far more wholesome subjects. Happily my daughter gave me the wake-up call in time. I was able to understand what had happened and managed to break free from the downward path on which I was heading.

## *Christ has Freed us*

We're inclined to be quite naive as to what freedom actually means to us. We usually claim to be free if we are physically free; that is, able to move around at will, go out and about when and where we want to, and are not physically locked in prison. Yet unfortunately many of us are actually locked into jails of sin, guilt, addictions and our way of life, along with our actions and behaviour. Many people are blissfully unaware of these kind of prison bars, which they themselves have erected. However, although they may be unable to pinpoint it, there will probably be some part of them which is aware of a certain loss of freedom.

Whether they will ever be able to fix it is difficult to say. It depends upon each individual, how introspective they are, how 'tuned into' God they are, and how much they value the freedom which is no longer theirs. Yet there's good news for those who are 'in prison'; the Good News of Jesus Christ. For when we turn to Christ not only is he ready and waiting to give us his help, but in so doing will free us from every shackle of our real or imagined imprisonment and restore us to the freedom which is our birthright.

St Paul tells us that:

'When Christ freed us, he meant us to remain free. Stand firm, therefore, and do not submit again to the yoke of slavery.'

St Paul is referring to the freedom to live and have our being as the Father's children on earth, the children whom he loves so devotedly. Furthermore, we are at liberty to proclaim the Good News and now have the freedom to evangelize on Jesus's Law of Love. God in his mercy has given us the great gift of freedom along with all the other gifts we receive from him.

We have, therefore, been exhorted to use it appropriately, and never to abuse it. We're constantly striving towards our goals in life and are often restricted, inhibited and held back in realizing them. But we're never withheld from the freedom to turn to Christ and to be loved and accepted by him, whenever and however we choose to do so.

This is the true freedom of Christ. No other can compare.

*The Joy of Love*

# ~ *Chapter Nineteen* ~
## In Search of Happiness

It's a well-known fact that most people spend their lives searching for, and sometimes achieving, some degree of happiness, at least for a period of their lives. Happiness is however, extremely difficult to define, and additionally it has an elusive quality that's quite hard to identify; to 'put our finger on'. Often when we try to recall our happiest times, we realize that they've been quite fleeting, although memories of these occasions still manage to lift up our hearts with joy. Sometimes even a sound, sight or smell can trigger a memory that we hold dear and associate with happiness and these sorts of sensory experiences can briefly enable us to feel that emotion again as our memories are re-kindled.

Additionally, we may find it a problem trying to recall what the circumstances and the occasion was, that made us feel such joy and actually this is both normal and natural, because true happiness can be initiated by the smallest of actions, gestures, words or circumstances. In fact, the search for happiness is akin to our search for God; desirable but sometimes elusive, challenging but a treasure and joy when accomplished.

Furthermore, it stands to reason that there would be such a close resemblance between the two lifelong searches, as they are undeniably bound together. We can only find true happiness when we find the Lord.

### The Happiest Days of our Lives

When two people embark upon marriage, there's an expectation that their wedding day will be one of the happiest days of their lives. However, what lies beneath this statement? The explanation is relatively simple. The special and sacred ceremony which takes place when a man and woman give themselves completely to each other with mutual love, and with the love and grace of God blessing their union, has all the ingredients for true happiness.

The key to the complete fulfilment of marital happiness is surely love; the love the two partners hold for each other and the love of God. Liam Kelly gives us these beautiful words taken from a marriage homily:

*'It is very consoling to know that this great partnership
Into which you are about to enter
Is a partnership that was designed by our Creator God
from the very beginning.
At the heart of God's creation is a love story*

*between a man and a woman.*
*God formed man and woman to be companions,*
*partners in a life-long journey of love.*
*And though that first love story is a love story gone awry,*
*from that moment on there has existed a wonderful*
*institution of marriage which is built upon*
*the partnership of a man and woman in love.*
*It is that partnership which you seek to form*
*by standing before God, before the community of the Church*
*as you promise mutual vows of life-long love and fidelity*
*to one another in the sacrament of marriage.'* [251]

### *Love is the Key*

The homily quoted by Kelly mentions the word 'love' no less than six times in this short passage. This is a good indicator of how important the author feels love is. The text is about the mutual giving and receiving of love. Love is generally key to happiness, joy and contentment. Matrimony is one such example of happiness flowing from love, and birth is yet another. We need only study the expressions on the faces of new parents to be able to clearly see huge love and happiness there, and for most people the role of grandparent is a natural extension of this.

---

[251] *Sacraments Revisited* – Liam Kelly, p. 167.

My mother was unenthusiastic about the idea of becoming a grandmother. She was relatively young at the time, and as I am an only child, her days of parenting and dealing with young children was definitely put behind her. Yet she describes the moment of setting eyes on her first grandchild as 'falling completely in love with him'. And in that moment I saw an expression of enormous happiness and contentment on my mother's face.

Even death, which completes the natural cycle of life, plays its part. When someone we love dies, we naturally feel intense *un*happiness, because the object of our love is no longer present. But that shared love can never be completely lost and will echo throughout time. Only in this way can our God-given love have a purpose which will endure for all eternity.

The Church explains to us that: 'true happiness is not found in riches or well-being, in human fame or power, or in any human achievement – however beneficial it may be – such as science, technology and art, or indeed in any creature, but in God alone, the source of every good and of all love.' [252]

---

[252] *Catechism of the Catholic Church* – Paragraph 1723.

It further goes on to explain that every one of us who has the desire for happiness has this desire because the Lord has placed it in our hearts. It's a divine emotion, and one which God has deliberately planted in us, in order that both we and it may grow and become ever closer to him. This in turn, enables us to give our love to the Lord, and to receive his unconditional love. However, God doesn't just return the love which we give to him. He pours out his love upon each and every one of us as free gift. We don't have to earn that love, nor do we receive it 'like for like' either. It's freely given.

### An Everyday Guide to Happiness

Although happiness is rather abstract, we're often quite poor at finding, protecting and preserving it. We're inclined to build up our expectations of any event or occasion which we feel would be a happy one, and this, of course, can result in anti-climax or even failure. We can be unwilling to accept situations, actions and people as they really are, because we anticipate greater, higher and more admirable results. This again can result in disappointment instead of the anticipated joy. Furthermore, we sometimes fail to appreciate the simple beauty of so many things in life – people, creation, kindness and unexpected pleasures of any sort.

If we could only take a moment to digest some of these experiences, we would instantly feel lighter and happier.

Many people entertain the idea that happiness is brought about by material gain. People sigh blissfully at the idea of a Lottery win which would give them a fortune, but the reality can be somewhat different. Furthermore, in trying to achieve riches we can become discontented with our own lot in life, and unhappy that we've not been 'lucky' enough to win a fortune. Surprisingly, this is a form of avarice which can destroy our beautiful and delicate spirituality, as well as counteract any chance of happiness.

It's worth mentioning that bad luck can play a part in anyone's life, but often it's a chain of events that have helped create ill fortune. Although I have had my own share of bad luck, I recognize that each of us must try to capture happiness as and when it occurs and endeavour to appreciate it to the full, no matter how fleeting it appears to be. Rabbi Jonathan Sacks asserts that we must, in fact, learn to transform our suffering as part of our own quest for contentment, and goes on to explain that:

'When bad things happen, use them to sensitise (sic) [yourself] to the pain of others. The greatest people I know – people who survived tragedy and became stronger as a result – did not ask, "Who did this to me?" Instead they asked, "What does this allow me to do that I could not have done before?" They refused to become victims of circumstance. They became, instead, agents of hope.'[253]

As part of our mission to achieve happiness, we should adopt a positive attitude towards life every day, giving thanks for what we have, instead of moaning about what we don't. O'Leary gives his perspective on positive thinking when he says:

'I imagine a line running across my mind, separating my thoughts. Below the line are the murky waters of complaining, fretting and anxiety. Above the line is where the positive and hopeful energies are waiting to be tapped into. It's at this point that I have a choice. I can remain a victim of my own negativity and descend into the self-perpetuating distress of the touchy ego. Or I can reach out of that swampy

---

[253] Rabbi Lord Jonathan Sacks writing in *The Times*.

place and find that firm and life-giving ground of positive thinking and letting go.' [254]

Likewise, we should learn how to forgive others and in turn, accept their forgiveness, if we're to attain happiness. It's a state of being which cannot shine through if we're burdened by anger or resentment against others. This weighs us down in the same way that sin can do, and an unforgiving person is generally not a happy one.

Our social interactions with others can often cause us pain; a chance remark, a hurtful comment or the realization that we've been excluded from something, are all examples of how we can easily become angry and hurt. This anger and hurt can, in turn, be channelled against another person, causing us to hold a grudge. We have to be able to let go of this grudge, and so feel the weight of our anger and pain roll away from us like a stone, as we forgive someone. After this, we can begin to feel contentment again. It's a process which we really need to go through.

In our quest for happiness, our social interactions are critical. We need to spend time with others as part of our service to them and the Lord, and in so doing we

---

[254] *Prism of Love* – Daniel O'Leary, p. 16.

should be able to *listen* to what they have to say, metaphorically step into their shoes, empathize, and if possible, take any necessary action required to help. If help is *not* required, then we can always just *listen*. This is a very important role. By attentively listening to someone else we're showing them that we care about them, and this makes that other person feel valued and nurtured. When we give of ourselves in this manner, the net result is our own inner contentment. Equally importantly, listening, empathizing and helping one another in this way sets a standard for us to stick to in our daily lives. The benefits we reap from this are truly valuable.

Generally, most of us feel uplifted when we receive praise for anything we've undertaken or achieved. We usually experience this as a warm glow of satisfaction which gives our day an extra boost. When we praise others we too derive a sense of happiness and well-being. Rabbi Sacks points out that all too often we ourselves eagerly await praise or congratulations, but strangely hold back in giving this to others.

Don't allow someone else to do the praising, he advises, do it yourself instead and make another person's day! In so doing it will also make your own day a brighter, happier one, which will contribute to your own well-being and satisfaction with life. [255] When we praise others, we are, in turn, thinking of them, and so we're able to benefit from a happiness 'double whammy'. This is because we're not only cheering them up but also ourselves into the bargain. Both Sacks and O'Leary, although coming from very different religious backgrounds, are clearly in agreement as to how we should try to find happiness in our lives, and what guidelines there are to achieve this.

Being our own person, the one God created us to be, achieves a sense of fulfilment most of us desire. And learning to appreciate the beneficial effect of laughter – even when this is directed at ourselves, plays a part in our quest for happiness also. Letting go of our failures and moving on in life to seek our successes, is another crucial component towards our state of well-being. After all, tomorrow is a new day, when everything often appears brighter. We can then put yesterday's events behind us as we start afresh. Finally, trust in God and his mercy and love. He will not fail you.

Interestingly, many of the factors which seem to be required for happiness have been thoroughly explored and discussed in previous chapters. Examples of this are of course, reconciliation, peace, positivity,

---

[255] Rabbi Lord Jonathan Sacks writing in *The Times.*

prayer, healing and creation. The sum total of these qualities and activities will always bring us nearer to the Lord and that, in turn, will provide us with that elusive longed-for happiness. Yet again this is essentially because they are critically linked. We can only know true happiness when we know the Lord.

## A State of Beatitude

Again I am reminded of that most wonderful of moments, when we're overcome by an intense sensation of happiness and euphoria and the feeling that everything is completely right in our world. This feeling is so beautiful, so shimmering with light and joy as to be extraordinary and it retains a deeply lasting impression.

Also, in my experience, it happens rarely. I could count the number of times that I have experienced this on one hand and my mother tells me that it has only ever happened to her twice in her entire lifetime. I am convinced that when this does occur, however we're being gently touched by the Lord and given a tiny glimpse of what our future life in Heaven will be like.

I was fascinated to hear, at a conference, a priest describing an almost identical experience of his own, which overcame him quite suddenly one morning.

He was convinced, he said, that he was in the presence of the Holy Spirit and was bathed in joy and light.

While the Eucharist can be described as the supreme sacrament in which we're given the gift of Jesus Christ, the moment of this utterly blinding joy, when we're touched by the Lord, can also be described as a supreme moment of happiness. This is when Christ is so close to us that he fills our entire vision.

'The natural desire for happiness,' the *Catechism of the Catholic Church* informs us, 'is of divine origin: God has placed it in the human heart in order to draw man to the One who alone can fulfil it.' [256] And this is not all: The *Catechism* makes it plain that 'beatitude makes us 'partakers of the divine nature' and of eternal life. With beatitude, man enters into the glory of Christ and into the joy of the Trinitarian life.' [257]

Simply put, each one of has an inbuilt desire to achieve and experience happiness, and this desire has been deliberately planted in the human heart by God, who knows that only he can truly bring it about.

---

[256] *Catechism of the Catholic Church* – Paragraph 1718.
[257] *Catechism of the Catholic Church* – Paragraph 1721.

The word 'beatitude' comes from the Latin *beatitudo*, meaning 'blessedness'; therefore, although human, we're empowered to receive this blessedness, well-being or happiness, which is a gift to us from the Father. This, in turn, makes us joyful participants in the life of Father, Son and Holy Spirit. Our ability to be blessed and to become ever more so, as we strive to reach that pinnacle of happiness which we call God, is a pure gift indeed. There is none other like it.

### *Radiant with Joy*

Pope Francis in his Apostolic Exhortation *Evangelii Gaudium* calls for a re-discovery of the benefit and the quality of joy. He is, however, at pains to point out that for some of today's Christians, that happiness which is a natural by-product of God's love appears hidden:

> 'There are Christians whose lives seem like Lent without Easter. I realize of course that joy is not expressed the same way at all times in life... Joy adapts and changes, but it always endures, even as a flicker of light born of our personal certainty that, when everything is said and done, we are infinitely loved.' [258]

---

[258] *Evangelii Gaudium* – Pope Francis, Paragraph 6.

In that infinite love we should be able to find huge joy and happiness, yet sadly, there are many people in the world who do not consider themselves to be loved by God. They have to seek out and grasp that joy, comfort and happiness purely for themselves, although usually with a bit of help from us, of course!

Critically, Pope Francis returns us to the point at which this chapter began: that is, happiness is about love, the love we receive from the Father and the love that we give to, and receive from others:

> 'Loving others is a spiritual force drawing us to union with God; indeed, one who does not love others "walks in the darkness" *(1 John 2: 11)*, "remains in death" *(1 John 3: 14)* and "does not know God" *(1 John 4: 8)*… When we live out a spirituality of drawing nearer to others and seeking their welfare, our hearts are opened wide to the Lord's greatest and most beautiful gifts.' [259]

Yet, when we love others with all our heart, we become vulnerable. We can easily be hurt, challenged and tested from time to time, especially when our human faults and feelings take precedence over our good intentions. There is perhaps no easy solution to

---

[259] *Evangelii Gaudium* – Pope Francis, Paragraph 272.

how we can avoid these problems, which occur as a result of our human nature, except to be sure in the knowledge that only love endures. When we love someone or they love us, Christ clearly becomes visible in that love. Pope St John Paul II states that:

> 'Man cannot live without love. He remains a being that is incomprehensible for himself, his life is senseless, if love is not revealed to him, if he does not encounter love, if he does not experience it and make it his own, if he does not participate intimately in it.' [260]

Every part of our human being is involved in love; our hearts, minds and souls and even our bodies. All our feelings, reactions and sensations play a part in the wonder of giving and receiving love.

The saying 'love makes the world go round' has a number of definitions, including having a strong feeling towards another person, being sexually attracted to that person and inevitably actually liking them very much! However, the resounding definition which appears to sum up love could well be:

---

[260] Encylical letter *Redemptor Hominis* Pope St John Paul II – Paragraph 10.

'Love is the feeling that a person's happiness is very important to you, and the way you show this feeling is in your behaviour towards them.' [261]

Love is intrinsically bound up with happiness; love is happiness and happiness derives from love. When we love we're made holy, wholesome and perfect in the face of that love, and when we receive the love of God we receive that supreme beatitude from him; perfect, wholesome love, which in turn generates perfect, wholesome happiness.

---

[261] The definition is generated by the author – *Julia Beacroft.*

# ~ *Chapter Twenty* ~
## In Whom shall I Trust?

A baby has utter dependence and total trust in the people who look after and care for it. It trusts that it will be fed and nourished with food and love, bathed, kept warm, sheltered and free from harm. Its cries will be answered and its requirements will be met. For a baby all of these basic needs are instinctive and it unconsciously trusts and believes that the appropriate care and love will be given.

It's well-known that bonding with one's baby is incredibly special, but the remarkable trust that a child places in its parents from the very beginning of its life, is equally extraordinary. By just observing a baby being fed, we receive glimpses of the love and trust the child bestows upon its mother, as it rarely takes its eyes off her face during the process. This is a truly moving sight and one which has struck me over and over again when my own children were babies and I was feeding them.

In fact, infants and small children *continue* to bestow the same level of trust in their parents throughout their childhood years. At this stage they believe that Mum and Dad are infallible. They unconsciously expect that their parents will continue to not only care for them, but make the appropriate life decisions for them.

Furthermore, they believe that their parents will always be able to come up with the correct answer to any problem or query! Understanding the bond of trust between a child and its parents, the Catholic Church informs those parents in the Baptismal Rite that:

'God is the giver of all life, human and divine. May he bless the father of this child. He and his wife will be the first teachers of their child in the ways of faith. May they be also the best of teachers, bearing witness to the faith by what they say and do...' [262]

## *Lessons in Trust*

We can understand why the 'church of the home' is given such a high profile by the Church itself, as parental influence is enormously significant in every family, usually until the offspring approach adulthood, at least! By the time this occurs, the basics of the Christian faith will hopefully have been instilled in them by teaching and example. Yet sadly, trust, which we're probably instinctively born with, is often eroded by life's experiences. Little by little every child learns that trust can be destroyed and wariness towards others may gradually set in.

A child's first experience of deception and betrayal may come from their siblings or comrades at school and they very soon learn to be cautious. How do we learn to trust another person again, when our trust has been destroyed? Sadly there are some people who are unable to restore this trust when they feel they've

---

[262] *The New Baptism Book,* p. 18.

been betrayed or deceived. Others may be capable of doing so, but whether to the same degree, however, is often uncertain. When our trust has been damaged, then we too are damaged, hurt, offended and guarded towards others, particularly the culprit involved. On occasion the betrayal may be so deep that the person is psychologically unable to allow themselves to trust anyone again. Yet following the example of Jesus Christ, we're called to love our neighbour as ourselves, and a vital part of that process also involves learning to trust others.

If we replace the word 'faith' with the word 'trust', then our understanding of the importance of trust in God's redeeming work and in our lives, is made clear. In his Apostolic Letter *Porta Fidei*, Pope Benedict reminds us over and over again of great works that were achieved and recorded in Scripture, due to absolute trust in the Lord:

> '**By faith,** Mary accepted the Angel's word and **believed** the message that she was to become the Mother of God.'

> '**By faith,** the Apostles left everything to follow their Master.'

'**By faith,** the disciples formed the first community.'

'**By faith,** the martyrs gave their lives.' [263]

Every one of these actions that Pope Benedict refers to, were achieved by a person or persons trusting fully in God. As a direct result, they were then empowered to carry out the Lord's work.

But trusting someone who's diametrically opposed to us on important matters can be challenging. We naturally warm towards, and trust those, who have the same or similar interests, beliefs and lifestyles as ourselves. Naturally, it gives us a common point of contact with that person. And yet despite this, not only are we required to try to understand their point of view, but also we need to allow ourselves to trust in the fact that their viewpoint could even be as valid as our own! Alongside this, it's important that we trust in God to provide us with some sort of understanding and empathy towards someone who is poles apart from us. This may sound fairly obvious, but in reality, it can take a fairly huge leap of faith to trust a person whom you feel is utterly wrong in some of their assumptions and beliefs. This is not to say, however, that we should

[263] Apostolic letter *Porta Fidei* – Pope Benedict XVI, Paragraph 13.

abandon our own philosophies – far from it – but we *should* be able to trust and form a bond of some kind, even with anyone who blatantly disagrees with us. Bearing this in mind, the Catholic Church similarly asks that we try to offer some acceptance and understanding, not only to other Christian denominations, but also to other global faiths as well:

> 'The challenge of difference, the task of meeting the followers of another religion in true dialogue, is the demanding one of combining genuine love and respect, and openness to unexpected truth and goodness, with a firm grasp of our own Christian faith and a readiness to be led by its light.' [264]

In this quote, the Catholic Bishops' Conference refers to 'genuine love and respect and openness to…truth and goodness' and there's no doubt that any of this could come about without some level of trust.

### *Scepticism and Suspicion*

To gain someone's trust is a prize worth striving for, but it can be an uphill struggle and may take a considerable time to achieve. However, the more arduous the task and the longer it takes, the sweeter the reward. For

---

[264] *Meeting God in Friend & Stranger* – p. 15.

when someone gives their trust, another person gains a gift of immeasurable worth and it should be recognized as such. It's unfortunate however, that the human race has a rather chequered history of abusing trust. In fact, if we quickly refer to the Scriptures we can easily see this. Sadly, we need read no further than Genesis to be aware of the greatest misuse of trust of all time. God in his love and generosity gave men and women the perfect context in which to live out their lives in peace, fostering harmony and love. Yet we 'blew it', as we were not content to trust God's judgement about what was best for each and every one of us. This of course, refers to the creation story where man's downfall is documented.

Although this narrative is fairly common knowledge, it doesn't prevent us, like Adam and Eve, from being left naked and defenceless, when we don't allow God to fully work in our lives. So often we fail to surrender ourselves to his wisdom and guidance. So often we just don't believe that our trust in the Lord will solve our problems or dilemmas and dispel our doubts.

In fact the Bible is littered with stories where trust is absent or misappropriated. Remember that despite the fact that his disciples followed Jesus, there were times when they simply didn't trust him! Due, no doubt, to their poor understanding of parts of Jesus's teaching. We're told that some of the disciples initially left everything and followed Christ, which would have shown an enormous degree of trust – to say nothing of a huge sense of adventure! But then their quarrelling among themselves, their desire for one-upmanship and their preconceived ideas about what they expected of the Messiah, at times contributed towards a lack of trust and conviction.

Thomas, who expressed his doubts about the post-resurrection Christ, will be remembered throughout history as the man who was unable to trust and believe in the power and the promise of Christ. Until his eyes had seen the actual risen Lord, and he had touched the wounds of Christ for himself, he stubbornly refused to believe. Jesus remarks upon this as follows:

'You believe because you can see me. Happy are those who have not seen and yet believe.' [265]

Whether we would fare any better today is highly debatable, especially as the modern trend appears to be one of less trust towards certain ideas and situations,

[265] *John* 20: 29.

particularly if they seem implausible. Of course, the disciples were not alone in showing a lack of trust when certain preconceived ideas were challenged. The rich young man, who so eagerly desired to commit his life to following God's commandments, and furthermore appeared to be well on his way to achieving this, falls at the last hurdle when Jesus advises him:

> 'If you wish to be perfect, go and sell what you own and give the money to the poor, and you will have treasure in heaven; then come follow me.' [266]

Sadly, the young man had to walk away as he was unable to totally trust the Lord and begin a new phase of his life. He heard the pronouncement of Jesus, he probably came close to believing the truth of it, but he was incapable of carrying out Jesus's wishes. He was materially rich but his faith in Christ and his trust were ultimately inadequate. Jesus's instruction demanded a huge act of faith from the young man, which sadly, fell far short of the mark. Would we have reacted in the same way as the rich young man, or would our belief and trust in the Lord have been strong enough to carry out his wishes?

---

[266] *Matthew* 19: 20 - 22.

Jesus himself must be fully aware of the problems which we, as God's children, encounter with the whole concept of trust. Although there's evidence to show that during his lifetime he acquired a following of believers, he 'knew them all and did not trust himself to them; he never needed evidence about any man; he could tell what a man had in him.' [267]

These words are most profound in that those who are sincere and try to follow the Christian path will encounter few difficulties. However, those who are insincere and are intent upon pursuing their own 'agenda' may find the notion of Christ knowing what 'a man had in him' rather worrying! To be quite clear about this – Christ is just as aware of what we 'have in us' nowadays over two thousand years later, as he was at the time of his life on earth. He recognizes when we're able to trust him and when we do not, and he is all too familiar with our human struggles to try to achieve this.

### Faint Heart never won God's Church

We live in troubled times. Wars, crime, materialism and substance abuse as a form of escapism, are becoming more and more widespread in our world. In a similar way the Church also suffers from today's troubles:

---

[267] *John* 2: 24 - 25.

instability, scandal, declining numbers of clergy and in some countries fewer members of the faithful. Yet 'courage is urgently needed in the Church of today; against the backdrop of declining numbers in many places and growing attempts to marginalise people of faith.' [268] It could be easy to lose heart in a Church where we sometimes disagree with its decisions. It could be easy to lose trust in a Church when we feel let down by it at times. With no effort at all we could lose faith in our fellow members of the Church when we're angry or disagree with them.

Yet we should remember that the Spirit is always at work within each one of us, even if we're unable to feel and recognize this at times. We need to pray for our clergy; our bishops, priests and deacons and we furthermore need to be able to pray for each other. The action of doing this is an action of trust; we trust that God will hear our prayers and will be a good shepherd for our Church, so that it may flourish and prosper. Our clergy also need our trust and support. They are our leaders in Christ. But of course, they cannot perform this function without God's help *and ours*.

We've looked closely at how our trust can be slowly but surely eroded and how for some people this

---

[268] *The Way of the Desert* – Andrew Watson, p. 143.

can occur quite quickly and easily, depending on the circumstances. However, our cynicism is wholly unproductive. We could, of course, journey through life being doubtful and distrustful of others, but this will only achieve the result of making ourselves unlovable. How can we be loved if we cannot allow another person to get close to us?

We also know that the Bible is scattered with snapshots concerning mistrust and deceit. However, these are counterbalanced by narratives describing scenes of enormous faith. When Christ raised Lazarus from the dead Martha did not say as she might have done "It's no use you coming here now! What can you do?"

Instead she expresses her belief that with Christ at her side all will be well:

> 'I know that, even now, whatever you ask of God, he will grant you…. I believe that you are the Christ, the Son of God, the one who was to come into the world.' [269]

We're in a great position to learn from Martha. Martha is aware of the stench of decay from the tomb

---

[269] *John* 11: 22 - 27.

where Lazarus has been laid to rest for four days. Yet her trust and belief in the Lord's love and mercy means that the fragrant aroma of Christ makes an overwhelming assault on her senses. We know that Jesus Christ raised Lazarus from the dead after a number of days.

With our love and trust however, Jesus can raise us to a new life whereby we're capable of any act, or speaking any word that will give love, life and comfort to another person. In so doing, we're contributing in our own small way towards the coming of the Kingdom.

In his Apostolic Exhortation *Evangelii Gaudium*, Pope Francis refers to both priests and laity alike resisting 'giving themselves over completely to mission and thus end up in a state of paralysis and acedia.' [270] The term *acedia* means spiritual apathy or indifference, which can further lead to cynicism and we must be beware of *our* cynicism preventing us from loving, close relationships with God and with others.

While all of us encounter both good and bad times, periods of great faith and phases of niggling doubts, there can be no question that the Holy Spirit

---

[270] Apostolic Exhortation *Evangelii Gaudium:* Pope Francis, Paragraph 81.

longs to remove our scepticism to bring us to the fullness of life in Christ.

However, in order for this to happen we must fully co-operate with him. Trust is a fragile and delicate plant, requiring nurturing and love, like our faith itself. Yet without trust we can soon find ourselves alone, wary and defensive.

God longs to penetrate our defences so that we can trust in him. Trust and belief: they are the very essence of life itself.

# ~ *Bibliography* ~

ALEI, D. 2003. Thy Kingdom Come. Walking in our Godly Inheritance. U.K.: *Sovereign World*.

ANONYMOUS. 2003. The Cloud of Unknowing (ed.) Evelyn Underhill. U.S.A.: *Dover Publications Inc.*

BARRY, W.A. 1991. Finding God in all Things – A Companion to the Spiritual Exercises of St Ignatius. Notre Dame, Indiana: *Ave Maria Press*.

BERNIER, P. 2003. Ministry in the Church – A Historical & Pastoral Approach. Connecticut: *Twenty-third Publications*.

COUGHLIN, P. 2009. The Fragrance of Jesus. Glimpsing the Kingdom through his Miracles. U.K.: *Kevin Mayhew*.

COZZENS, D. 2004. Faith that Dares to Speak. Minnesota, U.S.A.: *Liturgical Press*.

DALY, R. 1999. God's Little Book of Calm. London: *HarperCollins*.

FINLAY, J. 2003. Merton's Palace of Nowhere. Notre Dame Indiana: *Ave Maria Press*.

FLEESON, M. 2009. Life Journey. U.K: *Lindisfarne Scriptorium Ltd.*

FOWLER, J. 1988. Faith Development & Pastoral Care. U.S.A.: *Fortress*.

GREENE, G. 1940. The Power and the Glory. U.K.: *Penguin*.

GROOME, T. 2003. What Makes us Catholic – Eight Gifts for Life. New York: *HarperCollins*.

HAGAN, R.; KANE, I.; O'CONNELL, J. 2000. Faith Builder – A Basic Guide on how to Live as a Christian Today. U.K.: *Redemptorist Publications.*

HOPKINS, G. M. 1877 "Pied Beauty" in W. H. Gardner & N. H. MacKenzie (eds.) 1967 Poems of G. M. Hopkins. U.K.: *Oxford University Press.*

HUEBSCH, B. 2004. The General Directory for Catechesis in Plain English. U.S.A.: *Twenty-third Publications.*

HUGHES, G.W. 1985. God of Surprises. London: *Darton, Longman & Todd.*

JAMISON, C. 2006. Finding sanctuary – Monastic Steps for Everyday Life. London: *Phoenix.*

JEFFERS, S. 1987. Feel the Fear and do it Anyway. Australia: *Century.*

KELLY, L. 2000. Catechesis Revisited. London: *Darton, Longman & Todd.*

KELLY, L. 2001. Sacraments Revisited – What do they Mean Today? London: *Darton, Longman & Todd.*

KENDALL, R. T. 2005. Out of the Comfort Zone – Is your God too Nice? London: *Hodder & Stoughton.*

KNIGHT, J. 2004. Jesus – An Historical & Theological Investigation. London/New York: *Continuum.*

KÜNG, H. 2001. The Church. London: *Burns & Oates.*

LEONARD, R. 2006. Movies that Matter – Reading Film Through the Lens of Faith. Chicago: *Loyola Press.*

LYONS, E. 1987. Partnership in Parish – A Vision for Parish Life, Mission & Ministry. Co. Dublin: *The Columba Press.*

McKAY, M. 1993. Messages – The Communication Skills Book. Oakland: *New Harbinger Publications Inc.*

McMANUS, J. 2011. I am my Body. U.K.: *Redemptorist Publications.*

McMANUS, J. & THORNTON, S. 2006. Finding Forgiveness. U.K.: *Redemptorist Publications.*

MALONEY, G. A. 1993. Deep calls to Deep. A Christian Spirituality of the Heart. U.S.A.: *Dimension Books.*

MATTHEWS, I. 1995. The impact of God – Soundings from St John of the Cross. London: *Hodder & Stoughton.*

MEISTER ECKHART, 1979. Sermons & Treatises. Trans. M. O. C. Walshe. Shaftesbury: *Element.*

MEISTER ECKHART, 1981. The Essential Sermons, Commentaries, Treatises and Defence. Trans. E. Colledge/ B. McGinn. U.S.A: *Paulist Press.*

MERTON, T. 2003. New Seeds of Contemplation. Boston/London: *Shambhala.*

MICK, L. E. 2004. Living Baptism Daily. Minnesota: *Liturgical Press.*

NOUWEN, H. 1979. The Wounded Healer. London: *Darton, Longman & Todd.*

NOUWEN, H. 1998. Reaching Out. London: *Fount/HarperCollins.*

NOUWEN, H. 2003. The Heart of Henri Nouwen. New York: *Crossroad Publishing Co.*

O'LEARY, D. 2003. Prism of Love. God's Colours in Everyday Life. Co. Dublin: *Columba Press.*

O'MEARA, T. F. 2005. 'Lay Ecclesial Ministry – What it is and what it isn't', in R. W. Miller II (ed.) 2005

Lay Ministry in the Catholic Church.
U.S.A.: *Liguori, pp.67-77.*

O'MAHONEY, T.P. 2010. Why the Catholic Church Needs
Vatican III. Co. Dublin: *Columba Press.*

PATTISON, S. 2000. A Critique of Pastoral Care.
U.K.: *SCM Press.*

PATZIA, A. G. 2001. The Emergence of the Church –
Context, Growth, Leadership & Worship.
U.S.A.: *Intervarsity Press.*

RADCLIFFE, T. 2006. What is the point of being a
Christian? London: *Burns & Oates.*

RADCLIFFE, T. 2008. Why go to Church? The Drama of the
Eucharist. London/New York: *Continuum.*

RATZINGER, J. Pope Benedict XVI, 2008.
Jesus of Nazareth. Trans. A. J. Walker (2007).
London: *Bloomsbury.*

ROLHEISER, R. 1998. Seeking Spirituality. London:
*Hodder & Stoughton.*

SMITH, D. 1988. A Journey into God. London:
*Hodder & Stoughton.*

VANIER, J. 1993. Followers of Jesus. Dublin:
*Gill & MacMillan.*

WARREN, R. 2002. The Purpose-Driven Life – What on
Earth am I Here for? U.S.A.: *Zondervan.*

WATSON, A. 2011. The Way of the Desert.
U.K.: *The Bible Reading Fellowship.*

WILLIAMS, R. 2013. Choose Life – Christmas & Easter
Sermons in Canterbury Cathedral. London: *Bloomsbury.*

YOUNG, W. P. 2008. The Shack. London: *Hodder & Stoughton.*

YOUNG, W. P. 2012. Crossroads. London: *Hodder & Stoughton.*

### Vatican Documents

CATECHESI TRADENDAE. Catechesis in our Time – Apostolic Exhortation of *Blessed Pope [St] John Paul II*, 16th October, 1979.

CHRISTIFIDELES LAICI. Post Synodal Apostolic Exhortation on the Vocation and the Mission of the Lay Faithful in the Church and in the World. *Pope St John Paul II*, 30th December, 1988.

DEUS CARITAS EST. God is Love. Encyclical Letter of *Pope Benedict XVI*, 25th December, 2005.

EVANGELII GAUDIUM. The Joy of the Gospel. Apostolic Exhortation of *Pope Francis*. 24th November 2013.

EVANGELII NUNTIANDI. Evangelization in the Modern World. Apostolic Exhortation of *Pope Paul VI*, 8th December, 1975.

EVANGELIUM VITAE. Encyclical Letter on The Gospel of Life. *Pope St John Paul II*, 25th March, 1995.

LUMEN GENTIUM. Dogmatic Constitution on the Church. Second Vatican Council, 21st November, 1964.

PORTA FIDEI. Apostolic Letter of *Pope Benedict XVI* for the Induction of the Year of Faith, 11th October, 2011.

PASTORES DABO VOBIS. Post Synodal Apostolic Exhortation on the Formation of Priests in the Circumstances of the present Day. Pope St John Paul II, 25th March, 1992.

REDEMPTOR HOMINIS. Encyclical Letter of
Pope St John Paul II, 4th March, 1979.

SACRAMENTUM CARITATIS. Post Synodal Exhortation
on the Eucharist. *Pope Benedict XVI*, 22nd February, 2007.

SACROSANCTUM CONCILIUM. Constitution on the
Sacred Liturgy. Second Vatican Council,
4th December, 1963.

SPE SALVI. Encyclical Letter on Christian Hope.
*Pope Benedict XVI*, 30th November, 2007.

### Other Sources

CATECHISM OF THE CATHOLIC CHURCH, 2004.
London: *Burns & Oates/Continuum.*

GENERAL DIRECTORY FOR CATECHESIS,
Congregation for the Clergy, 2002.
London: *Catholic Truth Society.*

MEETING GOD IN FRIEND & STRANGER – Fostering
Respect & Mutual Understanding between the Religions.
2010. Catholic Bishops Conference of England & Wales.
London: *Catholic Truth Society.*

OXFORD ENGLISH DICTIONARY, 2006,
Ed. Sara Hawker. Oxford: *Oxford University Press.*

THE JERUSALEM BIBLE, 1966. London:
*Darton, Longman & Todd.*

THE NEW BAPTISM BOOK, 1978. Ed. Francis Dickinson.
U.K.: *Redemptorist Publications.*

THE ORDER OF MASS, New English Translation, 2011.
London: *Catholic Truth Society.*

THE TABLET, 8th February, 2014.

THE TIMES, Article by Rabbi Jonathan Sacks.

# ~ *Acknowledgements* ~

MY THANKS go first of all to my wonderful husband Patrick, who always believed in me and that I could write this book. He and my family have also been a great source of anecdotes too! *(Sorry....!)*

In particular I wish to thank not only my parish priest Father Kieran Kirby but also Father Brian Kenwrick and Sister Damian Cunningham for their love, friendship and advice over the years. I know that this has contributed towards this book. Thanks also to all the adults and children who I've prepared for RCIA and the Sacraments – and their parents. Their evident joy and keen insights have been my reward.

I was delighted to be able to use so many of *Joseph Hanrahan's* excellent illustrations in this book. In addition to having been a prize-winning art student, he is also a gifted musician as are other members of his family. If he's not in the music group at Mass, he's usually serving on the altar!

Thanks too to Adrian Wardle who has been a helpful and critical editor. During more than fifty years in publishing, he launched the Westminster Cathedral magazine, now known as *Oremus,* as well as our own diocesan newspaper *Catholic South West.* More recently he produced *The Daily Office of Our Lady* (The Syon Breviary) www.syonbreviary.co.uk

*Julia's next book, 'The Beauty of Holy Communion' – for parents of children preparing for Holy Communion – will be available later this year.*

---

*Front cover images by courtesy of NASA/Hubble (www.nasa.gov) and the Trinity Episcopal Church, Ashland, Oregon, U.S.A.*

*The author wishes to thank all who have kindly given permission to quote their work(s) in this book. We have tried to contact all copyright owners but without success in some cases. We respectfully ask them to get in touch with us at admin@sanciobooks.com*

# ~ QUESTIONS FOR GROUP DISCUSSIONS ~

### CHAPTER ONE – *Vocation, Vocation, Vocation!*
- Have you ever felt an unexpected and spontaneous urge to 'do something' which has had significant consequences for yourself and/or other people? Could you explain what this was? Do you think this urge came from God?
- What are *your* gifts? How can you use these for the benefit of others?

### CHAPTER TWO – *So What on Earth is Prayer all About?*
- Have you a special time and place to pray? Where, what and when is this?
- Which 'type' of prayer works best for you? Have you ever thought afterwards that God was right not to grant a particular prayer? Why?

### CHAPTER THREE – *How do we Become Fishers of Men?*
- In this time of the *New Evangelization*, how do you think we can reach out to others and help them to have a relationship with Jesus?
- Have you experienced of other people becoming unexpectedly interested when you were telling them a story about your faith or church life? What happened? Have you thought you may be called to a catechetical ministry?

### CHAPTER FOUR – *To Be or Not to Be Reconciled?*
- Which 'tools' do you use to prevent disagreements with others and to enable you to be reconciled with them? How effective are they?
- Have you ever changed your attitude for the better towards someone? How did you do this? How do you feel when you are forgiven by either another person or in the Sacrament of Reconciliation?

### CHAPTER FIVE – *Church + Faith = Christian?*
- Have you ever considered helping in a church ministry? Which would use your own particular gift(s) most effectively?
- Have you ever discovered a new meaning –previously overlooked – in the Liturgy of the Word?
- How strong is your sense of church community? Why or why not?

### CHAPTER SIX – *The Healing Touch*
- Doctors and nurses help to heal the sick. But all of us can heal others of such things as loneliness, despair, anger and sadness. How can we do this, especially now, in this time of the *New Evangelization?*
- In the RCIA programme, warmth, joy and healing are common emotions. Why do you think this might be the case? Can we take this out to others?

### CHAPTER SEVEN – *Losing that Lovin' Feelin'*
- Have you responded to the invitation to have God in your life? How?
- When you have suffered, are you angry with God or do you turn to him in consolation? (Do the *'Lifeline'* exercise.) Do you feel comforted by him?

### CHAPTER EIGHT – *Denying the Self*

• Do you do anything special in the period of Lent? Do you 'give something up' or do you do something extra?

• How do you see yourself? Have you ever challenged yourself on this?

• Have you ever thought about winning the Lottery? What would you do with the money? How do you think it would affect your life and the lives of those closest to you? Would the Lord have a part in this?

### CHAPTER NINE – *From Adversity to Positivity*

• If you have had adversity in your life, how have you coped with it?

• How can we make an adverse event into a positive one? Who gives *you* help?

### CHAPTER TEN – *All Things Bright and Beautiful*

• How important do you think our physical attractiveness is?
  What do you make of the concept of cosmetic surgery?

• Have you ever felt close to the Lord in nature?

• Have you ever considered the Mass in terms of beauty? Why may this be?

### CHAPTER ELEVEN – *A Change is as Good as a Rest*

• How well do you cope with change?
  Do you think change can be constructive?

• What changes have you observed in your parish over a period of time?

• What changes occur in each one of the sacraments?
  How are we affected by these?

### CHAPTER TWELVE – *Trying to Escape the Inescapable*

• Do you find talking about death difficult? Why? Have you been able to offer support and care for a bereaved person and if so, how?

• Do you let others to see you as you really are?
  Do you think it is important to do so?

• 'Christians of great faith approach the end of their lives in the confidence that they will be going to God and to life everlasting'.[1] *Do you?*

### CHAPTER THIRTEEN – *The Fullness of Life*

• Do you ever give thanks to God for being alive?

• How does God give each of us new life?

• How can we share in the life of Jesus?

### CHAPTER FOURTEEN – *Who do we Think we Are?*

• Do you think it's important to love yourself?
  How can this help our relationship with God and others?

• Have you ever watched the film '*Dead Man Walking*'?
  (This is a great example of someone who is the 'face of Christ' for another person. Show this film or excerpts from it, to your group.)

---

[1] Page 238

### CHAPTER FIFTEEN – *I Was a Stranger and you Made me Welcome*
- Is hospitality important? If so, why? How hospitable are you?
- Why do you think Jesus regarded hospitality as so important?
  Why was he so keen to respond to others when they offered it to him?
  Could the Eucharist be described as a gesture of hospitality? If so, why?

### CHAPTER SIXTEEN – *A Safe Haven of Peace*
- How do you feel about refugees? Have you ever had to take refuge?
  If so, where and why?
- Have you ever thought of the Lord as a refuge? How could he be one?
- Do you consider Mass to be a refuge? In what context?

### CHAPTER SEVENTEEN – *Cleanse Me from My Sin*
- Do you ever ask yourself these sorts of questions: 'What would God want
  of me?'; 'Would Christ approve of this particular thought?';
  'Would Christ be happy if I said what I really feel and want to say?' [2]
  If so, is your behaviour affected by such thoughts?
- Does your conscience help you in your decisions, speech and actions?
- Have you ever helped anyone who has been a victim of their sin?
  In what way?

### CHAPTER EIGHTEEN – *Born Free*
- How do we sometimes imprison ourselves? Can we set ourselves free?
- What kind of freedoms do you have in your own life? Do you value them?
- How did Jesus free us?

### CHAPTER NINETEEN – *In Search of Happiness*
- What makes you happy? How do you hold on to happiness? Is this possible?
- How do you help others to feel happy?
- What do you think of this statement? – 'Love is intrinsically bound up with
  happiness; love is happiness and happiness derives from love.' [3]
  Do you think it is true? Can we learn from it?

### CHAPTER TWENTY – *In Whom Shall I Trust?*
- Who do you trust and why? Have you ever had to win someone else's trust?
  How did you achieve this?
- To what extent do you trust in God? How can our trust in the Lord help us
  to achieve wonderful things? Have you ever experienced this?
- Can we trust God enough to allow him to penetrate our defences and enter
  fully into our lives? What do you think may be the result of this?

---

[2] Page 322, [3] Page 368.